Kuki Women

KUKI WOMEN

Hoineilhing Sitlhou

SYNERGY

SYNERGY BOOKS INDIA

(An imprint of Bookwell Publications)

New Delhi

First Published, 2014

ISBN:978-93-82059-20-2

Published by:
Synergy Books India
(An Imprint of Bookwell Publications)
24/4800 Ansari Road, Darya Ganj
New Delhi-110002
Phone: 011-23268786, 23257264
Fax: 011-23281315
E-Mail: synergybooksindia@gmail.com
bookwell@vsnl.net
Website: www.synergybooksindia.com

Printed at: Mudrak, 30-A Patparganj, Delhi-110091.

This book is dedicated to my beloved grandmother (L) Vahjahoi and my mother Zakimi

(L) Vahjahoi

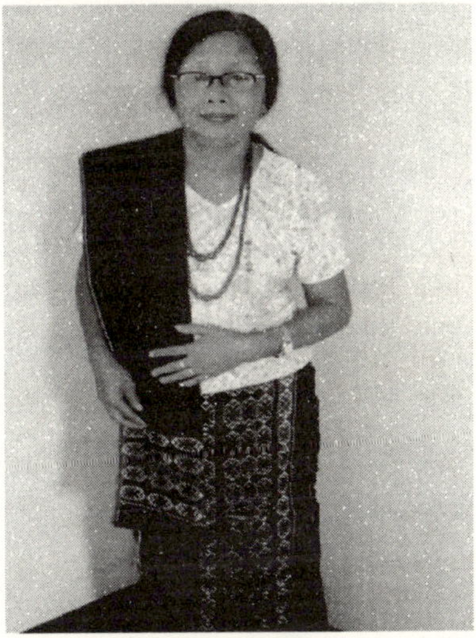

Zakimi

Contents

Foreword ix

Introduction xi

1. Behind the Scene: Prejudice of Kuki Chin-Zo Women in Manipur 1

2. Portrayal of Women in Folktales and Myths of the Kukis 43

3. Weaving: the Traditional Craft by the Kuki Women 61

4. Women in the Informal Economy: Unpacking realities of the Tribal Women Vendors of Manipur 94

5. Women Organisations and Collective protest: Nature, Scope and Challenges 123

6. Customary Laws of the Chikims with Special Reference to the Thadous 148

7. The Socio-Cultural lives of Vaiphei Women as defined by the Vaiphei Customary Laws 175

8. Status of Simte Women in Manipur 198

9. Health and Quality of Life: A case study among the Kuki women of Sapormeina, Manipur 218

10. Women's Health and Healthcare Accessibility: A Case Study of Kuki Women in Gelnel Village of West Sadar Hills 241

11. Representation of Kuki women in Thadou-Kuki films 262

12. Changing Pattern of Marriage System among the Thadou- Kukis of Manipur 275

13. Language and Gender: Linguistic Representation of Men and Women in Kuki Society 301

List of Contributors 319

Index 322

Foreword

There is a dearth of writings on the women of all tribes that falls within the umbrella of the Kuki society. Many students, particularly of the social science discipline, have often faced the dearth of materials on Kuki women. Even the available books, both by outsiders and insiders to the community, have a mere page or two dedicated to women. There is sadly, almost nothing for aspiring research scholars (who want to work on gender issues) to base their studies on. Therefore, a call was made to all interested persons to contribute in writing on any aspects (social, political, economy, religion, culture, education etc.) and perspectives (defined by profession and experiences) on women. The call received responses in terms of encouragement and contribution from scholars studying and working in different parts of the country. It is because of the efforts of these dedicated writers that the book has seen the light of the day. I also take this time to thank the respected members of the review committee – Mr. N. Annavaran (Assistant Professor in the department of Sociology, University of Hyderabad), Dr. Jangkhongam Doungel (Associate Professor and Head of Political Science Department, Mizoram University), Dr. Thongkholal Haokip (Assistant Professor in the department of Political Science, Presidency University, Kolkata), Nehginpao Kipgen (General Secretary of the U.S.based Kuki International Forum and a political scientist with specialisation in South & South East Asia), Dr. Paokholal Haokip (Assistant Professor in the department of History, Pondicherry University), Dr. Jangkhomang Guite (Assistant Professor in the department of History, Silchar University) and Khailen Haokip (Assistant Professor in Centre for Studies in Society and Development, Central University of Gujarat). Most of the essays in the book are based on primary data and has the privilege of being the pioneering study conducted in the chosen area of gender study. I thanked Kailen Singson for drawing the cover photo for the book. I sincerely hope that this book will be a beginning to many more studies on the Kuki women.

The book Kuki Women, is a tribute to all the women who silently worked behind the scene in the history of the Kuki society - the little girl who reluctantly gave up the opportunity to study so that her brother (s) could get education, the mother who selflessly toiled for her family to the point of shutting-off her own dreams, the competent wife who delights in her husband's success and remains to be content in the shadow of her husband, and lastly, to all the women who believed, fought and secured a visible place for themselves in the Kuki society.

Dr. Hoineilhing Sitlhou
Department of Sociology
University of Hyderabad

Introduction

The *Kuki Women* has thirteen essays written by thirteen authors. It deals with different facets of the intersection of gender and society in the context of the Kuki society. Before introducing the gist of each essay, it is pertinent to discuss the composition and identity issues of the Kuki society. The word Kuki is a generic term, which includes a number of tribes and clans. 'Kuki' refers to an ethnic entity spread out in a contiguous region in Northeast India, Northwest Burma, and the Chittagong Hill tracts in Bangladesh. The origin of the word 'Kuki', is not known but it first appears in Bengal in the writing of Rawlins entitled "Cucis or mountainers of Tipra" in Asiatic Researches in 1792 (as cited in Shaw, 1929, p. 11). The second record on the Kuki tribes in general appeared in the Asiatic Researches, volume VII, in a paper from the pen of Surgeon McCrea, dated 24th January 1799 (Macrae, 1919).

Kukis were already occupying the hill tracts of Manipur between the year 1830 and 1940 and Colonel McCulloch, the British political agent, settled them along exposed frontiers to act as buffers against other recalcitrant tribes (Johnstone, 1987, p. 26). Owing to McCulloch's 'buffer policy', the Kukis have been found settled in scattered pattern all over the Manipur hills. They now constitute an overwhelming preponderance in Churachandpur district, Sadar Hills subdivision of Senapati district and Chandel district. Otherwise, they are found mingling with Tangkhul (Naga) tribes in Ukhrul district, Mao-Maram-Paomai (Naga) tribes in Senapati district, and Zeliangrong (Naga) tribes in Tamenglong district (Gangte, 2007, p. 95). They are also found in Nagaland, Mizoram, Assam as also in Myanmar and Bangladesh.

"The British, using linguistic and cultural affinities and migration history as criteria, sub-divided and invented the 'Old Kuki' and 'New Kuki' appellations to group them (Arora & Kipgen, 2012, p. 435)." In the last half of the eighteenth century, the old Kukis first migrated from the Lushai land and settled down in Manipur and Cachar (Shakespear, 1975). The section of the Kukis who had been driven by the powerful Lushai clans and migration to Manipur around the middle of the 19th Century were called the new Kukis (Bhadra, 1975, p. 11). "Many scholars consider the differentiation between Old Kuki and New Kuki to be a misnomer, though some find merit in this subdivision (Arora & Kipgen, 2012, p. 435)." However, the classification was used by the state government of Manipur in classifying the various tribes of the Kukis. Under the Official Classification of Tribes in Manipur by the Directorate of Tribal Welfare & Backward Classes, 1981, the New Kukis of Manipur comprises of the tribes like Gangte, Hmar, Lushai, Paite, Simte, Thadou, Vaiphei, Zou, Ralte and Moyong under the same classification, whereas Old Kuki comprises of the tribes like Aimol, Chiru, Koireng, Kom, Anal, Chothe, Lamkang, Koirao/Thangal, Purum and Monsang.

In the present decade, ethnic identity assertion has caused redefinition of identities among the group who were originally classified as Kukis. "During the process of constructing and reconstructing the Naga political identity, some of the Old Kuki tribes, as mentioned earlier, were assimilated into the Naga fold. These tribes include Anal, Moyon, Monsang and Maring (Kipgen, 2013, P. 28)". Coupled with this, in the face of rising Naga insurgency and their use of coercion to further their cause, some of the old Kuki tribes joined the Naga ethnic group out of fear for their own security (ibid). Even amongst the group who were categorised as New Kukis, a new ethnic category was constructed as to bring together the three groups of people who were colonially named as 'Chin', 'Kuki' and 'Lushai', under one term 'Zo'

(Suan, 2011, p. 158-159). The justification was that the term 'Kuki' was a name imposed on them by the British imperialists' for administrative convenience and it was alien to them. But, the traditionalist pro-Kuki group wanted to retain the term as doing away with it would mean making much of history irrelevant to the existence of these particular group of people. The various essays in the book used the different categories—the Kukis, the sub-group of the Kukis or the newly constructed ethnic categories as 'Zo' or 'Chikims' or 'Kuki-Chin-Zo', but they refer to the same group of people.

Behind the Scene: Prejudice of Kuki Chin-Zo Women in Manipur is a study of the status of the Kuki-chin-zo women in the contemporary times. Western education have enabled the Kuki women of today to challenged the traditional status-quo as they started competing in the roles and positions which were earlier considered the exclusive rights and domains of the Kuki men. Women are seen to take over the roles of chiefs in villages and contest and won elections in urban areas. The essay includes case studies of the experiences of Kuki women who have excelled in sports, entrepreneurship, politics, academics and religious leadership. Based on the study conducted, it finally answers the question that the breaking down of the traditional barriers of the society by these women does not necessarily mean the doing away of the stereotype on women or the overall emancipation of the Kuki women.

Portrayal of Women in Folktales and Myths of the Kukis narrates five timeless folktales of the Kukis: *Lenchonghoi, Jonlhing, Ahsijolneng, Pi Chaiching* and the tale of the elephant apple. It analysed the contemporary relevance of folklores and mythical stories in determining the worldview and ideology of the Kuki society and their attitudes towards women in general. The study is a quest to unveil the following questions: What do the folklores and mythical stories reflect about the role expectation or status of women in the past? How are these roles translated in the mentality and societal expectation or in defining the 'ideal women' or the 'evil women' in the present society? What is the contribution of folklores and myth to the socialization process and in the social construction of gender relations in the society?

Weaving: the Traditional Craft by the Kuki Women is a social, economic and historical study of the practice of weaving in the Kuki society. The traditional *Kuki* women wove their cloths not for commercial purpose but solely for domestic use and it was a compulsion rather than a choice that they learn weaving as to clothe the whole family. Moreover, for a maiden, weaving is the yardstick for which her suitability for a wife or daughter-in-law is measured. But, a married woman who is an expert in the art of weaving, is honoured and given due recognition in the community. The techniques of weaving have also undergone changes to suit the demands of the changing times. The popularity of loin-loom and spinning wheel which is labour-intensive and time consuming is challenged by the development of technology in which weaving machines and computer technology is used. Weaving in itself reflects the close affinity between nature and culture in the Kuki society. Many of the designs of the traditional clothes were copied from natural elements like the python, the tiger, the rainbow, the horn-bill, the cucumber seed, etc. Lastly, it identifies the affinity among the many *Kuki* tribes by the origin, design pattern, uses and commonness of their textiles.

Women in the Informal Economy: Unpacking realities of the Tribal Women Vendors of Manipur discuss the contribution of women in the informal economy particularly the tribal women street vendors of Manipur. It highlights the plight of the tribal women street vendors in relation to their working conditions, needs, challenges faced by them, role within the family and society at large. Based on a fieldwork conducted in Manipur, Jaja Kipgen tries to contextualise the case of the Kuki women vendors and makes a connection between their situations to the patriarchal structure of the Kuki society. The preference of the male child for education in poor families leads to high dropout rate of girls who in the later stage have no alternative rather than to engage in the informal sector as street vendors so as to support their family.

Women Organisations and Collective protest: Nature, Scope and Challenges tries to understand and positioned the Kuki women collective protest within the larger theories and debates of social movement studies. It compares it to the case of the women participation in the Chipko Andolan in Uttarakhand and the Nupilan movement in Manipur. In the context of the Kuki society, the women collective protest were usually spearheaded by local based women organisations: one formed within the Church and the other at the broader societal level, which are operative on a need-basis to combat social ills like drugs or liquor sellers as also to protect the men folk from insurgents and armed forces. The temporariness and permanence of a protest is adjusted according to the demand of the situation and it is in this light that the writer presents a more detailed study of the Kuki Women Human Rights Organisations and Sadar Hills Women Union to understand the nature, scope and challenges of Kuki women collective protest in general.

Customary Laws of the Chikims with Special Reference to the Thadous is a descriptive study of the Thadou customs and cultures including marriage system, birth rites and treatment of the death as also the inheritance issues in the society. It critically analysed the customary laws of the Thadous and its prejudices towards Kuki women as it supports the patriarchal hegemony of the society. The writer makes a departure from the dominant assumption that elements of social changes in a society challenges and gradually does away with the tradition and customs of a society. She writes that customary laws are still relevant and prevalent in the present Thadou society.

The Socio-Cultural lives of Vaiphei Women as defined by the Vaiphei Customary Laws is a descriptive study of gender relations in the Vaiphei society as defined by customary laws. The customary law is normative in nature and act as a guideline for defining the various social institutions such as family, marriage and kinship in the Vaiphei society. Based on the analysis of these customary laws, it highlights the status of the Vaiphei women in the larger socio-cultural framework of the Vaiphei patriarchal society as also the impact of the waves of modernization and westernization in the form of education and Christianity.

Status of Simte Women in Manipur is an overview of the position of the Simte women in the Simte society. The customary laws plays a deciding factor in deciding the movement of a woman: from the selection of her marriage partner to the manner in which the marriage ought to be conducted or consummated or ended; to her responsibility and rights in different stages of her life. The writer Esther Lalremkim analysed the presence and participation of the Simte women in four important spheres of the society: political, religious, socio-cultural and economic, respectively. An interesting paradox in the case of the Simte women is that though they play a crucial role in the economy of the society, they are excluded from decision making process both within family as also outside, in Church and social organizations.

Health and Quality of Life: A case study among the Kuki women of Sapormeina, Manipur evaluates the general well-being and quality of life of women with special references to gynaecological problems. The essay is based on a fieldwork done among the Kuki communities residing in Sapormeina village of Manipur. In the Kuki society, the status of a woman is also determined by her child-rearing and child-bearing abilities. Infertility is unacceptable and a woman who is not able to bear a child is stigmatised and is considered a disgrace. Interestingly, though the blame for infertility is entirely on the women, the paradox is that there is a lack of health care for women reproductive health, gynaecological issues including proper postpartum treatment. Superstitious belief is also another factor that influences the local women to choose ethno medicine to allopathic medicine. According to the author, the factors like education, occupation, marital status, age-group determines and influenced the quality of life of the Kuki women as they determined their ability to be knowledgeable as also to negotiate and developed better health care system in the social structure.

Women's Health and Healthcare Accessibility: A Case Study of Kuki Women in Gelnel Village of West Sadar Hills is a study of the social determinants of the well-being of the Kuki women. The essay is based on a fieldwork conducted in Gelnel village of Senapati district of Manipur. Going beyond the biological model of health theory, it emphasised on the wider social perspectives that affect an individual well being and constraint women from improving the quality of her life. The author argues that the multiple burdens of production and reproduction make women more prone to ill-health as compared to her male counterparts. In most Kuki villages, access to health care facilities for women is determined by both structural and cultural factors. Firstly, there is the lack of resources in terms of finance and transport and communication. Secondly, the dictates of the customs and culture of a patriarchal society caused gender discrimination in which women are the last in the draw to receive education and health care facilities within the family.

Representation of Kuki women in Thadou-Kuki films studies the available Thadou-Kuki films in order to understand the gender relations in the Kuki society. At the onset, the author made the clarification that the Thadou-Kuki films are highly influenced by the Manipuri and Bollywood movies and this factor thin out the possibility of these films to be considered as representative of contemporary social reality of the Kukis. The essay narrates five popular Thadou-Kuki films: *Kum Som Kilungset, Jonlhing, Heno Neingailou hitam, Lhalihjaan* and *Ngaidam* for the purpose of analysis. In many cases gender stereotypes are re-confirmed in the films given where women are portrayed as dependent on men as 'damsel in distress', dedicated and sacrificial mother, wife and a resourceful homemaker. The chosen films shows that a woman as compared to man is more constrained by the values and the norms of the society and great importance is given to her reputation which is considered defining elements of her social identity. The films in order to cater to the demands of the masses tend to focus more on the dominant societal attitude of the 'ideal Kuki woman'.

Changing Pattern of Marriage System among the Thadou- Kukis of Manipur begins by discussing the various social agencies, customary laws, and practices that defined the traditional marriage system prevalent in the Thadou-Kuki society. Christianity and education were two factors that deeply impact the ideologies, concepts, laws and practices of marriage system in the society. Moreover, the institution of marriage is no longer the negotiation between two families but more of personal choice of the partners concerned.

Language and Gender: Linguistic Representation of Men and Women in Kuki Society is a contribution to the study of the relationship between gender and language by contextualising the case of the Kukis. Women are known to experience linguistic discrimination in two ways: in the ways they are taught to use language as also in the way general language is use to treat and define them. Likewise, the linguistic behaviour of men and women is gendered in varied forms in the Kuki society. The author analysed the conversational characteristics of the Kuki women in terms of epistemic modality, the frequent use of tag-questions, intonation, hedges, verbal hygiene, turn-taking and the differences in the overall purpose of communication. In order to understand the influence of cultural patterns, expectations of social norms and customs and gender stereotypes in the linguistic expression of the Kuki women, social and linguistic practices such as naming, adages, teknonymy, generic terms, evaluative adjectives, colour terms and necessity for politeness is studied.

REFERENCES

1. ARORA, VIBHA, KIPGEN, NGAMJAHAO. (2012) The Politics of identifying with and distancing from Kuki Identity in Manipur. *Sociological Bulletin*. 61 (3): 429-449.

2. GANGTE, T.S. (2007) 'Struggle for Identity and Land among the Hill Peoples of Manipur,' *Eastern Quarterly Journal*. Volume 4 Issues II, July-September.

3. JOHNSTONE, JAMES. (1987) *Manipur and the Naga Hills*. New Delhi: Gyan Publishing House.

4. KIPGEN, NEHGINPAO. (2013) Politics of Ethnic Conflict in Manipur. *South Asia Research.* 33 (1): 21-38.

5. MACRAE, JOHN. (1979/ 1801) 'Account of the Kookies, or Lunctas,' by, *Asiatic Researches,* Vol.VII, 183-198.

6. SHAKESPEAR, LT. COLONEL J. *The Lushai Kuki Clans,* Tribal Research Institute, Mizoram, 1975 (1912).

7. SHAW, WILLIAM. (1929) *Notes on the Thadou Kukis.* Published on behalf of the Government of Assam.

8. SUAN, H. KHAM KHAN. (2011) Rethinking 'tribe' identities: The politics of recognition among the Zo in the North East India. *Contributions to Indian Sociology.* 45 (2): 157-187.

Chapter 1

Behind the Scene: Prejudice of Kuki Chin-Zo Women in Manipur

Hoipi Haokip

Introduction

The notion of equality has exercised a dominant and emotional appeal in the struggle of women to free themselves from exploitation and oppression. Women, as in the past to the present day remained somewhat outside of history, although the centrality of the roles they play in contributing to domestic comforts in every society continued to be emphasised by feminist and commentators alike even in the 1790s. So also gender prejudice had long been woven into the fabric of human societies, sexism researchers have documented that women elicit predominantly positive sentiments but are often targets of prejudice. Yet for the Kuki-chin-Zo societies the term prejudice have remain an elusive subject. Most women of these societies fail to recognise the bias attitude embedded in its traditional customary norms and cultures and hence they refuse to recognise themselves as the prejudice lot. This denial has led to delusional perception among the women as the staunch supporter of the customary traditional laws which itself is manifested in the perceived outlooks within the society such as the importance given to sons over daughters, inheritance rights and the right to political leadership.

According to Laurie Rudman and Peter Glick (2005:154,156,162), "Women themselves may not realise sexism but instead may view male dominance as part of the natural order, at least until they have had their conscious raised is because gender prejudice is normative as to be invisible. Women are automatically allocated a lower status than men so much so that when they enter an occupation, the perceived status of the occupation can drop significantly. Thus, a powerful woman may make people uncomfortable because of the discordance between her ascribed status as a woman and her achieved status as a leader." S.T. Fiske and Stevens (1998: p. 181&163) notes that, "both of these scenarios could result in sexual discrimination. In one case, discrimination would result in not behaving like a woman should, and, in the other case, from behaving too much like a woman. Thus, ambitious woman may have to choose between being respected but not liked or being liked but not being respected".

Women in the Kuki-Chin-Zo society occupy a subservient position, whose main responsibility is to rear sons and daughters and raise them according to the values and morals of the society in which they lived. Most official histories marginalise the activities of women. But if one prods deeper into the oral narratives of the Kuki-Chin- Zo society, there are abundant references of women playing a crucial role in the histories of each family, clan, sub-clans and tribes. These historical facts have rarely been discussed explicitly, manifesting the insignificant attitude of the society. The pattern of excluding women's role is ingrain so deep that it persisted throughout the 20th century, making it all the more difficult to trace and problematic to transcend partisan division and articulate an autonomous narratives.

Gender prescriptions require women to be nice; when their leadership behaviour deviates from this rule, their evaluation suffers. According to John Stuart (Stuart, 1979, p.50-51), " power holds a smoother language, and whomsoever it oppresses always pretends to do so for their own good: accordingly when anything is forbidden to women, it is thought necessary to do so, and desirable to believe, that they are incapable of doing it, and that they depart from their real path of success and happiness when they aspire to it... the most depreciator of women will not venture to deny that of ages past, women, and not a few merely, but many women, have proved themselves capable of everything, perhaps, without a single exception which is done by men, and of doing it successfully and creditably." Likewise this article is in part to draw attention to some of the successful Kuki-Chin-Zo women who have risen above the social constriction and prejudices of the society.

I. Nature of Gender prejudice:

According to most social psychologists prejudice may be broadly defined as a negative social attitude toward members of an identified social group based simply on their group membership (G.E.M, Ste Croix, 2009, p. 22). Prejudice is an attitude directed toward people because they are members of a specific social group (Whitley & Kite, 2010, p. 22). Rupert Brown defines prejudice as any attitude, emotion or behaviour towards members of a group, which directly or indirectly implies some negativity or antipathy towards that group (Brown, 2010, p. 11). Eagly and Dickman (as quoted in Sniderman & Hagerndoorn 2007, p. 65), writes that " many , if not most of the important phenomenon of every day prejudice lie outside of the boundaries of the traditional framing of prejudice. Gender prejudice is a form of prejudice characterised by negative attitudes towards women and has followed the conception of being completely negative attitudes in nature (Pelinka, Bischof and stogner, 2009, 79)."

Gordon Allport (1979) acknowledged the functional nature of prejudice and identified both material gain and self enhancement as basic motivational processes underlying prejudice. He notes, "Outright greed is certainly a cause of prejudice most people want to be higher on the status ladder than they are". He observed that "there lies at the heart of any diversified and stratified social status the tempting possibility that economic, sexual, political, and status gains may result from the deliberate and even from unconscious exploitation of minorities. To achieve these gains prejudice is propagated by those who stand to win the most advantage". Men biased by custom, prejudice, and interest have presumed boldly the tendency to view women fickle therefore stating women as unfit to administer the state. The mere thoughts of acquiescing to a woman downgrade the positive attitudes that men typically have for women. This is highly illustrative among all societies but more so among the kuki-Chin- Zo groups and hence a woman likely to contest election or holding eminent position is always viewed with negative attitude and her morality as a woman is often questioned. As Mary Wollstencraft (1922, p. 19) points out "men keep from women all opportunities' of that cultivation of the understanding which infallibly leads to virtue, and by a singular want of logic hold them responsible for the moral deficiency which is the inevitable consequence".

To downplay the competence of women, men at all times and in every possible ways lay numerous forms of hurdles in her path. Thus, in order to prove her efficiency she has to overcome such criticism and judgemental attitude; in doing so backlash for female agency places women in a double bind. If they act competently and aggressively, they risk negative reactions for being insufficiently feminine. But if they are modest and communal, they risk being viewed as incapable of leadership (Rudman & Glick, 2008, p.163).

II. Brief Historical analysis of the term Kuki-Chin- Zo:

In order to comprehend the centrality of the word Kuki-Chin-zomi, it would be significant to outline a brief historical analyse of the background of how the expression Kuki-Chin-Mizo or Zomi came to be incorporated. The origin of the word is quite obscure, Colonial officers and ethnographers such as Reid 1942, Woodthorpe (1983, p. 238), A.G.E. Newland (1894), Soppitt (1893, p. 3), S.A Reid (1893, p. 238) had written diverse and numerous memoirs and monographs regarding about the origin of the term. In the meantime William Shaw (1929, p. 30) referred to them as the Thadou Kukis .

Regarding the term 'Chin', B.S. Carey & H.N.Tuck (1896, p. 3) asserted it as a Burmese corruption of the Chinese word 'Jin' or 'Jen' which means 'man'. Prof. F.K. Lehman (1963, p. 3), Prof. G. H. Luce (1954/1956, p. 26) term 'Chin'(Khyan in old Burmese) was derived from the Burmese word meaning 'ally' or 'comrade' and were of the view that the term might be from the Burmese word 'Khyan' which means 'basket'. It is a Burmese word (Khyan), not a Chin word. It is homologous with the contemporary Burmese word meaning basket'. Sir Arthur Phayre (1883) opines that 'Chin' was a corruption, through Arrakanese of klang, the word for a man and is believed to be given by Burmans. Sir J.George Scott (1932, p. 187) wrote, "the name Kuki and Chin are not natural, and have been given to them by their neighbours. Like others they do not accept the name given to them by the Burmese and ourselves; they do not call themselves Chins, and they equally flout the name of Kuki which their Assamese neighbours use. They call themselves Zhou or Shu and in other parts Yo or lai." The Chin Hills gazetteer recorded the facts that Zo (Chins) and the so called Kukis were one and the same race and that Soktes, Yos and Kamhaus were one people(Vumkhohau 1963: 297).

In yet another version James C. Scott (2010:14) in his book, 'The Art of not being Governed' he elaborated 'Zo' as a relational term meaning 'remote' and hence carries the connotation of living in the hills. Meanwhile eminent Kuki-Chin-Zo Scholars such as Pu Thawng khawhau (1955, p. 4), Pu Captain K.A. Khup Zar thang (1974, p.1) Khup Za Gou (2008) and Vumson (1986, p. 6) suggested 'Zo' as the correct term. Vumson in his book 'Zo History' theories that, "the author chooses, Zo as the designation of all people, because it appears to him that Zo, Yo, Jo, Cho. Sho, Khxou, or Yaw.....he believes that names such as Kuki and Chin which originated as abusive names should not be adopted as designation of a people".

Over and above these hullaballoo, the disagreement was further highlighted when Colonel John Shakespeare (1912, p. 8) clubbed them together referring it as 'Lushei-Kuki Clans', to quote his excerpt " the term Kuki has come to have a fairly meaning, and we now understand by it certain - clans, with well marked characteristics, belonging to the Tibeto-Burman stock. On the Chittagong border, the term is loosely applied to most of the inhabitants of the interior hills beyond the Chittagong Hill Tracks; in Cachar it generally means some families of Kuki. Now a days, the term is hardly employed having superseded by Lushai in Chin Hills, and generally on the Burman border all these clans are called Chin. These Kukis are most closely allied to the Chakmas, and the Lushais are most closely allied to their eastern neighbours who are known as Chin -"Nevertheless, there is no doubt that the Kukis , Lushais, and chins are all the same race". Hence, some reiterated 'Zo' as the correct idiom; while others are against it; creating a continuous ongoing debacle on the acceptable appellation to refer these groups of people, having the same socio-political, historical and cultural affinity.

Despite the numerous variant and theories over the question of correct terminology, today the accepted common term to denote these groups of people has been substituted by using 'CHIKIM' meaning Chin-Kuki-Mizo. Since this phrase has come to be widely accepted, without much contention, I have use the term Chin-Kuki–Zo in my article.

III. Portrayal of Kuki-Chin –Mizo or Zomi women:

The customary laws of the Kuki-Chin-Zo society are strongly influenced by the patriarchal family. An important point noteworthy of mentioning is the fact that traditionally since the man spent almost the whole year in hunting and raiding the maintenance of the home, hearth and the village was left on the shoulder of womenfolk. Consequently, a society which was always in the apprehension of possible social annihilation, the men folk undergoes training for the whole year; the maintenance of the home, hearth and the village was left on the shoulder of the womenfolk. Hence in such a society which was always in the apprehension of possible social annihilation, the craftsmen had to be basically utilitarian and every piece produced should serve the utilitarian purpose (Haobam, 1991, p. 207).

Kuki-chin-Zo society being a patriarchal society, the husband yearns for a sons and a wife who produces sons, establishes herself and her honour within the family and community. The birth of a son is a cause for great rejoicing, for the continuance of the family and clan name is assured. But the birth of a daughter is considered as loss for the family; for upon her marriage she takes the name of her husband and builds the family in his name. Though she did take part in the social, religious, political and economic life of the community her main principal function is as wife and mother. In the determination of genealogy, lineage is traced from the father's side. A man having no son is regarded as *'chimang'* meaning his lineage ceases and his descendent no longer related in the clan genealogy. Thus woman is often merely view upon as *'Chikhai'* which means 'bearer of children'.

Bertram & Carey (1932, p. 138), observe that "the women appear squatter than the men even, but are strong and lusty, and quite industrious and indefatigable as the Naga women, working hard all day wither at home or in the fields accustomed to carry heavy load". This comparison of the Kuki women may have arisen due to the fact that the Kuki-Chin-Zo people live in close proximity with each other; it may also have arisen due to the fact that despite the assumed differences between the Kuki-Chin-Zo people and the Nagas, they share some common socio-and culturally affinity.

IV. Customary Law and Impact on women

The general view that women in tribal society enjoy equal status with that of men holds true for the village people but when it comes to the workings of the customary law in society, women do not enjoy equal rights as that of men. In many instances women's roles and status were determined by social institutions, norms and ideologies. In the traditional society the economic roles of men and women were sharply distinguished because men were generally engaged in hunting and warfare while women were engage in domestic and agricultural activities. Women were not allowed to participate in politics, administration or in religious activities because those were regarded as men's domain. Simone de Beauvoir has with hindsight quoted aptly, "Woman has always been man's dependant, if not her slave; the two sexes have never shared the world in equality. And even today woman is heavily handicapped, though her situation is beginning to change. Almost nowhere is her legal status the same as men and frequently it is much to her disadvantage. Even though her rights are legally recognised in the abstract, custom prevents their full expression in the mores (Beauvoir, 2012, p. 18)".

In order to comprehend why and how women in the Kuki-Chin-Zo society are always back slotted in history by the society, it would best to briefly survey the customary laws, for a better perception of their namelessness and prejudice. There is no universally adopted definition of a customary law. It can be described as a set of rules through which tribal practices its culture and expresses its worldview. It is "an established system of immemorial rules which had evolved from the way of life and natural wants of the people, the general context of which was a common knowledge, coupled with precedents applying to special cases, which were retained in the memories of the chief and his councillors, their sons and their sons (sic), until forgotten, or until they became a part of the immemorial rules" (Barbora and Fernandes, 2008, p. 93).

Barbora & Fernandes (2002, p. 11) argues that while it is true that the tribal tradition of the Northeast gave more rights to women than caste societies did, the situation is changing in favour of patriarchy and at times patrilineal even in matrilineal societies. Left to themselves, education, religion and other social forces tend to adapt themselves to the dominant social norms that are by and large patriarchal. In the name of modernisation the State deals mainly with individual men in these societies that have for centuries depended on community ownership, on the egalitarian principle and on the gender based division of roles rather than power. As a result women in these communities have enjoyed a higher status than their counterparts in caste societies did, without being equal to men.

Modernisation that depends on the individual and profit based commercialisation, transfer all power to men. But social norms continue to assign to the woman the traditional role of looking after the household with very little or no control over the resources require for it. Thus customary law and tradition does not adapt itself to the changing reality. Despite the onslaught of modernisation, education, development and globalisation and adoption to Christianity, the Kuki-Chins-Zomi who embraced Christianity continued to keep intact the many elements of traditional customary laws of their society. The traditional political Institution of the Kuki-Chin-Mizo based on kinship system, continues to be enforced in strict accordance with the customary Laws. The village remains as the highest political unit among the Kukis and the chief exercise sole discretionary power. The traditional political institution of the Chief and his Council of Ministers function within a territorial jurisdiction, wielding its political authority and prerogatives in absolute term (Gangte, 1993, p. 124).

The office of the chief is '*Haosa*' and that of his wife is known as '*Haosapi*'. A woman is not permitted to meddle in the political affairs of the village. She is permitted to attend the Village Council meetings provided she is a widow and her son is still a minor, if not her son will represent as the head of the family, superseding the mother. Despite women playing an important role in various administrative system of the village, they were not directly involved in the running of the administration of the village. Only males were allowed to become the *Haosa* or chief and in the absence of the Chief the wife although was appointed as the chief, she was only a nominal head, the real power were exercised by the Council of members who were all male. Her main role as the *Haosapi* is to show hospitality to the members assembled in the *Haosa's* house.

The existing traditional act of divorce also confirms the derogatory role of women; even today, woman can be easily divorced on the ground of infertility, lack of male issue by men, adultery or incompatibility or on any flimsy ground. There is hardly any codified rule to strengthen her position as a married woman. She can be easily divorce or dispose over a few sums of money. Many instances even today are prevalent of such case where a young married girl is being divorce on ground of incompatibility. The members who initiate such divorce are all male and so the sentiments of the women are never taken into consideration. A girl being divorce is not paid any compensation rather the divorce compensation is handed to the parents or the male members of her family which may either be her brothers or her next male kin family. Her condition is one of a slave that is being sold and purchase according to the whims of the masters. She is deprived of not only her basic rights to express her opinion but financially have nothing to fall back to; she is left at the mercy of the men of her household. One instance in which woman had been unfairly treated and to which I have been a parley of such atrocities is, *'a girl name Jakim (name changed) was divorce by her husband after the birth of her first child simply because the parents did not favour her . The divorce settlement was an amount of Rupees 30,000 only, with the slaughter of a traditional and customary formality of one pig from the husband's side. The irony of the situation was that the petty divorce amount did not even reach the girl but was handed over to the eldest brother who spends it as he wishes'.*[1]

To add to such prejudices a married woman is sometimes discriminated on ground of her clan identity, she is often looked down by the in-laws if she belongs to a clan which is regarded inferior to her husband's clan[2]. The hierarchy of superior or inferior clan disrupted the stability and unity of the Kuki-Chin-Zo society to such an extent leading to a culmination of internal disintegration. Seilen Haokip (2010, p. 27) quote that , " unsavoury utterances, 'Kuki-siki', 'Kuki-makhai' (quarter-kuki, half-Kuki) over the candidacy of a Kom and a Paite for the post of a Kuki Minister , added fuel to fire. A rival party called Khulmi national Union was formed of various clans, excepting those associated with Thadou." The condition of such woman often is demoted to a rank of a slave, and the husband has no option since the mother-in-law is the matriarch of the house and her decision is unquestioned within the household matters. Such instances of clan distinction have been replaced by the economic and educational position she holds such as a salaried and educational background. Today, the question of seeking mother's brother- son marriage [3] no longer holds relevance in the quest for a prospective bride or groom.

Of all the most prejudiced of the customary laws of the Kuki-Chin-Zo people is the inheritance law. According to the customary law a woman is not entitled to inherit their father's or husband's property. They are governed by the un-codified customary laws and practices. Properties are always inherited by the males. She as a woman does not have any rights to claim any properties. The occupational status of the women also does not affect on the inheritance of properties though they may play an important role in the economy of the family. Daughters do not have the right to claim properties. A woman has access to the properties of the family within a certain extent but cannot inherit it. A woman as a wife and mother have the right over the properties as long as she remain under the roof of her husband but once she divorces or becomes a widow and goes back to her natal house, she lose the right to privileges which she had enjoyed previously while still living under her husband's house. Widow receives the land and house of her deceased husband to enjoy during her lifetime. But she has no right to alienate the said property. On her remarriage with a person of another clan other than her husband's the widow will forfeit her right to enjoy the property of her deceased husband; and if the parents die without a male issue, his nearest kin can inherit the property , therefore leaving her daughters at the mercy of the family members, uncared and unsupported.

There is always a strong feeling against women inheriting anything, and unless a woman has powerful relations, she will usually be entirely ignored at the division of the estate and even a widow will have hard work to secure any particular property which has been specially bequeathed to her by her husband on his deathbed. On the death of her husband the widow and her daughters live with the eldest son, or, if they continue to live in the house of the deceased, the eldest son is bound to provide for them and attend to all their wants, and they are a part of his establishment and assist him in the same manner as wives assist their husbands, by attending to all household duties and weaving wearing apparel (Carey & Tuck, 2008, p. 208). Customary Laws put woman in an economically insecure position. She inherits no property despite the fact that she has contributed to it through her unpaid labour. The widow is left at the mercy of the husband line and his heir controls what benefits she is allowed to get from the house. Women's inheritance right is depended upon the decision of men. Hence as a result instances intra family dispute arises within a family over the Inheritance issue. Even in areas where MLR&LR Acts[4] have been enforced and enacted, despite naming the daughters as the sole beneficiaries, on the death of the parents, the next kin supposedly to inherit the land can as per the Customary Laws demand his claim over the said inheritance. In some instances often the parents having no male issue resorted to selling off their land less it falls on the next kin of family

Although customary laws are codified in Mizo society in *'Mizo Hnam Dan'* it is clearly mentioned that ordinarily a woman cannot inherit property. However, if a person has daughters but no son, his daughters may inherit his property. In case of more than one daughter, the youngest daughter will be given first preference as in the case of sons [rule 109]. If a man dies without an issue, leaving behind only his wife, the court may take a share of the deceased's properties in favour of the widow as it deemed fit and proper [Rule109(4)]Rule 109(3) lays down that if the deceased's wife is ready and willing to remain in the house occupying the main bed and discharging the duties and functions of the mother, nobody should disturb her...if the mother tries to dispose of her husband's properties, the heirs may take the properties and distribute them. Thus, signifying that women allowed to inherit property under a strict supervision that they prescribed to the norms laid down by the Mizo Hnam Dan, and they were relegated to a mere caretaker of the property and not the owner; where she freely have the sole right and liberty as she deems fit.

In Manipur, the non-tribal women in the valley such as the Meitei enjoyed the right to inherit property, under the Hindu succession Act[5] but for the tribal women it is a far cry, the mention of it among the presence of men is abhorrent. Regardless of the Supreme court's verdict on property rights?; when women are fighting to assert their rights to which they are entitled; when various laws to sensitise the parliamentarians, planners, policy makers, administrators at the national,regional and state levels have been initiated. The position of women's right to inheritance remains static and no efforts has been undertaken by the so called lawmakers or dominant tribal leaders. They rather ignored the need for a change of societal attitudes towards women, the idea of women inheriting property is anathema for the men folk and hence although the world is progressing towards the goal of achieving equality, for the women of Kuki-Chin -Zo, until and unless equal access to property has been legally modified in the traditional customary law, equality would remain an elusive subject.

Similarly when a chief dies issueless, the chieftainship goes to the next kin of family. Likewise if the Chief dies leaving behind only daughters, the question of chief ship will pass to the next kin of family. But if the a son is born and is a minor the wife as a regent can uphold the position of the chief until the son came of age. Likewise if the chief dies leaving behind daughters then as in the former the next kin of family will assume the chief ship.

This inherently reflects that within a culture, one group may retain the power to define cultural values as well as the form those values should take. The powerful group establishes and maintains its dominance by rewarding those values that corresponds to its views and punishing those values that does not. The result is that minority groups and their cultural heritage are marginalised. The resulting discrimination consists of "discrimination and inequality..... Built into our literature, art, music, language, morals, customs, beliefs, and ideology.... to such a degree that they define a generally agreed- upon way of life" (Whitley &Kite 2010, p. 17).

Traditional Kuki life is dominated by religion and they are religious minded people. In the sphere of religion too, women are not allowed to participate, initiate or perform rites or ceremony, the office of the priest or thempu is officially held by a man, although instances of a women priestess or *thempi* have not been totally absent. Though customary laws do not recognised women officially as priestess, unofficial priestesses were common in every village. These priestess performed priestly function in the absence of the priest and when people were in dire need. Where such women acquire the knowledge to perform such religious rites and incantation remains obscure, however, according to Rev. Seikholet Singson (Kipgen 2010: 108), " usually the priest teaches his priestly rites called *'themthu'* to his son, but it was not permitted to teach him in isolation, he has to be accompanied by his sister or mother" this indicates the fact that the company of women was necessary for teaching and performance of religious rites; although women were not formally imparted the knowledge of traditional and religious rites they gradually developed the art of magical rites and treat people.

The Kuki-Chin-Zo women besides looking after the family, home and hearth also perform dual work in helping the men in the economic activities. Though men and women are in involve in the agricultural activities, women have more responsibility than men. Since agriculture is the main economy of the Kukis, women work side by side with their husbands, fathers and brothers in the Jhum fields. Due to her role in agriculture, traditionally a ritual known as *'Chang –Ai'* or (paddy rites) is committed solely to women, signifying her thankfulness as well as emphasising her role as the owner of the paddy.The house wife is the main performer of this ritual and its successful observance implies that the housewife is blessed and honoured even after death when she would be living in the world of the death (Gangte, p. 185; Goswami, p. 158) Although, in the pre-Christianized period the observance and the performance of *'Chang-Ai'* confirms women 's importance in the economy of the Kuki-Chin-Zo society, is her role in political and religious sphere complimentary to her? Here lies the dogmas of women's situation; She is exalted in the economic sphere and expected to labour hard with no gains whatsoever. Over and above this, women are also a part of the *'Loms'* (collective labor corps) working side by side along with men in groups, taking turns to work in paddy fields . It is only in rearing of poultry, pigs etc. which are considered as women's domain, she has absolute right without interference from her husband to sell animals reared by her. Every household among the Kuki-chin-zo society manages some form of poultry and piggery. This work is solely rest on the women, who reared and feeds the animals and fowls. As such the decision to sell abides on her. The money accrued from selling the animals are further utilised in the maintenance of the family such as for children educational purpose. According to Themneilhing of Motbung[6] village, 'she bought two piglets at an amount of Rupees 1500 each from the profit she accrued in weaving cloths. After 8-10 months, she sold it for an amount ranging from 8000-10000, depending on the size of the pigs. This money profited from selling her pigs and fowls are utilized on her children's education. While the small amount she received from selling fowls are meant for daily expenses.'

Another important method that woman use to boosts the family's economy is through weaving; traditionally every woman is expected to be skilled in the art of weaving, as she is the main supplier of the household clothing ,plucking the cotton, ginning, dyeing and spinning is prepared by her . Thus, the only area where a woman is allowed full liberation is in economic activity. Yet paradoxically for all her labour and acknowledgement bestow on her as the owner of the agriculture, she is left with no power to neither dispense land at her own whim nor accumulate wealth for herself, everything that she amass goes to her husband and his family line.

V. Western Education and its Impact:

Degree of literacy is one of the most important yardsticks of the degree of civilisation of a society. Evangelical influence opened up educational opportunities for women in Manipur. Literacy started in the hills with the advent of Christian missionaries who were responsible for reducing the tribal languages into written form by using the Roman script. It was primarily due to the efforts of the Christian Missionaries that the people of the hill area were opened to the benefits of modern education, however limited these might have been (Jayaseelan, 1996, p. 170). Under government patronage the Missions established a network of schools throughout each tribal area. In fact a school was established before a Church in most villages. While there were many government schools at major centres, throughout the tribal area of present Meghalaya, Nagaland, Manipur and Mizoram the responsibility for educational work was entrusted by the Government to the Missions for many years (Downs, 1994, p. 208). Barpujari (1978, p. 384) noted, "If the Missionaries would not have come to the rescue of the British administration by taking over the charge of the education of the tribes, progress of education which was slow in the hills would have been slower still. It will not be an exaggeration to say that Christianity and education developed in the Hills of the North East India like twin sisters".

Initially when the first school was established in 1897 in Ukhrul, by Pettigrew, only boys were enrolled; female were not enrolled to study in the school. Parents were adamant at the idea of sending their daughters to school. It took Pettigrew forty -eight years to succeed in convincing the parents to send their daughters to get education (Serto, 2004, p. 159). The entry of girls' education was recorded for the first time in 1909 (Pettigrew 1897-1922). Girls' education was started by Madame Alice Pettigrew who assisted him in teaching the girls not only how to read and write but teaches them the art of home maintenance, sanitary and cleanliness. Vocational trainings like sewing and knitting, gardening, cultivating, weeding and harvesting, etc were some of the important part of girl's education (Jally, 1989, p. 10). She worked untiringly for fourteen years to introduce girl's education. Mrs. Pettigrew found a way through the dormitory system by introducing night school, paving way for formal education (ibid, p. 151). With the shifting of the American Baptist Mission from Ukhrul to Kangpokpi in 1922-23 many tribes such as the Anals, Kukis, Chiru and Mao got western education (V.Phaning as quoted in Kinthuijinang, 2007, p. 206).

In order to find a possible means of educating girls, she sought the help of the Women Baptist Foreign Society which sent some money and with the amount; students were given scholarship of rupees three per month, enabling the girls to continue their schooling (Ningmasai, 1986, p.1-12) . Dr. Crozier and her wife also assisted in her endeavour for women's education. The arrival of Rev. Rostad and Elle Rostad was a great landmark in the field of women's education in South West Manipur. She started a school for girls in 1931-32, where she personally instructed them in practical subjects. Mrs. Rostad had to leave Imphal after the bombing of Imphal on 10th may, 1942. This was a serious setback towards the progress of girl's education as she was responsible for it under North East India General Mission (NEIGM) and has to close down its school in Churachandpur as the Japanese Army entered Manipur through Tiddim road. Though war came to an end in 1945, it took several years for the Mission to reopen its educational Institution (Jayshree, 2009, p. 157-159).

Prior to the establishment of the Ukhrul Mission and Evangelical School, the government authority had established one lower primary school at Sekmai in 1892 and at Mao in 1893 for the Hill people, and another for the valley people at Tera keithel in 1895 (Administrative Report of Manipur Political Agency,1891-92). In 1899, a girl's school was established at Moirangkhom for the first time in the state.

Only twelve girls were enrolled in the school (Singh, 1967, p. 15-18).

The KuKi-Chin group in the south of Manipur had the provision of educational facilities when the Thadou Kuki Pioneer mission started its ministry in 1910. Later the Thadou Kuki Pioneer Mission was changed into the North East India General mission (NEIGM) when it was transferred to Lakhimpur. Thereby a middle school was established at the mission centre. In 1930, the headquarter was shifted to Manipur (Ningzachin in Serto, 2004, p. 164)

The American Baptist Missionary established an upper primary school at Kangpokpi between 1922-23 and during 1928-29 one Upper primary school was established and another in Ukhrul (Singh 1867, p. 46-47). In May 1930 in Pettigrew's letter to his missionary friend, he mentioned that there were two Mission English Schools with 70 girls and 156 boys on the register, 30 Primary Schools with an enrolment of 150 girls and 408 boys and one K.G. School with 14 girls and 6 boys. These schools other than the schools at Ukhrul and kangpokpi were supported by the villagers out of the Churches fund (Jajo 1990, p. 20). In 1931, the North East India General Mission established one Lower Primary School in Churachandpur and in 1935 a high School for girls' was set up known as Tamphasana girls' High School. Gradually as the number of schools established expanded in the Hills from 1941-42, slowly a handful of girls were enrolled in such schools. There were 59 schools run by the American Baptist Missionary, which enrolled 589 boys and 277 girls. While the North East India General Missionary established 23 schools which enrolled 460 boys and 35 girls in the hill areas of Manipur. After Independence, the numbers of girls enrolled in schools gradually progress. However the percentage of tribal women is still very low compared to that of men.

In the field of education Kuki -Chin -Zo women are left far behind as compared to the male population. Initially when education was introduced, girls were not allowed to attend schooling due to ignorance and poverty. Apart from these drawbacks, there still remains a prejudice against girl's education, although parents are not poor (Jamini, 1989, p. 104). The Kuki-Chin-Zo regarded education for girls as unnecessary and waste of money since once they got married they will belong to other clan. Hence much of the girls in the Kuki-Chin-Zo society girls are often neglected as compared to boys in the matters of education. Besides the question of looking after the household task falls on the daughters so the most common answer regarding their schooling as noted by Chapman and Clarke was, "who would work if the girls were sent to school? When the missionaries persisted, they often replied, "We can't send our daughters to school: she is too useful at home, take my boy."(ibid.7)

Table - 1

Statistical Table Showing Figures of Students in the Hill Schools of the State from the Period 1908-21

YEAR	*BOYS*	*GIRLS*	*TOTAL*
1908-09	195	nil	195
1909-10	147	2	149
1910-11	164	1	165
1911-12	159	1	160
1912-13	111	7	118
1913-14	190	7	197
1914-15	190	7	197
1915-16	70	nil	70
1916-17	40	nil	40
1917-18	29	nil	29
1918-19	94	nil	94
1919-20	79	nil	79
1920-21	416	nil	416

Source: Extract from The Statistical record of The Directorate of Education, Government of Manipur.

The given table above indicates the small number of girls enrolled in schools as compared to the large turn outs of the boys enrolled from 1909-1921. From the period 1911 – 1915 the turnout of girls was comparatively on the rise from 1(one) to 7(seven). But from 1915 0n wards due to the ensuing of the 1st world war and the Kuki Rebellion, girls enrolled were nil, which persisted till 1921.

Table - 2

The table below indicates the percentage of Tribal women literacy, against male literacy according to the 1981, census.

	Persons	*Male*	*Female*
Manipur State	41.99	52.97	30.69
Manipur Central	42.61	54.55	30.50
Manipur South	61.50	72.12	49.71
Manipur East	42.54	51.12	33.27
Manipur West	37.76	47.24	27.99
Tengnoupal District	32.24	39.84	24.22
Manipur North District	26.08	34.53	17.11

Table 2

Literacy rate of Female against male literacy according to the 2001 census is given below:

Name of Scheduled Tribe	*% of Literate*		
	Total	*male*	*female*
Anal	73.9	81.6	66.5
Hmar	79.8	84.3	75.2
Kom	63.9	70.0	57.8
Any Mizo (Lushai) tribes	74.0	79.8	68.8
Maring	53.1	63.4	42.3
Paite	79.0	85.2	72.8
Simte	67.3	76.2	58.3
Thadou	57.1	64.5	49.6
Vaiphei	59.8	67.7	51.7
Zou		61.6	70.2
53.0			
All Scheduled Tribe	65.9	73.2	58.4

Source: Office of the Registrar General, India

The two tables indicate the slow rise of women's education, and the gradual narrowing down of disparity between the two sexes. Although the target of cent per cent of girls education has yet to be achieved, it is in the positive trends as compared from 1998 census to 2001. The two tables clearly outlined the disparity of boys and girls enrolled in schools. Indicating that education among girls is comparatively low as against boys. The two tables outline the fact that education plays a dominant role if women's status is to be elevated among the Kuki-Chin-Zo community.

Western education has to a large degree brought a change in the status and role of women on the one hand and on the other hand it has remained static, without doubt tribal women enjoy comparatively more freedom and less devoid of many constraints, however and somewhere they stand in between. Though tribal norms are somewhat liberal to womanhood, but yet again they are the least influenced by formal legislation. The emergence of women from the constricting bondage of prejudice is accorded to education; as more and more girls are enrolled in schools and colleges. It would today be absurd if a girl on ground of her gender be forbidden to attend school. But again a large number of women are not enrolled in higher education and other vocational and technical institutions in the rural areas. In the course of my field work I have come across instances where many girls sacrificed their higher studies, due to poverty so that their brothers could be sent to school, they are the last in the draw to receive education. They have to make way so that their brothers could be sent to school. Since the traditional and customary laws regarding men as the head and inheritor of clan lineage is deeply entrench in the social and individual psyche, of the people, man and woman within the family choose the boy child over the girl child.

VI. Glimpses of Kuki-Chin -Zo women as exemplary model

Despite the constraints of customary laws which curtailed and infringe the rights of women, the Kuki-Chin-Mizo women have slowly emerged from their cocoon of household duties with the access to education. Regardless of the prejudices against them, they have shown their mettle in the socio-economic and political field, displaying incredible feats in rising up against the numerous hurdles that traditions and customs had placed on her.

Below is a brief narrative of some remarkable women who has made a tremendous impact in the lives of the Kuki-Chin-Mizo people's outlook and had impacted the society towards a broader perspective. They have broken the notion of domesticity, challenging the narrow and pervasive outlook of men. These women although they have become a household name remain obscure due to the fact that their contributions have not been acknowledged as equally important as that of men.

Traditionally among the Kuki-Chin-Zomi people women cannot assume the post of chief ship; when a chief died, and if the son to succeed him is still a minor the next kin relatives such as the uncles will assume the post of chief as a regent until the minor son has come of age. Another provision is that the wife can also act as the regent; but generally the wife is superseded by the next kin of family. Woman assuming the role of political head has been a rarity. Since men do not want to be dictated by women as they believed that the latter are less intelligent in their view, and less knowledgeable in administrating the customary laws, therefore women are unfit to devote their time to the judgement passing as they are always busy in their household or fieldworks. Hence women's participation in social and political affairs is drastically curtailed in the Kuki-Chin-Zo society. There is hardly any women elected in the Village assembly due to the same reason forwarded by the men, meanwhile women on their part are also less conscious and interested in the political affairs.

Recently, after conversion to Christianity and introduction of western education, modern employment more women have prompted to take an interest in their role not merely as a wife but more of that of an equal partners, more and more women have decided to seize the role of a Chief in the name of the son as regent. They have become less daunted in grasping the mantle of leadership. Daughters educated has also initiated their rights to govern the village These women has overcome numerous hardship against the tides of opposition from their kinsmen and rivals in the maintenance of the daily administration of the village, and the day to day activities. It would not be an exaggeration to say that their achievements when compared to that of men are far more laudable, their sense of justice, diplomacy, and fairness, determination and knowledge of customary laws unparalleled.

For a society which have never permitted women in political affairs, administrative and sports, the feats of some of these women are a force to reckoned with, they have achieved what a normal man cannot achieve; breaking the age old traditional myths that 'women are unfit to rule or lead'. Unfortunately credit has never been in their favour; rather, the chauvinistic men at all cost often derided them with derogatory names such as '*numei jummoh*' (uncouth women).

Below is the achievement of some women who has broken the conservative notion that a women is meant to only look after the domestic affairs, thereby creating a niche for the future generation of women leaders.

(a) Emergence of Kuki-Chin-Zo women as Chief of village

The twentieth Century has witness more and more women taking up the position of a Chief as compared to the nineteenth century. This trend has rapidly been on the rise since the introduction of education. In the wake of such development, taking the daunting task of responsibility as a chief is no small feat. Some notable lady chiefs worth mentioning in Manipur is: Behiang *Haosapi,* of Churachandpur district, Saivom *Haosapi* of Saivom village in Tengnoupal district, Chassad *Haosapi* of Chassad village in Ukhrul district and Wakan *Haosapi* of Wakan village in Sadar Hills. Among these women the essay would like to include a short profile of lady chief of Wakan. Mrs. Lamkhoneng Haokip the eldest daughter of Singkhokhai and Domkholhing, of Maokot Village, Ukhrul district.

Married to Mr. (L) Letsei Haokip, Chief of Wakan, Sadar Hills studied till 9th standard until she got married in the year 1967. Her husband died at an early age leaving behind three minor sons and two young daughters. After her husband's dead she assumes the chief ship of Wakan village, as she narrated, '*when I first went to Wakan village to assume my position as the head of the village there were only a few houses, the condition of the villagers was pathetic, with no jeep able road, I had to journey for 3 to 4 kms on foot to reach the village, the village was so undeveloped that often I despair, but I took it upon myself to bring changes ; I ran from office to office, knocking the doors of every development departments to implement the necessary measures to transform my husband's village; some look down upon me; some snub me while others jeer behind my back; but I was undeterred. Today, my effort has been rewarded, the number of houses has increased and the condition of the people has improved since my first days*'. Her tale is a story of much hardship. Added to this her next kin of family always tried to undermine her position and decision. However she stood stoically and faced the ordeals, proving to her village that though she might be a woman, she is fit to rule as efficiently as men can. Slowly she gains the respect of her village people and through her she has established a government Lower primary school, Anganwadi centre, constructed a jeep able road, community hall. Besides looking after her children's need and sending them outside the state for schooling, she as a head of the Village performs the duty of a ruler, administrator etc. She is also one of the Women leaders of the Kuki Baptist Convention who has work tirelessly for the widows. In the year 1984-86 she was nominated as the recording Secretary of Women Department of KBC, and later in 1987 she was appointed as the President of the Women Department of KBC for two terms till 2000, she was appointed as the member of the KBC, Finance and property Committee. Through her initiative KBC Women fellowship was held from 1988 to 1993. Through her insistence the first Widow Camp was organised in 1991, at Chassad in Ukhrul District, since then annually Widow Camp has been organised to uplift and boost the morale of the widow. Although her son has now taken over the role of Chiefship much of the work had been carried out through this remarkable woman, Wakan Village has developed today through the efforts of her. Though she has decided to retire, she is still very much present and the de facto in making sure that the functioning and running of the village is carried out smoothly and fairly.

(b) Emergence of women in Politics

Women's participation in mainstream political activity has important implications for the governance in any country. In most parties, the women members are by and large thin on the ground if not invisible in the actual decision making bodies and rarely influence the more significant party politics. Most often, indeed they are relegated to the women's wing" of the party, and rarely made to concentrate on what are seen as specifically " women issues' such as dowry and rape cases, and occasionally on more general concerns like price rise which are seen to affect especially 'housewives'. Despite all this, only the foolhardy would suggest that women are unimportant in Indian politics today (frontline, 1999). Loni Lovenduski (2005, p. 16)opines that " as social patterns have changed, it has become easier to agree that women have rights as citizens that entitles them to participate in government, where those interests can be defended and advanced."

Kuki-Chin-Zo women's participation in politics is quite a paradox. In fact when compare to other Non-kuki tribes in Manipur such as the Nagas, they are more politically represented. All through the political history of the Kukis since 1960s, Kuki-Chin-Zo women have entered the arena of politics and contested elections. But this does not imply that they are not underrepresented. The pattern of underrepresentation persisted despite women's growing achievements in education, work and other areas of public life and despite growing numbers of qualified numbers of qualified women seeking political office. When a woman contests election she has less chance of winning since a number of factors act as hindrance. One main factor is the general tendency to view women as inefficient and incapable to handle the intricacy of politics. Due to such factors most women are less inclined to enter into politics.

Kazuki Iwanaga (2008, p. 4) argues that in the absence of facilitators the progress of women's achievement in politics will not take place or be slow, uneven or incremental at best. Facilitators can remove or reduce barriers that hinder women's political participation. They can broadly be grouped into three major categories; institutional, contextual and individually oriented facilitators. Mrs.Lhingjaneng Gangte was the first to be nominated in the legislative Assembly and Ms. Kim Gangte became the first women to be elected as Member of Parliament for Hill district, while Mrs. Nemcha Kipgen became the first women to contest election and won the seat as MLA.

(i) Mrs. Lhingjaneng Sitlhou-Gangte

Born on 18th December, 1938, at Tamenglong Head Quarter of Manipur West District, is the daughter of Jamkithang Sitlhou and Tingjahat belonging to the royal family of Thongdut state of Burma, presently the granddaughter of Maharaja of Thongdut State of Burma. Coming from a highly reputed family; she was one of the earliest Kuki-Chin-Zomi girls to be educated. She passed her matriculation examination from Tamphasana Girls High School in Imphal in 1955. In the year 1957 she completed her Intermediaries of Arts from Dhanamajuri College, and also bachelors of Arts from the same college in 1965. She is married to (L) T.S.Gangte, Director of Education in Manipur. Her interest and specialisation is in Social Work. She became the first woman to be appointed as a member of the Manipur Legislative Assembly for two terms from 1962-69. She was appointed as the President of the Tribal Advisory Committee by the Government of Manipur. Her other path breaking portfolios includes: advisory of the Education Advisory Board, Government of Manipur, Founder member of the Board of the Women's Bank (Imphal). She was also the Vice-president of All Manipur Tribal Women's Association. She is the only Tribal women to receive the Padmashri Award in 1875 by the Government of India in the field of Social Welfare during the Prime Ministership of (L) Indira Gandhi. She has also been selected as the women of the year in 1997 by ABI, USA. Her accolades and achievements are far ranging and wide, yet for all her achievement she has remain a silent figure today among the Kuki Society.

(ii) Ms. Kim Gangte

She is not only the first Kuki-Chin-Zo women to have triumph in the field of politics as member of Rajya Sabha(MP) but a model who successfully represent the tribal women of Manipur. Her achievement in politics is a boost for women, which has always been regarded as a monopoly of men. Her passion to work for the upliftment and empowerment of women and Human Rights issue motivated her to resign her job as a lecturer in Manipur University. She first contests the election in 1996 as an Independent candidate. However the fact that she was a woman was one of the reasons that act as a hurdle to her winning the election. Undeterred she continued her social work on Human Rights issue and finally her hard work and determination led her to win the election of 1998 as CPI candidate. Although she contested again in the subsequent elections of 1999 and 2004, she was unable to come out victorious. Presently she is the President of the Trinamool Congress Party in Manipur.

(iii) Mrs. Nemcha Kipgen

Her father died in the early years of her childhood and she and her two brothers were singlehandedly brought up by their widowed mother. Despite being a widow, her mother insisted that her only daughter should get access to education as par with her two brothers. This decision was objected by her uncle's whose belief was that a girl need not get any form of schooling. This was because of the patriarchal mentality among the Kuki-Chin Zo people that it was rather a waste of money and time to spend money on girls' education. Instead it would be much more profitable if a girl is taught the skill of weaving, cooking, and helping in the household chores as one day she would be married to another family, or tribe.

Despite criticism the mother believed that education would uplift her daughter from living a life of hardship and poverty. To enable her children to access schooling she work hard by toiling in the fields of her farm land and during the offseason sold rice pancakes in the bazaar. Due to her widowed mother's effort she completed her matriculate in Shillong and was immediately sent for a nursing training at Tripura Mission Nursing Institute in 1983 and hence completed her GNMS. As soon as she completed her GNMS (General Nursing of Medical Science) training she got a job at JNIMS (Jawaharlal Nehru Institute of Medical Science, Porompat) but as she was not satisfied with the manner of work, she quit her job and for a year open a pharmacy centre at Kangpokpi, eventually she landed a position in AIIMS (All India Institute of Medical Science) on July, 1991 and became the first Kuki women to become a staff nurse in AIIMS, which was a remarkable feat in those days. She got married in the year 1996. Though married she juggle her family life and her career efficiently from Delhi and sired a daughter and recently she adopted a son. From there on her career spiral upwards and she was appointed as the superintendent before she decided to venture into the field of politics. In the recent General Assembly of 2012, she contested the election amidst much competition and furore against three male competitors from Trinamool and Congress I.

Despite being a women, this did not prevent her from implementing numerous programmes for the upliftment of her society especially women. The first task which she deem of importance was providence of education to girls and boys alike in the far flung areas , specially the remote areas and the poor rural masses in her constituency, for she firmly believes that education was the only means of eradicating poverty and bringing empowerment to the downtrodden women whom the society fails to acknowledge despite their hard work and economic contribution, for the term, ' *numei*'(women) was often construed as a derogatory and inferior status, and a men in order to silent her would simply used such phrase as.' *Numei kithip in!*'(Women be quiet) or '*numei mila a thu kisei ding ham*? (How dare a mere women speak in public gatherings)' and *'numei in hou in a pulpit a loh thei louding ahi'* (women should not be allow to speak in the pulpit) again some are of the opinion that *'numei pulpit a Pathen thu asei kangai nom poi'* which literally 'It is absurd to listen to women preaching in the Church'. She felt that all communities should work together. A husband and a wife is part and parcel towards achieving these goals. She states that, 'When a husband looks down upon a women as inferior, that society could not progress'. For the development of the society it is imperative that a man should acknowledge the women's contribution and allow her to take much more initiative in the socio-cultural and political field. When the society is educated than the men would become aware of the need for changing much of the prevailing customary rights such as inheritance law, and thereby paving the way for socio-economic, political and religious prosperity and development in the Kuki -Chin -Zo society'

(c) Emergence of Woman as Ordained Minister:

Religion is a powerful agency in society and performs many important social functions. Religious institutions have until recently, been the most powerful agents and agencies of justice and injustice. They are arbiter of right and wrong, when they demonstrate prejudice of any kind, they give unstated acquiescence for everyone else to do it. Women who challenged the religious status quo had to cope, only with culture and tradition, 'but with the will of God' (Fiedler, p. xi). "The misfortune is compounded by the fact that repressing the contribution of women has been a deprivation of those very societies and cultures that have perpetrated this un wisdom and injustice" (Paludi & Coates, 2011, p. 134). Women of today who have a vision and vocation of ministry as women in religious leadership strongly wish a place at the table where the decisions are made for the future of women in the Church (ibid, p.135). One such woman who has strongly advocated equality of men and women in the religious institution is Mrs. (Rev) Dr. Kim Vaiphei, who has strongly voice her opinion against prejudice and discrimination meted out to women in Church. She is the foremost women among the Kuki-Chin-Zo women to have been ordained. She was ordained on 13th February 1997 by the Kuki Baptist Convention Assembly at United Sapermeina Baptist Convention. Prior to her ordination she was appointed as Women Secretary for seven to ten years respectively. She was then appointed to be the first women Pastor at KBC Centre Church, Imphal West on 1st Feb, 2001. Later, she was appointed as a Parish pastor supervising over 23 local churches in Sapermeina area having 9 local churches and One fellowship Church. She is one of the pioneer women to have declared openly in the church congregation, decrying the low position and injustices that woman has been forced to occupy. Prior to her being ordained, women has were debarred from occupying the Pulpit and preach the gospel, a woman can only preach in the women's department which is a separate department created solely for the women's religious growth and development. As Mrs Lhingneikim[7] commented, "I remembered how once we women were not allowed to stand in the pulpit and preach the gospel, nor be elected as the members of the deacon boards excepting women's department representation. It is only through her tenaciousness and boldness in affirming for women to have an equal status in the Church that today, women are allowed to freely preach the gospel among the Sunday gatherings.

Although the Kuki Baptist Convention (KBC), the church which ordained Mrs. Kim Vaiphei as the first pastor among the Kuki-Chin-Zo was acknowledged to be a champion of women's equal rights in the Church, ironically later she became the victim of male's bias within the same church. Though, she was the next in line for the post of president in terms of seniority and qualification, she was denied the chances to become the President of KBC, on flimsy grounds. This resulted in her breaking bond with the church. Had she not been a woman, the church members would not have discriminated her the way they did. Interestingly, a lot of the women try to find fault with her feministic attitude taking sides with the opinion of the men. While the men out rightly condemn her without any logical justification as someone who goes against the Christian teaching, the women were a silent spectator. The injustice meted to her on ground of being a woman, remain obscure and her frailties were exposed to demerit her.

(d) Kuki Women as a Social Activist

Across the social sciences as well as in history, women's contribution have been ignored, underestimated, or marginalised. Where women appear in history of the disciplines at all, they typically are featured as followers rather than leaders; their work is associated with the practice rather than theory; their ideas are devalued simply because they are ideas propounded by women. Rarely are women portrayed as original thinkers (Croco, 1999, p. 8). The essay has chosen two women, Miss Hevah and Miss. Lalam respectively, whose activities at a time when women's capacity was considered limited and resistance to women's intellectual leadership was pervasive among Kuki-Chin-Zo society. Ms. Hevah Haokip, Founder member of Kuki Women Organisation was actively involved in the inception of the Kuki Women Union, in the wake of the Naga-Kuki ethnic conflict, 1992-1993. The need for a women union body to help not merely in relief work but to be an organisation that would do something substantial for the hapless widows, women and children and the community in times of crisis was felt by a group of women. However no concrete idea could take place. It was under the initiative of women such as Hevah Haokip of Motbung, a law student, Mrs. Kimkhoneng, sister of Chief of Motbung and Mrs. Neikim and many others that the Kuki Women Union first materialise under a banyan tree at Motbung. According to Hevah Haokip, "since I was the only educated women, I was nominated as the Secretary, and hence the task of making a letter head, seals, typing memorandum fell on me. When we realise the pathetic attitude adopted by the State government, the Kuki MLAs, the political leaders of different association in the wake of this ethnic-conflict, these few women unanimously decided to take matters in their own hands; they resolved that they should set out to the capital state of India to redress the sufferings of our people to the Prime Minister'. On 6th October of the year 1993, they reached Delhi and finally met the Prime Minister Narasimha Rao, on 15th October. They submitted a memorandum along with the pictures of the Joupi massacre (Joupi is the name of the village in which many Kukis were killed during the Kuki-Naga clash in the 1990s). It was here that Mrs. Neikim gave a heart rendering soulful cry pounding her chest and wailing against the injustices, negligence and indifference attitude towards the Kukis of Manipur by the State and the centre, which made a tremendous impact'. Hearing the heinous crime committed and the pathetic condition of the State Governments failure to bring out a lasting solution, the PM underlined the memorandum submitted and immediately General Officer Commanding (GOC) 57th Brigade Mountain was dispatch to take stock of the matters at Motbung. So on December of the year 1993, the Kuki Women Union was formally established, with Neikim as executive member and Hevah nominated as the president from 1993 -2008. The formation of KWU (Kuki Women Union) was acknowledged by Kuki Inpi Manipur (KIM) in all areas of the Kukis from village to village. The head quarter of Kuki women Union was later shifted from Motbung to Churachandpur district.

Another woman who has endeavour to set up a Non-governmental organisation (NGO) regarded as a man's domain among the Kuki-Chin-Zo society is Ms Helam Haokip eldest daughter of Holjam and Lamkhongai Haokip of Urangpat, Saikul Division of Manipur is the founder and CEO of IRMA (Integrated Rural Management Association) in 2005. She completed her Master's of Science at Manipur University and after working part-time in different NGOs of Manipur, decided to set up her own NGO. She commented, "Since coming from a poor family my parents did not have the resources or the means to pay rupees fifty-thousand in those days for the post of supervisor, I decide to strike out on my own. As a young girl I had been actively involved in the society and had taken a keen interest in uplifting the status of women". In her effort to set up an NGO office she was assisted by her colleges who contributed book shelves, tables and chairs and a sum of rupees two thousand. Though her financial resources were limited she was not disheartened. Being socially inclined towards improving the lot of the underprivileged people among the Kuki-Chin-Zo community, especially women she link up with Nehru Yuva Kendra and initiated the formation of SHG in her village, the women were imparted Capacity building and skill development. These women were trained on the art of producing soaps and dish washing liquid based on environmentally safe components. Her training and workshop was met with a success and later the DRDA financial support she venture towards pocket mobilisation and formed another organisation called 'Women in governance' among like minded NGOs in different districts of Manipur in the hill areas, to ensure political empowerment. Her main aim and objective are ensuring participation of women in decision making such as Village Assembly, to stop violence against women, impart awareness among both men and women towards gender equality. She has participated in quite a number of international and cultural exchanges in foreign countries like Philipines, Bangkok, Uganda, Geneva and New York.

(e) Emerging trends of entrepreneurship

The number of Kuki-Chin-Zo women entering small scale entrepreneur work has increased significantly. They make a crucial role in the economic growth and development of local, regional and national economies. Yet despite their increasing numbers they have received little attention from academics into their experiences. In terms of business ownership there appears to be a great deal of consensus around the barriers that women face around the globe. Poor access to finance, home/work conflict, role overload, lack of business experience, lack of relevant skills and exclusion from men's business network are consistently cited as barriers to business ownership. Despite this, women continue to be successful perhaps because for many business ownership is viewed as a survival strategy that provides them with a personal and economic freedom they cannot gain through traditional forms of work (Fielden & Davidson 2010: 7).

Ms. Zoumuan Thangjom is another woman in the field of fashion who has paves a way for infusing new trends in clothing. She was one of the earliest and lone Kuki-chin Zo women whose love for fashion has today make a trend setting impact amongst the youths of Kuki-Chin-Zo society. She completed her Fashion designing Course at International Women's Polytechnic, Delhi in 1998. She was won numerous awards in the National Kut Competition for best designing. She not only designs but trained young girls, she has a number of employees working in her shop. She is the first among the Kuki-chin-Zo women to have formally undergone a designing course and thus decides opening her own shop. She not only employ a number of girls but also impart training in stitching and tailoring. Through her many unemployed girls had been able to acquire the skill of tailoring, thereby enabling them to earn their livelihood and support their families. Because of her success many parents who once has look upon fashion designing with disdain regarded it as economically beneficial form of financial stability.

(f) Emergence in Sports

Societal constraints on women's involvement in sports are reinforced in sports itself. Institutionalised sport is strongly masculine in its culture and organisation, itself; compared to men women hold fewer achievements in sports. Media coverage of sports has been reinforces its masculine image and is highly influential in promoting a view of sports that limits its appeal to women. The overriding message was 'real sports was not for real women'. (Frank &Collins 2003:104) This concept has always dominated the perspective of men as a result we find less number of women dominating the field of sports; their talents have always been subdued.

One finds that although women football, or volleyball are often played in the village tournaments, these women were included merely for the sake of amusement; no real efforts have been undertaken to sponsor or instil among the women the value of sportsmanship nor any formal training or institution have been taken up by the leaders and social workers for the inclusion of women in the field of sports. Those few women who have made a name for themselves have been entirely due to their tenacity and passion for sports, overriding parent's disapproval. Whatever clubs that existed among the Kuki-Chin-Zomi society are solely male club such as the Kuki Sporting Union, where only boys are the members, none so far had yet taken any initiative in establishing a women's club for the benefit of talented girls.

Many young girls have participated in the fields of different arenas of sports , representing their college and state in the national level, but yet none of them have been lauded for their achievements and thus their career has remain stunted before it could blossom; quite untraceable and unnamed, for the society deemed it as . Even Magnificent Boxing Champion, MC.Mary Kom, five time world champion has remarked,'my father was furious when I took to boxing- a taboo for women so also football is regarded as a men's sports. I have decided to include a young women named Melody Haokip, whose participation in women's Football as a member of Eastern Sporting Club has made success, but whose achievements have not been by and large largely acknowledge by the Kuki-Chin-zomi community; whose potential in scaling the world of sports is something one looks forward, given the right appreciation and sponsorship by the community. Her achievement has shown that if women's skill in sports is hone suitably, they too can achieve marvellous feats and laurels.

Miss Melody Phaljaneng Haokip hails from Y.Thingkangphai village, Sugnu area of Chandel district in Manipur. Born on 14th January of the year 1985, she hails from a simple family. Fortunately, her parents have always backed her in her passion for football. As a young girl, she was more of a tomboy who loves outdoor sports, playing with young boys rather than girls. Although she has often played in numerous village tournaments, clubs and associations, her career in football was finally given a fillip when she represented Manipur Football Women's Team in the 32nd National Games from 13th to 22nd December, 2002 at Hyderabad and her team won the Trophy of the women's final Match between Manipur and playing for Eastern Sporting Cub, Women's Football. She participated in the AFC U-19, Women's Championship, from 16th March to 14th April 2002 at Goa, and successfully completed a football Camp for U-19, Women's Team at Nehru Stadium, Fatoorda in Goa, which was organized by the National Olympic Committee for Germany and Deutchen Auswartigen Amt. along with the All India Football Federation. Presently, she is women police constable, and she joined her service since 2007 and remains a Coach for Eastern sporting Union in Manipur.

Conclusion: The aftermath

Though the society may not have acknowledged their contribution, these women were the harbinger of change. Their initial hardship in overcoming the numerous hurdles was no less worth mentioning. Consequently despite the fact that women constitute half of the electorates, Kuki-Chin-Women is grossly under presented in the state policy making. Presently only one scheduled Tribe women represented as opposition party in the Legislative Assembly Men refused to acknowledge them and as much as possible suppress them politically, socially and religiously. The obstacles to women's empowerment in the socio-economic, religious and political fields are varied and it maybe structural, institutional, political and cultural factors. Cultural including traditional attitudes towards women leaders, has a significant influence as it works as a control mechanism for social, political and economic institutions. In a society where the public are of the opinion that men made better leaders that women, relatively low proportions of women are forthcoming to contest for elections; where women have not been inducted in the village councils as members, it remains a difficult tasks for women to break the age old traditional attitude that women are best suited to household work and if seeking for government jobs, the teaching profession or white collar jobs are the best options.

The question then is if the tendency to have a narrow outlook over certain jobs, position persists, why are parents willing to send their daughters outside of the State to work in companies and other allied jobs which are viewed as unfavourable and unsuitable for women. The most probable answer is for economic benefits only, as the traditional agricultural means of production have become obsolete in these ever changing modern scenario; options and means of using women as a means of securing economic welfare have preceded the attitude of men. It can thus be acknowledged that prejudice that existed among the Kuki-Chin-Zo women is well shielded behind a screen of social and economic mobility. The hidden facets of bias are too deeply engrained in the minds of the people that it has been but a slow and difficult process for the women to truly be empowered in the true sense of the term. For an outsider, the Kuki-Chin-Zo women seem to enjoy a lot of social and cultural freedom without any restrictions. However, there is a veil of discrimination which is so elusively hidden for the outsider to discern clearly. To conclude as Sweetman (2000, p. 5)acknowledge, "education cannot be assumed to lead women attaining leadership positions in parliament, good quality education does play a role in building women's capacity to become leaders in society. Education is needed so that it encourages independent, critical thought, fosters self-confidence, and provides young girls with a vision of what they might become."

References

1. A Thadou-Kuki divorce proceedings initiated on 23th Feb. 2010 at Haokip -Veng, Imphal East, Manipur

2. An observation made on the tales narrated during my childhood days of my aunt and my mother who both belong to the clan beside the Haokip clan.

3. See TS.Gangte's: The Kukis, William Shaw': The Thadou Kukis, Shakespeare's The Lushai Kuki Clans.

4. Manipur Land Revenue and Land Reforms Act , 1960 was enacted by the Parliament to consolidate and amend the law relating to land revenue in the state of Manipur and to provide certain measures of Land reform. Before the enactment of the State land laws, the Assam Land & Revenue regulation Act, 1886 was applied to Manipur by a State Durbar Resolution, The MLR & LR Act, 1960 intends to bring about uniformity in distribution of land throughout the State. However, section 2 of the Act says, "It extends to the whole of the State of Manipur except the hill areas thereof."

5. According to the Hindu Succession Act of 1956, daughters of a "Hindu" male dying interstate (i.e without leaving a will) were equal inheritors along with sons of only their father's separate property.

6. Interviewed of Mrs. Themneilhing on Feb.2011 as part of Microfinance Socio-Economic Impact Analysis for WSDS (Weaker Section Development Society) at Motbung, Manipur

7. Interviewed of Mrs. Lhingneikim, on 23th May 2013, A Former Kuki Baptist Church, Women Society Treasure at Haokip-Veng, Imphal, Manipur

BOOKS

1. BARPUJARI, S.K. (1978) Educational Development in the Hills of North east India: A general Background. Ed. In: *Social and Economic Profile of North East India,* Delhi: Scholar Publishing House.

2. BOUTEN, JACOB. *(1922)Mary Wollstonecraft and the Beginning of Female Emancipation In France and England,* Amsterdam: H.J. Paris V/H Firma A. H. Kruypt.

3. CAREY, S. BERTRAM & TUCK, H. N. TUCK. (1932), *The Chin Hills,* vol.1 Tribal Institute of Aizawl.

4. CAPTAIN KHUPZA THANG. (1974) *Zo Suanh Khang Simna Laibu* (Genealogy of the Zo (Chin) Race of Burma, Tedim.

5. CHAPMAN, E & CLARKE, M. (1968) *Mizo Miracle,* Madras: Madras Christian Literature Society

6. DEVI, JAMINI. (1989) *Education in Manipur,* Imphal : Rai Pravina Brothers

7. DEVI, JAYSHREE NGANGOM. (2009), History of Women's Education in Manipur upto 1947, Unpublished Ph.D. Thesis, Dept. of History, Manipur University.
8. DOWNS, S., FREDERICK. (1994) *Essays on Christianity in North India,*New Delhi: Indus Publishing Company.
9. FERNANDES, WALTER & BARBORA, SANJAY. (2002) *Changing Woman Status In India: Focus On The North East,* Guwahati: North Eastern Research Institute
10. FERNANDES., WALTER & BHARAL. *Gita, Customary Law-Formal law Interface: Impact on Tribal* Culture in: T.N.Subbha, Joseph Puthenpurackal & Shaji Joseph Puykunnel,(2008), *Christianity and Change in North east India,* eds. New Delhi: Concept Publishing Company.
11. FIELDEN, L.,SANDRA, DAVIDSON, J., MARLYA. (2010), International research handbook on Successful A women Entrepreneurs, ed.UK: Eward Edgar Publishing Limited.
12. GANGTE, T.S. (1993) *The Kukis of Manipur- A Historical Analysis,* Delhi: Gyan Publishing House.
13. GOSWAMI, TARUN. (1985) *Kuki Life and Lore,* Haflong: North Cachar Hills District
14. HAOBAM, SHYAMSUNDAR. (1998) *Arts and Crafts of Manipur, In: Sanajoaba, Naorem (ed.) Manipur-Past and Present, Vol.3, New Delhi: A* Mittal Publication
15. HONPI, NENGZA CHIN. (1983) *An Autograph Anecdote.*
16. JAYASEELAN, L. (1996) *Impact of Mission Movements,* New Delhi :Scholar Publishing House (P) Ltd.
17. ROBERT, REID. (1893) *Chin-Lushai land,* Calcutta: Aizawl Tribal Research Institute.
18. COL. SHAKESPEARE, J. (1912) *The Lushai Kuki Clans, London:* Macmillan & Co. Ltd.
19. JEUTI BAROOAH. *Property and Women's Inheritance Rights in The Tribal Areas of The North east* In: Walter Fernandez and Sanjay Barbora (2002) *Changing Women's Status In India,*Guwahati: North eastern Social Research Centre.
20. KIPGEN, G., TINGNEICHONG. (2010)*Women's Role in the 20th Century, Manipur- A Historical Study,* Delhi: Kalpaz Publication.
21. KHUP ZA, GOU. (2008) *Zo Chronicles,* New Delhi: A Mittal Publication.
22. LEHMAN, FREDERICK, K. (1963) *Structure of the Chin Society,* Illinios: Illinois University Press.

23. LUCE, PROF., G.H. (1956) *Phases of Pre-pagan Burma,* London: Oxford Press

24. MAREMMEI, KINTHUIJINANG. (2007) *Ethno History of Chiru Tribe of Manipur,* Ph.D. Thesis, Manipur University.

25. MANGOLJAO SINGH, TH. (1965,1985) *Western education in Manipur,* Vol.1,Imphal

26. NEWLAND, A.G.E. (1894) *The Images of War: Services in the Chin Hills,* Calcutta: Thacker and Spink.

27. NINGMASAI, S. (1968) *Tangkhul Naga Baptist Church Women History,* Ukhrul.

28. PHAYRE, SIR ARTHUR (1883) *History of Burma,* London, Trubner & Co., Ludgate Hill.

29. REID, S.A. (1893) *Chin Lushai Land,* Aizawl Calcutta : Aizawl Tribal Institute

30. ROBERT REID (1893) *Chin-Lushai land,* Calcutta: Aizawl Tribal Research Institute.

31. JALLY, R.R. (1989) The Baptist Church In Manipur in: Serto, Manilei(2004), *Education and Social Change Among the Kom Tribe of Manipur,* Ph.D. thesis, Manipur University.

32. SCOTT J., JAMES (2010) *The art of Not Being Governed,* New Delhi: Orient Black Swan(p) Ltd.

33. SCOTT, SIR J. GEORGE (1932) *Burma and Beyond,* London: Grayson and Grayson.

34. HAOKIP, SEILEN (2010) *Rhetorics of Kuki nationalism: A Treatise,*New Delhi: Lustra Print.

35. SERTO, MANILEI (2004) *Education and Social Change of The Kom Tribe of Manipur,* Manipur University: Unpublished Ph. D. Thesis, Department of Education.

36. SOPPITT, C. A. (1976) A *Short account of The Kuki-Lushai Tribes of the North East Frontier,* Firma-KLM Pvt. Ltd. Meghalaya

37. SWEETMAN, CAROLINE (2000) *Women and leadership,* Oxfam international, Oxford, UK.

38. THANGKHANGIN, S. (1979) "Why must we be called Zomis?" in Zomi Today, Zomi Press, Churachandpur.

39. THANG KHAW KHAI (1955) *Zo Khang Simna Laibu,(Genealogy of the Zo)*

40. VUMSON (1986) ZO History, Aizawl.

41. VUMKHOHAO, Profile of A Burma Frontier Man, Indonesi: Kilatmatdju Press.

42. PETTIGREW, WILLIAM. Twenty Five years Mission, 1897-1922,in Ukhrul Mission School, Ukhrul

43. WOODtHORPE, R.G. (1983) *The Lushai Expedition*, 1871-72, Delhi: Spectrum Publication, Delhi.

Online sources

1. Allport, Gordon (1954), The Nature of prejudice, Cambridge, M.A. Addison-Wesley. Viewed on 18th May,2013 (http://www.amazon.com)

2. Beauvoir, de, Simone(2012) Knof Doublesday Publishing Group, Viewed on 28th May, 2013 (Http: www.Free ebooks.net./category/multicultural-and-gender-studies/4)

3. Bouten., Jacob, (1922)Mary Wollstonecraft and the Beginning of Female Emancipation In France and England, H.J. Paris V/H Firma A. H. Kruypt, Amsterdam, viewed on 25th May,2013(http://www.Free ebooks. net/category/multicultural-and-gender-studies/3)

4. Brown, Rupert (2010) Prejudice and Discrimination, USA: Wiley-Blackwell Publishing House. Viewed on 29th April, 2013,:(http://www.books.google.com.)

5. Sniderman, M.Paul & Hagerndoorn, Louk (2007) when Ways of Life Collide, Princeton University Press, United Kingdom. Viewed on 5th June, 2013 (http: www.books.google.co.)

6. Fielden, L.,Sandra, Davidson,J., Marlya eds.(2010), International research handbook on Successful A women Entrepreneurs, Edward Edgar Publishing Limited, U.K. Viewed on 15th June, 2013(http://www.books.google.com.)

7. Gordon, A. Laurie & Glick, A. Peter. (2008), The Social Psychology of gender: How Power and Intimacy Shape Gender relations, New York: Guilford Publication. Viewed on 25th April, 2013 (http://www.books.google.com)

8. Halloway A. Paul, (2009) coping with Prejudice: 1Peter In Social Psychology Perspective, Germany: Mohr Seibeck. Viewed on 28th April (http://www.books.google.com)

9. Iwanagi ,Kazunagi (2009) Women's Political participation and representation in Asia: Obstacles and Challenges, Nordic Institute of Asian Studies, Norway. Viewed on 9th June,2013 (http://www.books. google.com)

10. Lovenduski, Loni (2005) Feminizing Politics, Polity press, UK, viewed on 12th June, 2013(Http://www.books.google.co.in.)

11. O., Crocco, Davis, O.L., Jr.(1999) Sending the Future to their will: Civic Women, Social Education and Democracy, eds. Rouman &

Little field Publishers, INC, USA. Viewed on 13th June, 2013 (Http://books.google.co.in)

12. Paludi, Michelle, Antoinette (2011) Women as Transformational leader,: From Grassroots to Global Interests, vol.!,. Viewed on 13th July, 2013 (http:// www.books.google.co.in)
13. Pelinka, Anton, Bischof, and Karin Stogner (2009) *Handbook of Prejudice*, ed. Viewed on 1st June ,2013, 2013 (http:// www. Books. google. Co. in.)
14. Sweetman, Caroline (2000) *Women and leadership*, Oxfam international, Oxford, UK, Viewed on 28th May,2013 (http: www./ /books.google.com)
15. Tess Kay, *Women Sports and Social Exclusion*, In: Michael, F. Collins &Frank (2003) *Sports and Social Exclusion*, London: Rout ledge. Viewed on 28th May,2013 (http://www.books.google.com)
16. Whitley, E., Bernard Jr. & Kite E. Mary (2010), *The Psychology of Prejudice and Discrimination*, 2nd ed. Wardsworth Cengage Learning,USA. Viewed on 30th April, 2013 (http:// www.books.google.com)

Interviewed

1. Mrs. Hevah Haokip, leading founder member of Kuki Women Union on 20th April, 2012 at Motbung, Manipur
2. Miss Helam haokip, Founder of IRMA(Integrated Rural management Association) on 28th April.2013, at her Office in Chassad Avenue, Imphal, Manipur
3. Mrs. Kim Vaiphei Haokip interviewed on 12th Oct. 2012 at Langol, Imphal west, Manipur
4. Mrs. Lamkhoneng Haokip, Chieftainess of Wakan Village, Interviewed on 14th March, 2012 at Wakan Village, Sadar Hills
5. Mrs. Lhingjaneng Gangte interviewed on 3rd April 2012 at Old lambuland Imphal, Manipur
6. Ms. Melody Phaljaneng Haokip interviewed on 9th April, 2013 at Paona bazaar, Imphal Manipur
7. Mrs. Nemcha Kipgen, MLA of kangpokpi Constituency, interviewed on 27th Feb. 2013 at lamphel, Manipur
8. Ms. Zouman Thangjom interviewed on 5th April, 2013, 2013 at Old Lambuland, Manipur

Other sources

1. Frontline (1999), vol.16-issue 20, sept.25th -0ct.08.
2. Administrative Report of Manipur Political Agency1891-92

Chapter 2

Portrayal of Woman in Myth and Folktales of the Kukis

Hoineilhing Sitlhou

Introduction

If one reflects back at the most popular fairytales: Snow white, Cinderella, Sleeping beauty, Rapunzel and many others, what do all these female characters in the story have in common? In truth, they are much more than innocent narrative of childlike fantasy. Female always play the central figure in these stories and in the stereotypical roles they played out. Cinderella was a character who was submissive, hard-working and good-willed despite the ill treatment meted to her by her step-mother and step-sisters. Despite her circumstances, every day of her life, she would look out of her window and dream of the day her prince charming would come to whisk her away. Like her, Rapunzel, Snow white and Sleeping beauty were captives in different situations and circumstances and in short, 'damsel in distresses'. The evil characters were also played by the women as 'step-mother', 'step-sisters' or 'ugly-witch' etc. Men on the other hand were portrayed as being strong in terms of will power and physical strength, and they always come to rescue the women characters that were prone to treachery. The side-effects of these fairytales are that they propagate the myth of male superiority and at the same time serve to justify the existence of inequalities between women and men.

Like fairytales, folktales and myth are important element of popular culture and extremely influential on human consciousness. Kuki folktales interestingly often centralised around women beauty, wisdom and resourcefulness. There are off course, women who are evilly inclined and capable of doing more harm than an army of men like the character of the 'step-mother', 'the evil witches', 'demons' or 'the dejected lover'. There are many folktales that explicitly deal with women's roles, actions and contribution. The essay analysed the contemporary relevance of folklores and mythical stories in determining the worldview and ideology of the Kuki society and their attitudes towards women in general. It asked the crucial questions: what do the folklores and mythical stories reflect about the role expectation or status of women in the past? How are these roles translated in the mentality and societal expectation or in defining the 'ideal women' or the 'evil women' in the present society? What is the contribution of folklores and myth to the socialization process and in the social construction of gender relations in the society?

(1) The Kukis

The origin of the word 'Kuki', is not known but it first appears in Bengal in the writing of Rawlins entitled "Cucis or mountainers of Tipra" in Asiatic Researches in 1792 (as cited in Shaw, 1929, p. 11). The second record on the Kuki tribes in general appeared in the Asiatic Researches, volume VII, in a paper from the pen of Surgeon McCrea, dated 24th January 1799 (Macrae, 1919). The Encyclopedia Britannica, Volume 13 of 1963 records the Kukis as "a name given to a group of tribes inhabiting both sides of the mountains dividing Assam and Bengal from Burma, south of the Namtaleik River" (Encyclopedia Britannica, 1963, p. 511). The research will focus on the Thadou dialect-speaking group of the Kuki community. The language belongs to the Tibeto Burman family according to Grierson in his famous linguistic survey of India (Grierson, 1990). History of this group is shrouded in oral traditions including folklores and folktales. The origin of this group like other cognate Kuki group is traced from a cave known in the local dialect as *'khul'* (Rizvi, 2006, p. 15).

(2) Literature Review: Oral Tradition and Women History

Different strands of narratives simultaneously existing in a society plays an important role in shaping the identity of a person or the community as a whole. Identities, "...are both imposed and self-made, produced through the interplay of names and social roles foisted on us by dominant narratives together with the particular choices families, communities, and individuals make over how to interpret, and resist, those impositions as well as how to grapple with their real historical experiences (Alcoff, 2003, p. 3)."

In some ways, the social order in the Thadou-Kuki society today has come to resemble an onion, each layer of which is a different age group. With the demise of the extended family, the segregation between generations has only gotten worse. The significance of the older populace in most tribal societies permeates beyond the boundaries of familial relations to a wider network of the society. They are important carriers or reservoirs of age-old traditions, reminders to our cultural heritage, and observers to a society in transition. These elders have been involuntarily, self-appointed recorders of the past since ancient times. It was only with the coming of the colonial missionaries, a century ago that the age-old and time-tested oral tradition found another medium of expression in the written word (Sitlhou, 2011, p. 22).

In a society like the Thadou-Kukis, which does not have a written literature before the advent of British Imperialist, oral tradition plays an important role in their understanding of their own history, social customs and social structure. Myth, stories, folktales, histories, gossips, informants' account and legends are passed down by word of mouth. Thus, for a society with no written records, myth becomes history to form a probable or acceptable presumption of origin from which they can derive their identity and understand their origin and history (ibid).

Myth means a traditional story accepted as history, serves to explain the worldview of a people. According to Mircea

Eliade in 'Myth and Reality,' 'myth' means a 'true story' and beyond that, a story that is a most precious possession because it is sacred, exemplary, significant (Eliade, 1964, p. 1). Today, that is, the word is employed in both the sense of "fiction" or "illusion" and in those families especially to ethnologists, sociologists and historians of religions, the sense of sacred tradition, primordial revelation, and exemplary model (ibid). Although the actors in myths are usually Gods and Supernatural beings, while those in tales are heroes or miraculous animals, all the actors share the common trait that they do not belong to the everyday world (ibid, pp. 10-11). The story narrated by the myth constitutes a "knowledge" which is esoteric, not only because it is secret and is handed on during the course of an initiation but also because the "knowledge" is accompanied by a magico-religious power. For knowing the origin of an object, an animal, a plant, and so on is equivalent to acquiring a magical power over them by which they can be controlled, multiplied, or reproduced at will (ibid, p. 15).

To understand the state of the society in the pre-colonial period, oral narratives are an important means of understanding the past. "Oral traditions make an appearance only when they are told. For fleeting moments they can be heard, but most of the times they dwell only in the minds of people (Vansina, 1985, p. Xi)". Jan Vansina (1985, p. xi) wrote, "Whether memory changes or not, culture is reproduced by remembrance put into words and deeds. The mind through memory carries culture from generation to generation". He continued, "Ancient things are today. Yes, oral traditions are documents of the present, because they are told in the present. Yet, they also embody a message from the past, so they are expressions of the past at the same time. They are the representation of the past in the present (ibid, p. xii)." Oral narratives can be treated as the collective voice of society, the voice of tradition (Chatterji, 1985, p. 269). "Originality of style and innovations in the means of expression are not considered important in the narrative in the same manner as in modern fictional literature, where originality is a value in itself (ibid)."

According to Arlette Farge, "in restoring the history of women's cultural, social and political identity, we must avoid limiting it to two unchanging, unrealistic images: that of a past which is gone forever and that of a present paralysed by tradition. History is full of contradictions, of alternating currents, of overlapping events where consistency and inconsistency both have a place" (Farge, 1992, p. 21). Jules Michelet, "...saw in the relationship between the sexes one of the driving force of history modulated by the latent conflict between Woman/Nature and Man/ Culture. Woman may be a power for good when her natural nature takes the upper hand, but becomes a force for evil when she usurps political power and steps out of the private sphere. Then history is disturbed and woman becomes a witch" (as cited in Perrot, 1992, p. 2).

(3) Beauty with Brain: The Story of *Lenchonghoi*

Lenchonghoi was a girl of enchanting and incomparable beauty. She had seven brothers. She had a desire to possess the bright radiance of the sun (*ninel*) and the cool white glow of the moon (*lhanel)* to add to her beauty. She believed she could attain perfection only if she had both these two celestial objects as her attire. She longed and pined for them. Her seven brothers with all their affection for her were determined to fulfil her wish. The seven brothers set out to procure the sun and moon's radiance for their lovely sister. They carried with them provisions of food for their journey. They would come back to their sister *Lenchonghoi* for replenishment of their food package when it gets over. Now, the brothers being aware of the attractiveness of their sister were very protective of her and had built ten doors leading to the inside of their house. They would sing outside the house in the following way:

KaU KaU Lenchonghoi jo, kotpi tho som nei hon no bu chun sagi mechun sagi abei tai!

O sister! O sister *Lenchonghoi!* Open for us all the ten doors of the house. The seven packages of boiled rice and the seven packages of curry that you packed for us is exhausted.

On hearing her brother's voice, *Lenchonghoi* would open the door and replenished their provisions for them. The seven brothers would then get back to their quest again.

When their brothers were away from the village, an ogre *Khalvomtepu* came from another village and visited an old widow and tries to be amorous with her. The cunning widow in order to save herself directed him towards the beautiful *Lenchonghoi.* She also taught him how to approach her. Since, she was in the same neighbourhood; she knew the song which *Lenchonghoi's* seven brothers used to sing to make her open the ten layered doors for them. Accordingly, *Khalvomtepu* went to *Lenchonghoi's* house and sang the very same song in front of the door. *Lenchonghoi* could easily make out that it was not one of her brothers because *Khalvomtepu* had a hoarse and raucous voice. She did not open the door. Disappointed, *Khalvomtepu* went back to the old widow and reported what had happened. The old lady instructed him to drink urine so that his voice would improve and *Lenchonghoi* might not be able to differentiate it with those of her brothers. *Khalvomtepu* went back and sang the song again. This time *Lenchonghoi* opened the doors thinking that the singer was one of her brothers. *Khalvomtepu* abducted her forcibly but not before properly closing all the doors of the house.

When the brothers came back to get their provisions, *Lenchonghoi* was no longer there to open the door for them. They inquired and were told that their sister had been forcibly abducted by the *Khalvomtepu.* They got furious and vowed to avenge their sister. The seven brothers took a vow in the following words:

Ka U Lenchonghoi phu ka lah jou dingle kot pi tho som palvang ing nge!

If I can charge through the ten doors of our house, it is a sign that I would be able to avenge my sisters' abduction and bring her back. The brothers tried to break their way through the doors one after another. In the process, six of the brothers' tried dying. The youngest one managed to break down the doors and get to the hearth of the house. He smeared ashes all over his body and transform himself into a bird. He flew hither and thither in search of her lost sister. One day while flying above he saw some youth working in a jhum field. He went near them and sang to them the following songs:

Ka gal la lomlhang kon ho, kaU Lenchonghoi na mu uvem!

O you dear young folks who are working in the jhum on the other side of the brook, Have you seen my sister *Lenchonghoi?*

They replied that they have seen her very conspicuously and she might have by now reached the land of her mother and father. The bird flew away and came to a village where she saw a woman weaving on her loom and sitting on the platform of the house. The bird came closer to the weaver and perched on the bamboo branch near her. He put the usual question to her saying, 'O you below me who is weaving! Have you seen my sister *Lenchonghoi?'* The lady weaver replied: if you happened to be my younger brother of bygone days, come down and drink this water from this mug which I am using to moisten my loom's threads.

The bird came down and drank the water. The woman was actually *Lenchonghoi* herself and both of them were overjoyed to see each other. *Lenchonghoi* kept the bird in a safe place away from the sight of the *Khalvomtepu*. In the evening, khalvomtepu returned home from hunting bringing with him several deer that he had killed. He gave them to *Lenchonghoi* for cooking. After cooking, *Lenchonghoi* threw a small piece of meat to her brother in his hiding place. He told *Khalvompu* that he was offering the piece to a meat eating insect. *Khalvomtepu* imitate her by throwing a big chunk of meat in the same direction. It hit the hidden boy on the nose that resulted in bleeding. *Lenchonghoi* was afraid that the beast might find out about his brother. So, she made up a story: 'by throwing that piece of hot bone you have hit the pot where I have kept the blood. The pot is broken and the blood I stored is split'. *Khalvomtepu* then commented: 'Oh! It smells like human blood and also like that of a beast. I don't understand why?' She quickly replied: 'The smell of human must be of me, a human being; and the smell of beast must be of you, who is a beast'. He seemed contend with the answer. In the meantime, the hidden bird slowly regained back his normal human form. One day, *Lenchonghoi* requested *Khalvomtepu* to drink wine with her. She kept two big jars of wine and challenge *Khalvomtepu* that she could drink more than him. She had secretly made a hole in her wine jar so that she would not get drunk. Everything went as planned and *Khalvomtepu* drank the wine till he was completely drunk. After confirming *Khalvomtepu's* unconsciousness, the siblings ran away from the place. They made few preparations before leaving. *Lenchonghoi* put a louse in a wooden mortar and instructed the louse to response on behalf of them. She also put a winnowing bamboo platter and told the platter to fan *Khalvomtepu*. She collected all the seeds with magical powers which belong to *Khalvomtepu*.

After a while, *Khalvomtepu* regained consciousness, he called out only to be answered by the louse and when he asked for the fan the platter winnowed him. When he realized what had happened from an old woman, he was furious. He pursued them, and in no time was about to reached them. Seeing him approaching towards them, *Lenchonghoi* threw all the magical seeds which create water, fire, gorges, thorns and ropes to stop him. In order to avert the magical powers of the seeds, he commanded them not to be effective on him as he was the real owner. Therefore, it did not work on him.

A duel took place between *Lenchonghoi*'s brother and *Khalvomtepu*. They fought relentlessly till both of them were completely exhausted. They were observed from heaven by the god and goddess. The goddess said, "Whom should we help? Should we help *Khalvomtepu*, who is like a dog, or the younger brother who is a human being? God said, "Whether in the hills or the village, a dog eats everything he finds but humans who are the descendants of Manmasi[1] would not eat anything without first offering a portion of their meal to the gods and goddess. Therefore, we should help the human.

God then said to the younger brother below on the earth: "O Human being! Hear me. Cut a leaf of palm plant which has tongue-shaped leaves and which is growing beside you." Accordingly, the younger brother cut the leaf, the tongue of *Khalvomtepu* got cut and he died instantly.

After the death of *Khalvomtepu*, *Lenchonghoi* and her brother returned to their home. They collected the skeletons of their dead brothers. Then, they collected clean leaves, unspoiled by excrements of birds and beasts. They also drew clean water unpolluted by droppings of birds and beasts. Spreading the leaves on the ground, they put the skeletons of the dead brothers on the leaves, they mixed the life giving seeds in the water and sprinkled it on the skeletons, and the six dead brothers came to life again. They lived happily ever after. The seven brothers tried to complete their quest of meeting the request of their sister. After much effort, they were able to acquire the radiant glow of the moon for her sister. As a result the moon became pale in her appearance. But the brother failed to take away the radiance of the sun, so it attains its brightness till today.[2]

(4) The Haughty Beauty: The Tale of *Jonlhing*

Jonlhing was another girl of unrivalled beauty. She was aware of it and it made her vain. She was in love with a young man by the name *Nanglhun.* The story has it that she compared herself to many elements of nature. This is evident from the song made by her:

Ka chung toni nang sangin ka em joi,

Gamlou sonchengpha sang ka dong joi;

Chunga toni nang chunga che um lou,

Setlei chungchon kei chunga che um lou.

In the song, she says she is more radiant the sun and her skin is more delicate and softer than the new bud or shoot from the trees or plants of the forest. The gods were angry with her for comparing herself to the Sun and she became affected with leprosy like disease. She then realised her folly and the last two lines reflect her repentant heart. She retracted her words by saying that there was none as radiant, bright and beautiful as the sun in the sky, but down on earth, which was her dominance, there was none prettier than her.[3]

(5) A Girl Worth Fighting For: The tale of *Ahsijolneng*

Ahsijolneng was a lady known for her beauty, charm and good nature. Till today her name is used as a synonym for beauty and character combined. She was the daughter of a chief of a great village. Suitors from all walks of life and from far flung areas came to woe her. *Ahsijolneng* chose a young man by the name *Changkhatpu,* a good but poor man. She had been told in her dream that she would be married to a man from a poor family and instantaneously she knew that in *Changkhatpu* at their first meeting. Her parents rejected the proposal as they had expected her to accept a man from a more affluent family. They rebuked *Changkhatpu* saying that he should have look for a bride from his own rank. But he kept begging the chief for his daughter's hand in marriage. Finally, the chief agreed that if *Changkhatpu* was capable of performing three difficult tasks, then he would give consent to the marriage.

The first test was to collect a bag full of sesame, without missing a single seed, which had been scattered in an empty space in the chief's agricultural field. A flock of birds came to his aid and they filled the bag with the sesame seeds in no time. *Changkhatpu* had been kind to them in the past and this was the birds' way of showing him their gratitude. He had made a watering hole for them to drink from.

The second test was to fell in one day all the trees growing in the chief's field. There were so many big trees in the field that it would not have been possible even if all the villagers united to perform the task together. *Changkhatpu* was worried but the winds assured him their help as he had been helpful to them in the past by giving them direction on where to blow. *Changkhatpu* made marks in all the trees to make it easier for the winds. At night, the winds in the form of a gale blew down all the trees in the chief's field.

The third test was to place a big boulder in front of the chief's house. This was an exercise which was not possible even for the whole villagers put together. This time *Changkhatpu* was really worried and started shedding tears. The cloud came to him and instructed him that they will lift the boulder for him and he should stand underneath the boulder and act as if he was lifting it. Together, they succeeded in lifting and moving the boulder in the chief's lawn.

Everyone in the village was awestruck by his feat and the reluctant Chief was now compelled to hand over his daughter's hand in marriage to *Changkhatpu*. The chief arranged a great feast in honouring the marriage as also to bless his daughter with her new found husband. The story did not just end there; the couple still had to fight another obstacle in order to stay together. While on their way to *Changkhatpu's* house, *Ahsijolneng* realised that she had forgotten to take her favourite red *ponve* (wrap-around) and red cornelian bead. *Changkhatpu* offered to go back and pick it up for her. He built a small lodging for her in the tree before going back to her parent house. Meanwhile, *Lhominu*[4] took the form of an old lady and deceived *Ahsijolneng*. The *Lhominu* sucks the blood out of *Ahsijolneng* and threw her body away. She then took the form of *Ahsijolneng* and impersonates her. When *Changkhatpu* came back he noticed the difference in personality but there was nothing that he could really do. The narrative says that *Ahsijolneng* spirit took the form of a gourd and grew in the front yard of *Changkhatpu's* house. When *Changkhatpu* realised that it was the *Lhominu* who took the form of his wife, he beheaded her. The dead of the *Lhominu* released the spirit of *Ahsijolneng* from her bondage and she regains her true self once again.[5] They lived ever after.

(6) The Benevolent Maiden Spirit: The tale of *Pi Chaiching*

The Kukis have a special name for a particular type of grain found in the field. In the paddy field, sometimes one or more stalks refuse to be pregnant with grains. It remains in that form, refusing to change with the changing times, unlike its counterpart who had moved on to the next stage by bearing grains of rice. These stalks were compared to an unmarried woman. They were named *Chang-nungah,* meaning maiden lady. In the lore of the Kuki people, this *Chang-nungah* has an interesting significance. They were considered as a harbinger of good fortune and harvest. Accordingly, they were revered and adorned as if a woman and the priest performs a special ritual to appease it to bring blessing to the field owner's family. The purpose of the ritual is to invoke blessing as also to foresee the fate of a family in terms of prosperity in a given year.

Legend has it that this practice was due to a story, which involved an old lady and two orphaned siblings. In the story, an old woman visits the village of the two siblings. She begged from door to door but no one was willing to accommodate her. Finally, she knocked on the door of the two children who told her that they had nothing to offer her. The old woman assured them that if they let her in, she would find a way to relieve them from their hapless condition. The children, in return, welcomed the old woman to stay with them. They shared with her whatever little they had and treated her well.

From that day onwards, the old woman stayed with them for good. When the siblings went to the field, the old lady would close the doors and spread a mat called *dop* on the floor of the house. She would spread out the mat on the floor everyday for that purpose. She would sit on the mat and then shake her entire body after which a strange thing used to happen. From her body, rice grains would keep dropping until the spread-out mat would be full with grains of rice.

This ensured an abundant supply of rice and a comfortable living for both the children. The old woman was affectionately called grandmother *Chaiching* or *Pi Chaiching*. Their living condition gradually improved and in due course of time, they became very well-to-do and did not have to worry over daily sustenance. During every harvest, they always reaped a bumper crop many times larger than their land holdings. They became very influential within their village.

One day, grandmother *Chaiching* told her grandchildren, "My grandchildren, when you are tending the field, do not let any weed grow unattended, because when you do that something sticks in my teeth and I cannot sleep at night due to the pain." The siblings had meanwhile become vain in their newfound affluence and status. They did not heed their grandmother's request but mischievously defied it. They intentionally let the weeds grow in the paddy field. *Chaiching* would groan in pain throughout the night as the siblings would watch her squall and even made fun of her in the morning.

During the harvesting season, *Pi Chaiching* requested her grandchildren again, "My grandchildren, until and unless you have gleaned every single stalks of paddy, you should not burn it." Once again, the children chose to disobey her. They burned the paddy pile before the harvesting was over. *Chaiching* cried the whole night in pain and could not sleep. She said, "My whole body is burning." In the morning, *Chaiching* confronted her grandchildren and told them that, she had enough of the ill-treatment meted to her. She told them, "From this day onwards, you are not going to see me anymore. Nevertheless, I am going to tell you something, which you should always bear in mind and never forget. From now onwards, whenever the harvesting season arrives, I will appear as a *Chang-nungah* or rice-maiden. If you heed my biddings and follow my instructions, then you will always be rich and prosperous but poor otherwise." Then she told them how to tend the special paddy stalk or *Chang-nungah*.

This is the reason why in the olden days and even in the recent past, there was a belief that whenever a *Chang-nungah* appears in the field, they considered it as the spirit of the paddy and believed that it would bring them fortune and good health if they tend to it according to the instructions given by *Pi Chaiching*.[6]

(7) The Bad Mother: The tale of the Elephant Apple

A married couple carrying their child went into the jungle to dig for yams. At one place they found some ripe elephant apples and ate the fruit and made up loads of what remained but found them too heavy to carry. The husband said, "leave some of the fruit," but the wife replied, "No, the fruit is very sweet, we won't leave it. More children will be born to us from the womb that bore this. Let us leave the child and take the fruit". So they left the child in a yam-hole and carried the fruit home. The child cried and cried and was found by a *Lhominu*[7]. The *Lhominu* thought to herself, "I will bring him up and eat it". However, when the child was all grown up, he become aware the intention of the *Lhominu* before she could kill him. He killed the *Lhominu* and went in search of his real parents and confronted them. Then, his mother was filled with remorse at what she had done to him. She cut in half an elephant apple and blew her nose and put the phlegm and the combings of her hair into it, and said "for your sake, my child, I am doing this". After this, they forgave each other and dwelt together happily ever after. Legend has it that it was from that day that the hair combings are to be found as the fibres of the elephant apple and the rheum of the nose is its kernel.[88]

(8) Conclusion: Tradition Mirrors Society

Human being's dependence on the social environment begins long before they are born, with the folkways and mores governing his parents' courtship and marital selection, with the customs concerning pregnancy, with the whole system of cultural practices surrounding the family (Davis, 1981, p. 201). It is through socialisation that a person learns social behaviour or what it means to be a boy or a girl or what is expected of them by the society. According to Kingsley Davis, "the heart of socialization is the emergence and gradual development of the self or ego. It is in terms of the self that personality takes shape and the mind comes to function. The self develops out of the child's communicative contact with others (ibid, p. 208)." Therefore, socialization can be defined as that process that every individual goes through in life in which the helpless infant gradually becomes self-aware, knowledgeable person, skilled in the ways of the culture into which he or she is born. For Ogburn and Nimkoff, "socialisation is a process by which the individual learn to conform to the norms of the group (Ogburn et al, 1979)." The cultural norms that are followed are the 'standard desired' by the group.

The child is socialise by several agencies and institutions in which he participates like the family, the school, the neighbourhood, the occupational group and by social class, caste, religion and religion. In the context of the Kuki society, folklores also play a crucial role in the process of socialization or a person's upbringing. Stories are narrated to children by the adult members in the family and these folklores become ingrained in the child psyche very early in life. Little girls are taught to model their life, values and imagination like the so called 'ideal woman' in folklores. Characters like *Lenchonghoi, Ahsijolneng* and *Jonlhing* became the parameters in which to measure the 'ideal woman' or 'perfect woman'.

The folklores and myth contributes and determines not only the worldview and ideology of the Kukis, but they also represent the stereotypes of both men and women. They reproduced and emphasised gender related issues including gender roles and how women are represented in a particular society. Theories stressing on the social construction of gender emphasised how we learn the gender roles that relate to our biological sex through our interaction with social structures, such as the family, schools, the media and so on (Oakley, 1981, p. 297). Men also expect ladylike character in their woman. The conventional personality type of Kuki women ought to be soft-spoken, quiet, graceful and refined, polite, humble, obedient as against to qualities like assertiveness, ambitious and economically independent according to popular vote.[9] Women are understood to be vulnerable beings that constantly need to be protected even if they are as resourceful as the *Lenchonghoi* like character. Therefore, it is difficult for the independent minded Kuki women to find a space in the Kuki society.

Women's status in society remains defined by their family functions (both actual and supposed) in a way that does not hold for men (Oakley, 1981, p. 297). In the family 'mothering' is and the reproduction of healthy children is seen as the ultimate role of women (Oakley, 1974, p. 69). Irresponsible mothers who do not fulfil their duty as a mother or a cold hearted mother who forsake her children are often compared to the mother in the story of the elephant apple. As the story goes, the belief is that they would come to repent their action one day. Old Women or grandmothers as also old men are suppose to be a harbinger of good luck. Coupled with the belief as in the story of *Pi Chaiching,* is the fact that the Kuki society is a gerontocratic society in which grey hair is highly respected as a sign of wisdom and experience.

Oral tradition are told and retold and they dwell in the minds of the people. It is carried forward from generation to generation. It shapes both the individual and the social consciousness as well as reflects and reinforces social beliefs and behaviour. It becomes the collective voice of the society or the voice of tradition. Folklores and myth becomes the dominant narratives influencing the way a person construct his or her identity or cultural identity or social identity. As Eliade says Myth is a traditional story accepted as history as it serves to explain the worldview of the people in a society. This is particularly true for the case of the Kuki society which has no written history of their own in which myth gives them a sense of history.

Sherry B. Ortner (1996) discusses the tendency to associate women with 'nature' and 'the domestic unit', and men with 'culture' and 'the public entity.' Thus activities such as politics, warfare and religion are seen as the province of men. As in the case of fairytales, in folktales, men are portrayed as the more powerful gender in terms of wit, courage, valour and physical strength and as the rescuer of women from their condition of distress. Much as it is true that they serve to entertain and preserve culture, some folktales tend to justify the existing inequality between women and men in the society as they re-affirm to women the status of the weaker sex in the society.

Notes

1. The first human being created by God
2. This is a revised version of the Story of Lenchonghoi as recorded by Tarun Goswami in his book, 'Kuki Life and Lore'.
3. This is a translation of the thadou version of the story in the text book Thimthu Le Jaila (Thadou Kuki Literature-X).
4. A mythological being with supernatural powers and is half tigress and half a woman.
5. This is a translation of the thadou version of the story in the text book Thimthu Le Jaila (Thadou Kuki Literature-X).
6. As recorded by Hoineilhing Sitlhou in her doctoral thesis, 'Land and Identity: A Sociological Study of the Thadou Kukis of Manipur'.
7. A mythological being with supernatural powers and is half tigress and half a woman.
8. As recorded in William Shaw's book, 'Notes on the Thadou Kukis'.
9. Sitlhou, Hoineilhing. 13th August, 2008. 'Women's Role in the Community: In the Context of Kuki Society,' *Kuki International Forum* in http://kukiforum.com/2008/08/women-role-in-community-in-the-context-of-kuki-society/ (accessed 31st May, 2011)

References

1. Alcoff, Linda Martin, Eduardo Mendieta (ed). *Identities: Race, Class, Gender and Nationality*, Blackwell Publishing, 2003.
2. Chatterji, Roma. *Folklore and the Formation of Popular Consciousness in a Village in the Purulia District of West Bengal*, Thesis submitted to the University of Delhi for the Degree of Doctor of Philosophy, Department of Sociology, Delhi School of Economics, Delhi-110007, 1985.

3. Davies, Kingsley. *Human Society*, Surjeet Publications, Delhi. 1981.
4. Eliade, Mircea. *Myth and Reality*, George Allen and Unwin Ltd., London, 1963.
5. Encyclopedia Britannica, William Benton Publisher, USA, Vol. 13, 1963.
6. Farge, Arlette. 'Method and Effects of Women's History', in Michelle Perrot's edited book, 'Writing Women's History', Blackwell, Oxford, 1992.
7. Grierson, G.A. *Tibeto Burman Family, Part III, Specimens of the Kuki-Chins and Burma Groups, Linguistic Survey of India*, Vol. III, Low Price Publications, Delhi, 1990.
8. Goswami, Tarun. *Kuki Life and Lore,* North Cachar Hill District Council, Haflong, 1985.
9. Macrae, John. 'Account of the Kookies, or Lunctas,' by, *Asiatic Researches,* Vol.VII, 1979, 1801, 183-198.
10. Oakley, Ann. *Housewife,* Allen Lane, London, 1974.
11. Oakley, Ann. *Subject Women,* Martin Robertson & Company Ltd., Oxford, 1981.
12. Ogburn, William F. and Nimkoff, Meyer F. *A Handbook of Sociology,* Eurasia Publishing House, New Delhi, 1979.
13. Ortner, Sherry B. *Making Gender: The Politics and Erotics of Culture,* Beacon Press, Boston, 1996.
14. Rizvi, S.H.H. et al. *Kuki-Chin Tribes of Mizoram and Manipur,* B.R. Publishing Corporation, Delhi, 2006.
15. Shaw, William. *Notes on the Thadou Kukis,* Journal of Asiatic Society of Bengal, Published on behalf of the Government of Assam, 1929.
16. Sitlhou, Hoineilhing. Land and Identity: A Sociological Study of the Thadou Kuki Tribes of Manipur, Thesis submitted to Jawaharlal Nehru University for the Degree of Doctor of Philosophy, Centre for Study of Social Systems, School of Social Sciences, New Delhi-1100067, 2011.
17. Thimthu Le Jaila /Thadou Kuki Literature-X (a text book for class X under the board of secondary education, Manipur), Published by Thadou-Kuki Literature Society, Manipur, 2002.
18. Perrot, Michelle (ed.). Writing Women's History, Blackwell, Oxford, 1992.
19. Vansina, Jan. *Oral Tradition as History,* James Currey, London, 1985.

Chapter 3

Weaving: The Traditional Craft by the *Kuki* Women

Ngamkholen Haokip

Weaving is, without doubt, the most developed and advanced of the varied crafts practised by the *Kuki* women. The traditional *Kuki* women wove their cloths not for commercial purpose but solely for domestic use. They learnt the art of weaving from their very early age of six to ten. They wove varieties of cloths of various designs and motifs by using of Loin Loom. The varieties of cloths include shawls, wrappers, skirts, scarves etc. The production of cloth was infact a very lengthy process spanning across over a year. It started with sowing of cotton seeds in a Jhum field. Ginning separated cotton from its seeds, carding process cleaned the material, spinning drew out and twisted the fibres of cotton and thus produced thread. The thread was winded for sizing, and then the process to weave was started. They used locally available leaves, flowers, grasses, clay, ash, burnt creepers, fruits and rhizomes etc. to produce different colours. The required tools or implements for the whole process of weaving were made by the men of the family. This essay attempts to discuss the role of *Kuki* women in the art of weaving textiles in *Manipur*, and also to identify the affinity among the many *Kuki* tribes by the origin, design pattern, uses and commonness of their textiles.

"Numei ponkhong theilou chun aji-acha te ipiti phalbi adousah ding ham?"

Research Scholar, Department of Visual Art, Assam University: Silchar Email: pupatimes@yahoo.com

How would a woman, without the knowledge of weaving, keep her family warm during the winter season?

Introduction

Clothing is one of the basic needs of mankind. Cloth not only cover our body parts but also protects us from hazardous elements, such as rough surface, insect bites, splinters, thorns, cold and heat. The weaving of indigenous textiles has come to replace the use of tree barks and animal skin. The dress remained as an emblem of the community. The type of cloths depends on physical structure, environment, geography and social norms. Different ethnic groups have different techniques of weaving. With the advance of modern technology every ethnic group also developed their technique of weaving. For weaving, looms like loin loom (see Plate 32), suspended loom, throw and fly shuttle loom (see Plate 33), pit loom, jacquard loom and frame loom (Association, 2010) are use in India.

Textiles have a long tradition in the world. Indian tribal textiles are one of the oldest in the world, dating back to the Indus Valley civilization (Peters, 2013). India is the second largest textile industry in the world after China. It provides employment to maximum number of the people next to agriculture. Textile is one of the main industries of India. It constitutes the single largest industry in India (Dr. P. Chellasamy and N. Sumathi). Cotton, woolen, silk, readymade-garment; hand-crafted, jute and coir textiles are the textile industry segment of India (India, March, 2013).

The traditional *Kukis* used mainly Loin loom. Of late shuttle loom and computerize technique of weaving have been newly introduced among the *Kukis*. Weaving occupy an integral part of household duty for the *Kuki* women. The tools needed for weaving are made by the menfolk. Equal percentage of married and unmarried women took part in weaving. Traditionally, a girl child in the age group of 6 to 10 years learned the process and the practice of weaving by the use of *Aige-Hoh*[1] (Haokip 2011) and then after obtaining the skill they started weaving by the use of *Pat-sum*[2]. In this regard Milui Lenthang (Lenthang, 2005) elaborated that

"In the past, the *Kuki* young girls learned the process of weaving by the used of *Ai-ge,* and then wove with *Patsum* and thus produced small cloth. They wove usable cloth only after they know the process properly. This way, they produced different cloth for man and woman through their creativity. They also introduced various designs of clothes. Therefore every clan/tribe has their own traditional cloth with reference to their custom and culture. The people are named as *Kuki-Chin-Mizo* and they are the descendants of one family."

By helping the senior weavers they picked up the technique before they can start full-fledged weaving on their own. Thus, they learned the skill of weaving in different designs from their tender age. Every woman knew the art and processes of weaving, but there were some exceptional women who excelled in the skill. A young girl expert in weaving was highly honoured in the village and was the preferred choice for a wife or a daughter-in-law.

The traditional *Kuki* women wove dresses only for their domestic use and not for commercial purpose. The women are superb artists of the loom (Guite, 2010). The *Kukis* produced cottons in their fields. William Shaw (1997) states, all these (the) clothes are woven from cotton which is grown on their lands and spun by women. They also purchase major part of their need of yarn either through the co-operatives or from the local shops. Those who produce cotton in their fields have to pass through different stages before it can be used for weaving. Their handloom and handicraft product depends on materials available in the agricultural field and forest. The *Kuki* traditional cloth designs may be invented or first produced by the men but it is the women who have developed them.

Kukis of Manipur

In Manipur, the *Meitei,* the *Kuki* and the *Naga* are the three main ethnic groups. The hill area of Manipur is occupied by various tribes of the *Kuki* and the *Naga* ethnic groups. The Kuki groups are indigenous people, (Haokip, 2008) who trace their origin to mythical *Khul* or *Khur*[3], a subterranean dwelling understood and commonly referred to as a cave. Presently, they settled in Chittagong Hill Tracts of Bangladesh, Chindwin region of Myanmar (Burma) and North East region of India (Assam, Nagaland, Manipur, Mizoram and Tripura). Under the provisions of Article 342 of Indian Constitution, the *Khul* or *Khur* origin people are listed in Schedule Tribes of Manipur as *Aimol, Anal, Chiru, Chothe, Gangte, Hmar, Kharam, Koireng, Kom, Lamgang, Maring, Mizo, Monsang, Moyon, Paite, Purum, Simte, Sukte, Tarao, Thadou, Vaiphei* and *Zou* etc. Lal Dena (Loncheu, 2013) quotes that

"One of the worst victims of British colonialism and perhaps the most misunderstood ethnic groups were the people who are called *Chins* in Myanmar and *Kukis* in India and Bangladesh. Though called by different names, one cannot deny the fact that the people are one and the same race; for their appearance, manners, customs and language all point to the conclusion that they originally came from one common ancestry and a place which they variedly called *Sinlung (Chhinlung), Khurpui* or *Khul* which may be located somewhere in and around the Stone Forest and *Kunming* in *Yunnan* Province in China. They were once a single ethnic entity in their original homeland."

Status of Women in *Kuki* Society

The position of *Kuki* women in socio-cultural, economic and politics sphere have come to be appreciated of late. Only a few writers and scholars penned the status and role of women in *Kuki* society. The world-wide issue of "Woman Empowerment" impact the status of *Kuki* Women in different aspects like socio-cultural, economic and politics. The advent of Christianity with modernization and the introduction of education are also the transforming factors. The written materials or records may be less, but *Kuki* women were not un-honored in the society.

The role of *Kuki* women is most distinctive in the field of art and craft. In the past, the *Kuki* women who bore off-spring, who performed *Chang-Ai*[4], who were considered beautiful, who possessed great singing skills and who were well-versed in art and craft etc. were highly honored and acclaimed in the society. Women also played an important role with regard to the traditional institutions of *Lom*[5] and *Som*[6]. Good and dutiful *Som-nu (*Lady of the *Som*) earned admiration from the village-folk. Such a *Som-nu* exhibited good moral character and also meted out equal treatment to all her *Som-pas* (boys of the *Som)* without any bias. The main objective of the *Som* was to acquire the customs and war tactics besides staying together. It was also useful in meeting emergencies like fire, war, theft etc. In this sense, the service of women in *Som* was their indirect contribution towards socio-political issues. Women also learned all household works and also hospitality in practical at the *Som*.

In *Lom*, the responsibility of women is to carry all the agricultural implements including wrap food of *Lom* members on the way to the field. The duty of *Lom-pas* (male members of the *Lom*) was to carry wood and bamboos for construction of house or household implements of the village members who could not carry by their own due to heavy weight or large size. In this way, both men and women contributed to the benefit of the family/society. Thus, the *Lom* and *Som* were the centres of learning and service to the society. However, the status and role of women in the *Kuki* society is debatable. In the words of *Paokhohao Haokip* (2013) "It was also burdensome for the family as well as the *Som-nu* who had to take utmost care to look after the comforts of the *Som* members." With the advent of modern civilization the practice of Som is not to be found and no more applicable in the present *Kuki* society.

In a state like Manipur, where identity politics is strong, the *Kuki* women too played an important role in it through weaving of their cloths. Dr. P. Chellasamy and N. Sumathi (Dr. P. Chellasamy and N. Sumathi) coined the cotton textile industry as *Swadeshi* industry because it was developed with indigenous entrepreneurship and capital and in the pre-independence era the *Swadeshi* movement stimulated demand for Indian textile in the country. Like the *Swadeshi* industry movement, the indigenous people of Manipur too have their respective movement in weaving of their cloths. The *Kuki* women also produce their traditional cloths in the perspective of market and identity. The *Kuki* women now produce a large number of their traditional cloths in varied designs and wear such as muffler, waist-coat, neck-tie, purse, carrying bags etc. Their hand woven traditional cloths are sold in different place of India. They have also introduced new styles and designs in different attires. The *Kuki* women have also succeeded in fusing traditional designs and motifs with modern techniques and modern fabrics in producing fashionable and these can be worn by anybody and everybody. The weaving product of Kuki women also plays an important part in identification and popularity of their identity to the world.

History of weaving

The history of weaving is as old as their culture. Ncy Doungel (Doungel, 2009) believes that weaving was started right from the time, the people settled down on this earth[7]. Vanlalruat (Guite, 2010) traced the origin of weaving back to 500 BC. Whatever the origin and year of introduction of weaving, weaving was practiced right from the time of their earliest period of their settlement. The tribal weavers in Manipur mostly used the loin looms. They used the loin looms because they did not possess the knowledge of other methods of modern weaving. After the *Meiteis* in the valley became adept at weaving in fly shuttle loom in 1900 (Bhadur, 2000), some cooperative societies of Churachandpur District introduced it in 1983 financed by the state government.

According to the invocation (Lenthang, 2005) given here, the clothes are already in used after "The Flood" mentioned in the Bible.

Nihchen ponsil hungkon dohna thiemthu (Narrative on the Origin of Weaving)

Chunga hungkon doh patchon silpon chun
Leiduppi-leithaopi mun a hung chun lang
Leisanpa sahlhongpi chunga kon in pu houvin
Hinjui yin, pa houvin hinjui in
Kholkip-kholjang mihemte leh sahiem te lah ah
Khindal lin hungpangin, hoidal lin hungpang in
Pondum, ponlhe, pon mongvom, chuleh pon geisen chun
Sim leija, hin mano-in, maleija hin mano-in
Pusha-pasha in hinjūi in
Mitpha-hapha in hinjui in
Tidam ludam in hinjui in
Manmasi chate ding in.

Free translation

The cotton cloth, originated from above,
Come and fall in the land of honey and milk
May the good fortune of the ancient fathers accompany
You from the abode of *Leisanpa*[8]
May you be a protector and shield
Of all the human and animals of *Kholkip-kholjang*[9]

May you produce *Pondum, ponlhe, pon mongvom* and *pon geisen* cloths

In the whole world

May the good fortune of the ancient fathers accompany you

May your eyes and teeth be good
May your body and head be sound,
For all *Manmasi*[10] *[Kuki]* descendents

The staple yarn was imported to Manipur in 1950s and the tribal people began to use it as well. The tribal weavers used four-ply acrylic wool in 1960s and 1970s. They split this four-ply wool into one or two-ply wool for weaving. They also used one and two-ply wool yarns to weave their cloths conveniently in assorted colors during 1980s. Today, some sections of tribes have acquired the art of weaving by using the fly shuttle loom. Above all, they were free from the hard and poor method of vegetable dye. In the past, the *Kuki* weavers did not have the skill in needle works. But nowadays, some embroidered textiles are also produced by them.

The *Kuki*s cultivated cottons in their field from time immemorial. From the incantation (Lenthang, 2005) the legend is that, the *Kuki*s are always cultivating cotton in their field wherever they settled.

Vantho thosagi leitho thosagi a
Vantham jolla hungkon doh silpon patchon chun
Hiche Pi Ngaite nuchan
Vo, kong chan hinvop chun
Sim lei ah nahin chingin
Mal lei ah nahin chingin
Najing in simlam ahin lon
Mal lei ahin lon
Napah in sim lei van hinsallin

Free translation

Seven layers of heaven and seven layers of earth
The cotton cloth, originated from above
Pi Ngaite and her daughter
Treasured it
Sowed it in the east
Sowed it in the west
Your leaves spread across the east and the west
Let your blooms beautify heaven and earth

Method, techniques and tools:

Ginning is carried out by a locally made wooden machine called *Pat-heh*. The roller is geared to move in opposite direction. The roller in motion by means of a crank attached to the end of one of them moves by one hand in the crank and with the other feeds the machine with cotton. Another process is *Pat-sai* (carding). The implement is a simple and small bow consisting of a bamboo piece to which a carved string is attached to give it a shape of a bow. The operation is simple and it cleans the cotton by thickening method. Thus, cleaned cotton gets ready for spinning (see Plate 34). One of the most common processes and implements was *Mui* (Spinning wheel). Cleaned cotton slices are spun in a local-made spindle called "*Mui*". It is simple spike made of smooth, straight, thin and hard wood or in some cases an iron needle. One end of the spike is invested in the centre of a round flat spindle whorl. The other end of the spike has a notch for the purpose of holding the thread. Thus the "drop spindle" is spun with the right hand against the thigh and turns it by rotating, while the cotton piece is held in the left hand. The strand of cotton being spun passes from the left hand to the spindle. The yarn thus produced is wound round the wooden or iron spike from time to time and thus works as bobbin. Winding is the process of transforming yarn from wanks to bobbins by locally made instrument call *Pat-lam.* The machine is a drum like structure with a wooden stand. The drum consists of a circular wooden rod and two wooden discs which are pinned at two ends of the rod.

The process of sizing is also one of the traditional forms of weaving. The process is very simple; a quantity of boiled rice with starch is squeezed through a cloth strainer in a tube of cold water. The dyed or the white yarn is taken through the solution and womb sound on two bamboo poles stretched properly to dry. The dried sized yarn is then cleaned from any size particle or dirt on it.

To shape a cloth, the two threads the warp and the weft are interlaced in a right angle. The longer thread called *"atung"* (warp) is hold by front-bar and the altitude thread called *"aphei"* (weft) is woven on it by shuttle. The designs are woven in a desire colour of thread intermingle with the weft or colour-weft alone. Some cloth designs have no colour weft.

In this type of cloths, the designs are woven from colour-warp and the colour-weft itself. It is also depends on the heald-bar. Heald-bar plays the role of selector to weave the designs by selecting continuously one after another. The more designs in cloth needs more heald-bar. Weaving of *Saipikhup* (see Plate 9), *Thangnang* (see Plate 26), *Khamtang* (see Plate 27) needs more than five heald-bar. To weave simple and plain clothes only one heald-bar is needed. Some designs like flowers and animals are weaving by the process of copied and weaved. This type of weaving needs only one heald-bar but the designs are crafted by hand process.

The traditional *Kukis* used mainly the technique of Loin loom. For the *Kukis,* weaving tools were and still constitute one of the most important assets for women. The *Kuki* women used to take their weaving tools with them when they get married or shifted from one village to another. They carried weaving tools and implements if they happened to migrate or move temporarily to any place. They could easily set up the loom wherever they were, without much difficulty.

The Loin Loom had a continuous warp of manageable length and warp beam was attached to two upright posts. The breast beam was attached to the back leather belt. The shed was affected by the half – head process operated by the hand. The breast beam was almost in the weaver's lap, when the warp rose at an angle of 350 degree up towards the warp beam. The shuttle was shot through by hand, and the weft was beaten up with sword. There was no specific weaving site for the loin loom and the weavers could weave anywhere, whether it was in the verandah or inside the house or any open site.

Some of the tools used for this type of loin looms called *"Thilbu"* is known by different names among the closely related tribes of the *Kuki*s are shown below:

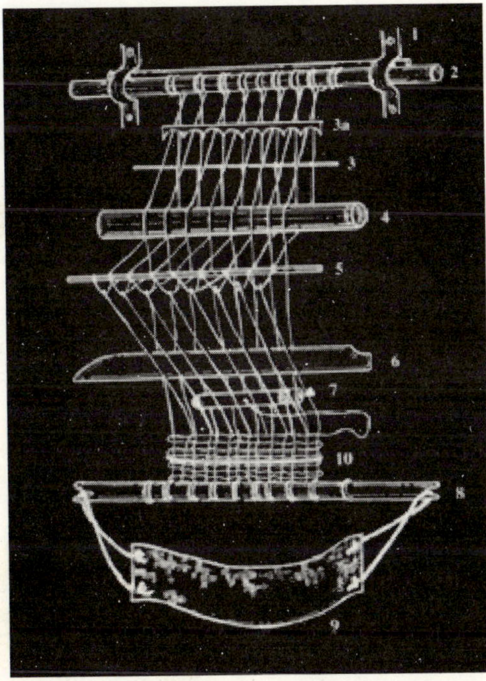

m

The cloths of *Kukis* produced in Loin-Loom have its advantages and disadvantages. The main disadvantage of Loin Loom is that it is very time-consuming. It can take weeks and even months for weaving a particular cloth. Again, it is labour-intensive. Weaving by carrying the entire load of the loom complete with all its tools and implements in the loin by the women in sitting position for long hours is not conducive to their health. Moreover, the loin loom-produced cloths do not fetch high prices in comparison to machine-produced cloths which are more attractive. As such, the use of loin loom is not very profitable for the weavers. However, the finesses and durability of loin loom produced cloths is its distinctive feature. Buyers who have a good knowledge of the higher quality of loin loom-produced cloths vis-à-vis machine-produced cloths will prefer the former and will even pay a good price for it. The *Kuki* women are not only advanced in

Table: Loin loom implements in different dialect

Tribe	1	2	3	4	5	6	7	8	9
English		*Front Bar*	*Bamboo-bar*	*Heald-bar*	*Sword*	*Shuttle*	*Breast-bar*	*Back-strap*	
Aimol		*Tarakol*	*Tukket*	*Tinbu*	*Chukshee*	*Tiem*	*Khotheng*	*Tasake*	*Kongvon*
Anal	*Nakeso*	*Ata*	*Nhaiyin*	*Teyer*	*Anha*	*Tringdar*	*Takhol*	*Ata*	*Anham*
Chiru	*Serui*	*Robuchena*	*Taije*	*Robu*	*Tana*	*Reteim*	*Thori*	*Kaikongke*	*Kongbon*
Chothe	*Luyam*	*Yetpu*	*Najet*	*Utong*	*Tana-Chei*	*Teem*	*Huitheem*	*Apamna*	*Kongnamphai*
Gangte	*Tahgui*	*Puonkam*	*Tiengchang*	*Pumlong*	*Taanah*	*Tiem*	*Khohthei*	*Kokla*	*Kongduop*
Hmar	*Hruol*	*Puon nangna*	*Taizel*	*Tinbu*	*Tanhana*	*Tleam*	*Khothei*	*Kolsake*	*Pheivon*
Kharam		*Tarkol*	*Tajel*	*Tinbu*	*Rana*	*Tatem*	*Kouteng*	*Taskei*	*Kouvon*
Koireng	*Takairongrui*	*Tairikol*	*Taijel*	*Timburu*	*Rinachung*	*Tatem*	*Khotheng*	*Kasake*	*Kongvon*
Kom		*Thamder*	*Tajel*	*Tarum*	*Trairanha*	*Tartem*	*Kothei*	*Konbei*	*Khongkhai*
Lamgang		*Daktalang*	*Datai*	*Timbu*	*Tarnadatai*	*Tatem*	*Yelshi*	*Da*	*Namphei*
Maring		*Satan*		*Rabu*	*Traiyel*	*Tathlem*	*Tathal*	*Taban*	*Namphei*
Mizo	*Themhrui*	*Themtlang*	*Tukrek*	*Thembupui*	*Hwahchawi*	*Themtleng*	*Khawhtehi*	*Themkawl*	*Kawngvawn*
Monsang		*Lasung*	*Tijir*	*Tumbu*	*Ronha*	*Chomder*	*Takhur*	*Lasong*	*Kongki*
Moyon		*Rasung*	*Taijir*	*Tumbur*	*Runa*	*Tumber*	*Takhur*	*Rasung*	*Ramphak*
Paite	*Tahkhai*	*Siamlehna*	*Chiangtang*	*Longpi*	*Nahvoh*	*Chiampek*	*Khohthei*	*Kolka*	*Kongduap*
Purum		*Nampon*	*Neiyet*	*Timbu*	*Tanathing*	*Tlim*	*Worthengla*	*Aikungkeng*	*Kongnamphai*
Purum (Kom)	*Takairui*	*Taru*	*Tajel*	*Timbu*	*Ranabok*	*Ritem*	*Kotheng*	*Taske*	*Kongvon*
Ralte	*Themhrui*	*Themtlang*	*Tukrek*	*Thembupui*	*Hwahchawi*	*Themtleng*	*Khwahthei*	*Themkawl*	*Kawangvawn*
Simte	*Tahvoh*	*Naahkam*	*Chiangtang*	*Lowngpi*	*Nahtawi*	*Chiam*	*Khohthei*	*Kolka*	*Kawngkuap*
Sukte	*Tahkhai*	*Siamhelh*	*Ciangtang*	*Lowngpi*	*Nahvawh*	*Ciampek*	*Khawhthei*	*Kolka*	*Duap*
Tarao		*Labuhshung*	*Shung*	*Taibhu*	*Shung*	*Kuktrim*	*Taithal*	*Labushung*	*Lamphai*
Thadou		*Achungkam*	*Tulet [Tuhdet]*	*Pumlong*	*Tanna*	*Lhem*	*Khothei*	*Tainam*	*Kongdop*
Vaiphei	*Tangkhangkol*		*Tangkhang*	*Tiangchang*	*Tinbu*	*Tana*	*Tiampek*	*Khothei*	*Kolka*
Kongduap									
Zou	*Thahkhua*	*Siamlehna*	*Chiangtang*	*Longpi*	*Nahtoi*	*Chem*	*Kholong*	*Kolka*	*Kongdop*

Source: (Bhadur, 2000)

loin-loom weaving, but they also apply the aesthetic values of their traditional cloth in different ways. In this regard, mention may be made of the application of needle works in the *Kuki* textiles. In the past, the *Kuki* weavers did not have the skill in needle works. But nowadays, embroidery has also come to be used in the textiles. The latest development in the field of weaving among the *Kukis* is the use of computer technology[11]. *Ms. Roslyn Khongsai* is one such *Kuki* artist who has introduced the novel concept of computer technology to the *Kuki* textiles.

Dyeing

Dyeing was one of the processes of obtaining the desired colour of cloth. The traditional dyeing techniques of the traditional *Kuki*s differ from region to region. From locally available tree leaves, flowers, grass, clay, ash, burnt creepers, fruits and rhizomes etc. they produce all types of primary and secondary colour. While dyeing black color, the solution of *Mukangpan/Mopi* (strobilbathus-flaccidifolius) plant leaves was used. They repeated the same process of dyeing so as to concentrate the color and to obtain black-colored textile. Some tribes used *Tournefortia-candolii* leaves to prepare red color. But the *Kukis* mostly extracted the red dye from a creeper plant known as *Sonsan (Thadou), Patsanlo (Gangte/Vaiphei)* and *Muthi (Hmar)* plant and also from the leaves of tea plant. Turmeric was the most common source of yellow dye. The traditional *Kukis* crushed the tuber of turmeric plant, dip it into water, stirred, and boiled the turmeric solution to produce yellow dye. The crushed bark locally known as *Hmaiphi Thing* and *Inkum Thing* were mixed in a vessel containing water and heated until the content is boiled. Dipping in this liquid produced navy blue cloth. The indigo dye was obtained from the plant *Strobilanthes-flaccidifolius* grown by them (Shaw, 1997). Today they have abandoned all these traditional techniques of dyeing because the industrial yarns are available in their local markets.

Origins of designs

The different cloth designs of *Kuki* are manufactured by copying the beautiful shades and colours of snakes, animals, birds, landscapes, atmosphere, agricultural products etc. (see Symbol-A-I). Commonness of its designs and names shows their affinity. Their unique creativity in weaving can be better understood by knowing their origin. Designs of the *Kukis* may resemble with other allied *Kuki* tribes who are settled in Bangladesh, India and Myanmar (Burma). There is also a possibility of sharing and borrowing with other ethnic groups of their neighboring.

The different designs and techniques of weaving are not imported from outside of Manipur, but are passed on to different generation after they came out of *Khul/Khur*. When the *Kuki* (*Songthu/Chongthu*) group of people came out from *Khur/Khul* a tiger obstructed them at the gateway. One of their leaders wove a cloth in the same pattern and colour of tiger. With the help of the cloth the leader crossed the gateway. The tiger considered him to be one of its fellow tigers and therefore did not kill him. Then the leader killed the tiger with his spear. Therefore the whole family came out safely (Bhadur, 2000). Different versions of the same myth are prevalent among the *Kuki* tribes. The name of the cloth is *Laijiang* or *Ponchial Rulpuiyek* in *Aimol* (see Plate 28), *Ponthal* in *Koireng* (see Plate 8), *Thompui* in *Kharam* (see Plate 29).

Another version pointed to the pattern of snake (python) in their traditional cloth (Haokip 2011) (see Symbol-H). There was a creative woman who wove near the stream. While she wove, she saw a python nearby. She crafted what she saw in the cloth. From that very pattern the cloth is woven till today by the weavers. Vanlalruat (Guite, 2010) mentioned that it was during some 500 BC. Another version to this belief was that of Ncy Doungel (Doungel, 2009) "weaving was started when they settled on this earth. It was also believed that when they came out of *Khul/Khur* they killed a *Sampi* (big snake/python) and cut it into pieces. While carrying the cut pieces, womenfolk wove the pattern of snake in their cloth design." But the name of the cloth is different from each tribe. *Nuhmeipun* by *Kom* (see Plate 6), *Khamtang* by *Thadou, Ponchial Rulpuiyek* in *Aimol, Ponthal* by *Koireng.*

As *Thangnang* and *Khamtang* designs are copied from the snake pattern, the Kukis belief that wearing of *Thangnang* and *Khamtang* considered dangerous while crossing the big rivers. Therefore, according to the legend, while crossing the river water, (Lenthang, 2005) the *Kukis* chant the invocation to cross safely.

Chunga Pathen leh noi a Pathen
Chule tuikul lengpa leh tuikul lengnu
Heimol dingpi mun lhung dingin
Tuiting jol pumchunga nu-naote leh mipite kahung uve
Ajeh chu Kapu Lengoukhup chanu
Tingman in Silpon chung leh chenpon pat chungah
Hi tuikul te Thangnangjem le Khamtangjem
Navo dohsah chu silpon in hin nei in
Chenpon in hinnei in
Sim lei hinluo dingin chung khopi a cheng
Manmasi chate kahiuve
Tuikul lengpa leh tuikul lengnu in
Hoidal in hung pangin tindal in hungpang in
Mitphat-haphat nading
Tidam-ludam nading in
Manmasi Chate nei mano lhungsah un

Free translation

God of heaven and God of earth
And king of *Tuikul* and Queen of *Tuikul*[12]
To reach our destination in the hills
We, the people, with our women and children cross the river
Because *Tingman,* the daughter of our forefather *Lengoukhup,*
Wove on the cloths *Thangnang* and *Khamtang* designs

From the pattern of the python

Wearing the cloths as shawls
Wearing the cloths as wrappers
We are the sons of *Manmasi [Kuki]* from the northern city
For occupying the eastern land
May the King of *Tuikul* and the Queen of *Tuikul*
Be our protector and defender
For goodness of our eyes and teeth
And soundness of our body and mind
Lead us, the *Manmasi [Kuki],* to our destination

The origin of *Changmai-mu* (Cucumber Seed) in their cloths was the sole and amazing creativity of women (see Symbol-B). While showing the seeds of cucumber in the field she was very fond of the seed (Haokip, 2011). And therefore the pattern or design of cucumber seeds was woven in many of their cloths. Another origin of *Kuki* cloth was the colour pattern of rainbow. The many colourful yarns used for *Puandums* evolved from the colours of the rainbow (Guite 2010). There were different designs woven in the cloth depending on the tribe's concept and uses. Though *Vaphol/Pholva* (Horn Bill) (Haokip, 2013) which is so much connected with their culture had disappeared (Haokip, 2013), the *Kukis* crafted the feather of *Pholva* pattern in black and white motif on their cloths (see Plate 11).

The cloth called *Thangnang* and *Saipikhup* has the design of *Gosem-jang*[13] (see Symbol-G) and diamond-shaped design. The diamond-shaped design has two versions, the design of *Changmai-mu* (cucumber seed) and the belly portion of the python. The origin of most commonly used cloth *Saipikhup* have a different myth to trace with its literal name "elephant-knee". According to the legend narrated by Chochon (Haokip C. , 2013), the design of *Saipikhup* was woven from *Sampi-khup* (*sampi*=python, *khup*=downward facing) pattern. The literal meaning of original name "*Sampi-khup*" is "back side of python". From the word Sampi/Saipi and they called it *Saipi-khup*. Therefore, the name of the cloth become *Saipikhup* meaning *saipi*=elephant and *khup*=knee (Bhadur, 2000). Giving attention to the Kuki cultural history, we found elephant only in the folktale of "*Chemtat-te Pu*". The *Saipikhup* cloth is used as under garment by *Aimol, Koireng, Kom, Purum (Kom)* and *Thadou*. The *Thadou* people also used *Saipikhup* cloth as a shawl of two type's viz. *Pasal-Saipikhup* (for male) and *Numei-Saipikhup* (for female). The *Thadous* skirt *Khamtang-Saipikhup* (see Plate 14) was newly introduced. The style of the cloth is almost same with *Aimol* skirt- *Saipikhup*. The traditional *Khamtang* of the *Thadous* has only the pattern of snake.

Social and political aspect

Among the tribals of Manipur, there are some social norms as regards the practice and use of certain cloths. According to the traditional belief of *Kukis,* girls are not allowed to touch certain cloths of man. The menfolk as hunters are also not allowed to touch any lower garment of women. It is their belief that a man who touches the lower garment of women cannot hunt. There are also some clothes to be worn only by Chiefs, wealthy/successful persons and good warriors/ hunters. In the past only the Chiefs and heroes worn *Saipikhup* among the *Thadous* (Haokip U. J., 2011).

In the olden days some cloths were not allowed to be woven by the commoners (Goswami, 1985). Only the chiefs and officials, and their families were allowed to weave. It was also forbidden to put on these cloths while crossing a big river. It was feared that the cloths might attract the Snake King to the weaver. Ncy Doungel (Doungel, 2009) also noted that

> "...in the olden days a village priest will perform a ritual "*Lhalho*" to the women who wove *Thangnang* and *Khamtang* before they start and after finish. Because it was believe that the sound of weaving while they wove echoing to all nock and corner and the snakes will search for the place of weaving. Therefore, as *Khamtang* bears the pattern of snake sick women's doesn't wear it. *Khamtang* and *Thangnang* are also not worn while crossing river. If the women who wove were in any unhealthy condition, priest has to perform a ritual to cure her with an incantation."

The incantation was (Goswami, 1985)

> "(The name of the weaver) *amah in apon khon hi Taneng, Tachin Neichong umaho khon patna akhon ahi, ati alun dam le hen amit ahan phatlo hen*"

> This woman (the name of the weaver is mentioned) has woven this piece of cloth. In the past such cloths were woven by *Taneng, Tachin* and *Neichong*. May the weaver's head and body remain hale and hearty. May her eyes and teeth remain sound.

Textiles came to be associated with social and ritualistic events from the very early times. The continued existence of this craft helped in decentralization of the social and economic power and also provided with enough employment to the people.

Different traditional cloths of the *Kukis* are used for different occasions such as death, marriage, traditional festivals and religious ceremonies (see Table 2). There are a lot of similarities in the texture, design and motifs of clothes among the *Kuki* tribes. Each of the tribes (tribes as recognized by the government) claimed the clothes belonged to their respective tribes. They interpreted differently to strengthen their claims of originality. But, some tribes accepted that they had borrowed from others. This shows their affinity and same origin of oneness. Th. Thomsong's (Thomsong, 2011) explanation "there is a lot of sharing and borrowing culture within the *Kuki* tribes and with other ethnic group in Northeast India or its neighboring countries" is true. Mutua Bhadur (Bhadur, 2000) mentioned the *Moyon* and *Monsang*, who formerly belonged to one tribe, use the cloths under common names. But after the differentiation into two discrete tribes in 1956, they began to rename the previously used cloths in their respective dialects which differ slightly. Not only may the tribe recognition result, the dividend polity played by unwanted host in *Kuki* society is the primary reason.

Among the *Kuki* traditional cloths, *Pondum/Puandum* is typical and very popular in their tradition. It is used in different occasions such as death, festivals and it is also used to honoured a successful person. Both men and women of different tribe of the *Kukis* use the cloth in different ways. The *Thadou* tribe uses *Pondum* (see Plate 30) on the occasion of death. Where any mature person died, (Kimjalam, 2013) the *Thadou* women wore it as a lower garment or as a wrapper. They also present *Pondum* to the death person to show their love and respect which they called it *Thi-tomna* or *Thi-khuna*. The cloths presented by the mourners are not to be buried with him or her; the bereaved family presents it to the near and dear ones of the departed person. According to the customs of *Thadous, Pondum* was necessary for covering the dead body (Sitlhou, 2011) in murdered cases. Among the other *Kuki* tribes, *Gangte, Mizo, Paite, Simte, Sukte, Vaiphei* and *Zou* also have *Pondum,* but they do not use it on occasion of death. The design, colour pattern and its uses are different. New and various designs of *Pondum* also introduced by different tribe in different patterns. The *Paite BA Puandum* (see Plate 21) is one such beautiful and momentous cloth. Introduced in 1952 (Bhadur, 2000) it is specially meant to honour educated persons whether academic or professional. It is a mixture of black, red, blue and green with *Tungmaimu* (Hangsing, 2010).

As clothing plays an important role in recognition of identity, identity politics for recognition and popularity prevailed in Manipur has a great impact on *Kuki* traditional weaving of cloths. The *Kuki* women too played an important role in identity politics through their weaving of cloths. It can be observed that, during *Naga-Kuki* ethnic clash of 1990s, the traditional cloths of *Nagas* and *Kukis* are not worn by both the group. Other ethnic groups of the same state also avoid wearing of *Kuki* and *Naga* cloths as the counterpart group can attack because of the cloth he/she wear. *Seikholet* narrated that (Seikholet, 2013) "one *Meitei* man (my client) was almost to be attacked by my villagers because of his wearing *Naga* cloth....in 1990s, no one wears the *Naga* or *Kuki* cloths...our physical looks are similar and a person who wear this cloths can face attacked from either group". Therefore, the demand of traditional cloths has gone down in 1990s. Not only demand in market outlook, according to their traditional belief, uncompleted work of craft and weaving was taboo. If a craft person died before he/she complete the work they called as *"Tohsam*[14]*"* and that incomplete craft was not completed by other craft-person or used it. The traditional *Kukis* does not start new craft or weaving during war or rainy season because anything can be happened to the craft-person. Therefore, the *Kuki* women also not practiced weaving during this ethnic clash, and the development of weaving was effected in some of their area.

Soon after the *Naga-Kuki* ethnic clashes in 1993 in Manipur, development in weaving revived rapidly. In contradiction to earlier developments or practices, weaving now focus on identity classification or identity politics for recognition. Now the *Kuki* women produced varied and good number of their traditional cloths by different techniques of weaving for identity recognition and popularity. The most development of weaving by *Kuki* women can be the post-ethnic-clash[15] weaving.

Conclusion

Besides catering to the domestic needs of the family, the *Kuki* women devoted their time to acquire the techniques and know-how of weaving. As the popular saying of the *Kukis* goes "*Numei ponkhong theilou chun aji-acha te ipiti phalbi adousah ding ham?*" The literal meaning is "How will a woman, who is ignorant about the art of weaving, keep her family warm during winter?" It implies that every true *Kuki* woman knows or must know how to weave. Therefore, the art of weaving is an indispensable trait of a *Kuki* woman, and a woman who has such skill is highly appreciated and honoured in the society.

Loin-Loom, the traditional weaving technique of the *Kukis* has its advantages and disadvantages. Some buyers preferred the product of Loin Loom than the product of Shuttle Loom. The product of Shuttle Loom is easily available and at a reasonable price. It is chosen by most buyers (rich and poor) for use on the occasions, auspicious ceremonies, rites and rituals, festival and other ceremonies. Needle work or embroidery textile is another new and interesting feature in their cloths. Moreover, modification and modernization of weaving technique, cloth designs and materials used have a great impact on traditional *Kuki* weaving. Their innovation in weaving are connected with their local status, participation in decision making, identity politics and creativity in art. The *Kuki* women now produce a large number of their traditional cloths in varied

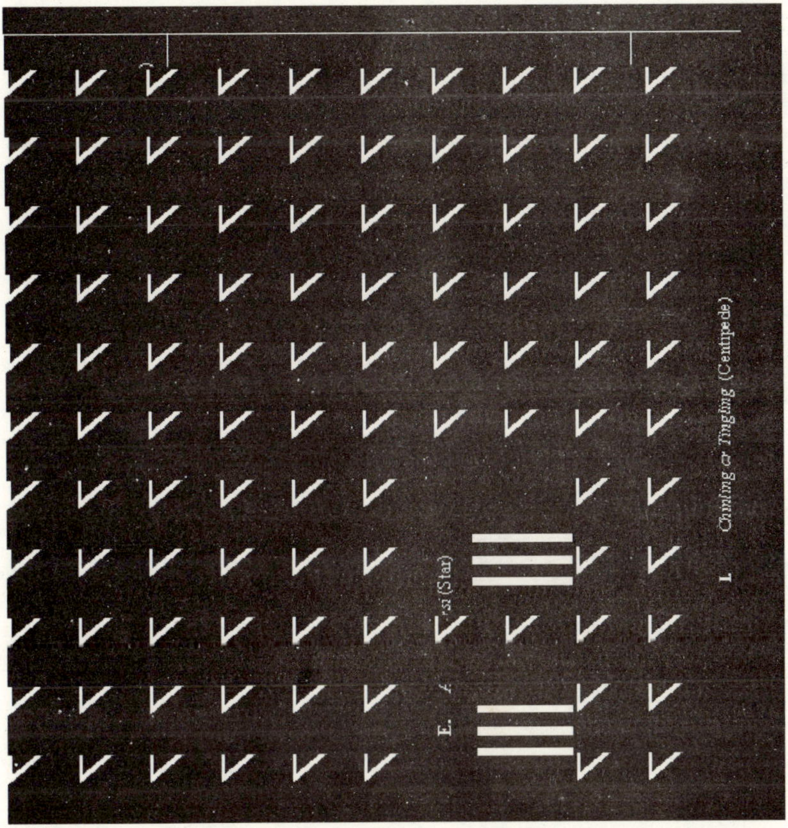

Symbols use in cloths

designs and wear. Their hand woven traditional cloths are sold in different places of India. They have also introduced new styles and designs of their cloths in different attires such as muffler, waist-coat, neck-tie, carrying bags etc.

The essay pursued randomly argues that the *Kukis* of Manipur have their own art of weaving. The traditional cloths of the *Kuki* group are very distinct from the *Naga* group. The former uses such designs or patterns of *Changmaimu* (cucumber seed), *Sumtung* (traditional pounding/grinding machin), *Tiengka* or *Thalka* (Arrow), *Vagol-mit* (Eye), *Ahshi* or

Table 2: Cloths of the *Kukis* used by different tribes, men and women

Sl. No.	*Tribe*	*Men*	*Women*
1.	Aimol	*Ponte@, Diaram, Amthal, Ponchial Rulpuiyeak$, Ralngam Buchun, Muikhamjal^*	*Saipikhup#. Senchal@, Arsian**
2.	Anal	*Lungvin#, Anal Bu, Wahrak Akal Bu*, Jatha@*	*Akhum Ahno#, Lungvin#, Wahrak Akal Bu**
3.	Chiru	*Apa Ponte*, Bangpui Pon, Ponrobo, Lindu*, Ponhang*	*Nupang Ponve#, Aarsi Ponve#. Jidit Ponve#. Longdi Aam, Khongkhit, Nupang Ponte*, Aimo Suivo**
4.	Chothe	*Awa-ampee*, Leingam Busun̆*, Phurup Aam*, Purum Pan*, Theiru-aam*, Chaotanam, Uikengchung/Uikeaam*	*Uikengchung/Uikeaam, Purum Nik#. Tongkaap#, Chaotanam/Hangsa-Hangset*
5.	Gangte	*Puandum*, Thansuohpuan**	*Puandum*, Thansuohpuan*, Paunlaisen#*
6.	Hmar	*Thangsapuan#. Hmarpuan#*	*Paunlaisen#. Hmar-am#, Hmarpuan#. Ngotekher#. Thangsapuan#, Mithipuan#. Thangsaopaunbat, Ngotlong Polang Pun khat@, La-um@. Polang Ketang@. Saipikhup#.*
7.	Kharam	*Thompui Basal Ponsil@, Ponjadum@, Ponsenjal*, Thompui Lukhom, Tasaje, Thipusa Kongsoi, Thipusa Kongsoi.Thompui Lukhom#, Ponbel Thuibao#, Ponbel#, Thompui Nuimaisa Ponsil**	
8.	Koireng	*Morvon, Ponsan*^, Ponthal^*	*Ka-a-am, Thaitei, La-um*
9.	Kom	*Pasepun*, Pukhamjal*, Punchai*, Lukhom^*	*Punkophoi#, Puntre#, Kekir#, Numeipun*, Koram.*
10.	Lamgang	*Takarbu*, Takar Bunglapol*, Takarlap**	*Takarbu*, Takar Bunglapol*, Takarlap*, Lamthin#, Nikti#, Diphun#, Woisen#, Takar Kinik#*
11.	Maring	*Khoinganlu$, Langphai#, Karkhop#, Kungvere*	*Karkhop#, Kungvere*
12.	Mizo	*Ngotekherh, Puandum, Thangsapuan*$*	*Ngotekherh, Puanchei#, Hmar-am#*
13.	Monsang	*Elerpiin pon*	*Elerpiin pon, Edung Enhii#, Echang#, Ekam Enhii@, Atrim Enhii#, Ethii Enhii, Changkha Enhii, Savang Jur Enhii.*
14.	Moyon	*Kurkam Peen*, Wangjam Piin*	*Tudilili#, Tingpi#, Changkak, Tengpi Enhii.*
15.	Paite	*B.A. Puandum*$, Puandum*, Ngotekherh*, Thangsuah Puan*$Puandum*, Ngotekherh*, Paunlaisen#, Gungal Puan#, Kheaupheau#, Malam#, Aksipak#, Lianbuangthuam#.*	

Sl. No.	*Tribe*	*Men*	*Women*
16.	Purum	*Kotana*, Uikengchong*, Thalkuiam#, Ampun Hengkung sapa, Tangngam Basun*, Thamachet*, Purum Pal*, Laidil*, Pheeseng*, Paluplamhor*, Awamphi, Tungdap*	*Ekuok Punbil#, Ahopunsan#, Khentral#, Lamlangphanek#, Sandolik#, Sipersibup#*
17.	Purum (Kom)	*Ponjaldum, Ponthal Lukom, Amachal Lukom, Koram*, Nahong*, Puandum*, Aipui Ruko*	*Sairem Ponlang*, Mukhamjar@, Khamtang#, Chalakok-in#, Saipuikhup#, Ponvolchel#, Jamsil@*
18.	Simte	*Puanlaisan* Puandum#*	*Khangthah-Puandum#, Santeleniih#,*
19.	Sukte	*Puandum*, Tanching, Paunlaisen**	*Paunlaisen*, Zonik#, Khephlu#, Nikvom#, Nikphei#*
20.	Tarao	*Leijing*^, Punthelona**	*Punthelona*, Lukphaivum*, Punsil#, Phurekthing#, Punshiljee#, Lungakkhu#, Leingamshun**
21.	Thadou	*Saipikhup*, Mongvom*, Pondum*	*Saipikhup*, Thangnang*, Nineljem#, Khamtang#, Saipikhup#, Pondum*#*
22.	Vaiphei	*Puandum**	*Khengkoi#, Thanso Punvek#, Gol-luipon#*
23.	Zou	*Silpaun*, Pasal Paundum, B.A. Paundum*, Ngongon, Kangthapaun**	*Puandum#, Zoulamnik#*

Hints:
@ = Wrapper **# = Lower garment/Skirt** *** = Shawl** **$ = Meritorious/High Status** **^ = Elders/Chiefs**

Ahsi (Star), *Thal* or *Gulngam-Thal* (Bow), *Gosem-jang* (Bamboo pipe of a *Kuki* musical instrument), *Gulpi* (Snake), *Chingling* or *Tingling* (Centipede). Therefore, the common affinities of the *Kukis* (*Khul* or *Khur* origin people) in their traditional cloth designs, origin, symbols and uses are classic. Further, the weavers (*Kuki* women) also play an important role in identity politics. The *Kuki* cloths are now widely recognized and popularly used all over the world.

Notes

1. Bark of plant (rhizome family) shredded into thin strips.
2. Short strands of thread generally of 10/12 inches cut out from the edge of woven cloth and tied together to make long strands.
3. There were different theories about the so called *Sinlung, Khul or Khur*. Different writers mention it but no one described that the cave is a large natural underground chamber or what it is? The most common belief is that it is located in the present Yunnan state of China. *Khuplam Milun Lenthang* statement "...*Manmasi [Kukis]* are not a human born by cave i.e. neither not the son of cave nor the people of cave" shows that they are not the descendants or sons of cave, but they are passing through the cave. Therefore, all the people originated from cave are generally described as *Chin-Kuki* by varied writers.
4. *Chang-Ai* is a celebration of bounteous rice harvest in which the lady of the family is honored.
5. A *Kuki* traditional institution concerned for economic life of the individual and the community in the village. Akin to a modern youth club or philanthropic organization giving free services in helping each other freely is one of the principles of *Lom*. For the younger members it is the learning school for all physical works.
6. *Som* is another *Kuki* traditional institution for youths of the village to stay together and learned their rich custom, culture, war tactics etc. *Som* is also concerned for any emergency like fire, war, thieves inside the village. The main objective of the *Som* was to acquire the customs and war tactics besides staying together.
7. The *Kukis* came out of a cave called *Khul/Khur* which is believed to be under-earth,

8. *Leisanpa* is a man-Emperor of the earth. *Leisanpa* is the man "Adam" the first man according to the Christian Holy Bible (Genesis 1:27).
9. The literal meaning of *Kholkip-Kholjang* is "the place where all living beings lives", i.e. what we called the earth. According to Dr. Khuplam Milui Lenthang this is the earth after the flood mentioned in the Old Testament of Holy Bible (Genesis 6,7 & 8). Another version by William Shaw in his "Notes on the Thadou Kukis" claimed that it is located above *Kaithenmangpi* in Manipur on the right bank of the *Imphal River*. At the time of the flood the *Thadous* say they collected at *Kholkipkholjang* where every living thing took refuge. He also noted that the upper portion of this place of refuge is known as *Kholkip* where all the animals are said to have congregated, while the lower portion is spoken of as *Kholjang*.
10. Dr. Khuplam Milui Lenthang is one of the person who belief that the *Chin-Kuki-Mizos* are one of the lost tribes of Israel-the descendants of *Manasseh/Manmasi*. Therefore, the Author, Dr. Khuplam Milui Lenthang used the term *Manmasi*, which is none other than *Kukis*. The author's version of *Manmasi* is not accepted by all.
11. This is my suggestion that, the used of traditional designs in this computer technology needs more technical research.
12. *Tuikul* means water or river. According to the legend described by Dr. Khuplam Milui Lenthang, the king and the queen of water or river were male python and female python.
13. The bamboo pipe of a *Kuki* musical instrument.
13. The *Thadou* term *TOHSAM* means incomplete work which was impossible to continue by other, used when someone died before completing his/her works (especially in craft), that incomplete work or craft was called *TOHSAM.*
14. Weaving after *Naga-Kuki* ethnic clashes of 1990s.

References

ASSOCIATION, A. I. (Ed.). (2010). *All India Artisans and Craftworkers Welfare Association*. Retrieved May 24, 2013, from http://www.aiacaonline.org: http://www.aiacaonline.org/pdf/handloom-weaving-extended-documentation.pdf

BHADUR, M. (2009). *Art of Textile; Manipuri Textile from Bangladesh and Myanmar*. Imphal: Mutua Museum.

BHADUR, M. (1997). *Traditional Textiles of Manipur*. Imphal: Mutua Museum.

BHADUR, M. (2000). *Tribal Hand Woven Fabrics of Manipur*. Imphal: Mutua Museum.

BHADUR, M. (1994). *Tribal Textile of Manipur*. Imphal: Mutua Museum.

DOUNGEL, N. (2009). *Puchon Pachon (Customary Practices of Thadou-Kuki)* (Second ed.). (N. Haokip, Trans.) Imphal: Tribal Research Institute, Imphal.

CHELLASAMY, P., SUMATHI. N. (n.d.). *Indian Textile Industry*. Retrieved May 28, 2013, from Fibre to Fashion: http://www.fibre2fashion.com/industry-article/pdffiles/indian-textile-industry.pdf

GOSWAMI, T. (1985). *Kuki Life and Lore*. Haflong, Assam: North Cachar Hill District Council.

GUITE, V. (2010). *Tribal Folk Costumes and Crafts*. Delhi: Akansha Publishing House.

HANGSING, T. (2010, February 09). *Zogam Online*. Retrieved 05 30, 2013, from Zogam Online.com: http://www.zogamonline.com/columns/thathang-hangshing/3146-documentation-on-the-zoumi-culture-and-tradition.html

HAOKIP. C. (2013, June 1). Writter. (N. Haokip, Interviewer) Facebook.

HAOKIP. N. (2011, December 18). Artist/Craftsman. (N. Haokip, Interviewer, N. Haokip, Editor, & N. Haokip, Translator)

HAOKIP. P. (2013). I Have a Dream: My Vision of New Kuki Society. In T. Haokip, *The Kukis of Northeast India: Politics and Culture* (p. 165). Delhi: Bookwell.

HAOKIP. P. (2006). *Re-discovery of Traditional Institutions of the Kukis in Manipur; with special reference to Lawm and Sawm*. Serampore: Unpublished Thesis submitted to Senate of Serampore College/University, Serampore.

HAOKIP, P. (2013). Reinculcation Traditional Values of the Kukis. In T. Haokip, *The Kukis of Northeast India: Politics and Culture* (p. 189). Delhi: Bookwell.

HAOKIP, P. (2008). *Zalen-gam The Kuki Nation*. New Delhi: KNO.

HAOKIP, U. J. (2011, October 20). Village Elder. (N. Haokip, Interviewer, & N. Haokip, Translator)

INDIA, C. C. (March, 2013). *A Brief Report on Textile Industries in India*. Corporate Catalyst India, Corporate Catalyst India. New Delhi: Corporate Catalyst India.

KIMJALAM. (2013, January 27). Village Elder. (N. Haokip, Interviewer, & N. Haokip, Translator)

LENTHANG, D. K. (2005). *Manmasi Chate (Kuki-Chin-Mizo) Thulhun Kidang Masa.* Moreh: Hill Tribal Council.

LONCHEU, N. (2013). *Bawmzos: A Study of Chin-Kuki-Zo Tribes of Chittagong.* (P. L. Dena, Ed.) New Delhi: Akansha Publishing House.

MUTUA BHADUR, Y. SANTABAI. (1996). *Tribal Art of Manipur.* Imphal: Mutua Museum.

PETERS, A. (2013). *The History of Tribal Textiles.* Retrieved May 28, 2013, from Fibre to Fashion: http://www.fibre2fashion.com/industry-article/7/673/the-history-of-tribal-textiles1.asp

SEIKHOLET. (2013, January 04). Businessmen. (N. Haokip, Interviewer, & N. Haokip, Translator)

SHAW, WILLIAM. (1997). *Notes on Thadou Kukis* (1929 ed.). (J. Hutton, Ed.) Guwahati: Spectrum Publication.

SITLHOU, HOINEILHING (2011). Continuity and Change: The Setting of a Customary Court Amongst the Kukis. In N. H. Lunminthang, *Kuki Society Past, Present, Future* (pp. 364-378). New Delhi: Maxford Books.

THOMSONG, T. (2011, March 17). Historian & Politician. (N. Haokip, Interviewer, & N. Haokip, Translator)

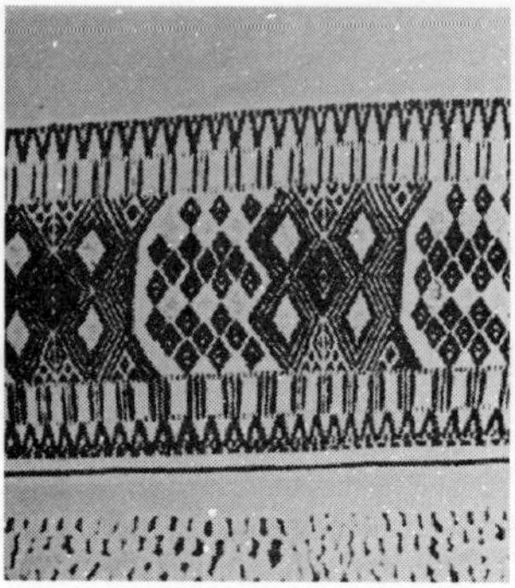

Plate 3. *Ponthal Lukom*: Purum turban (Bhadur, 2000)

Plate 4. *Saipuikhup:* Purum skirt (women) (Bhadur, 2000)

Plate 6. *Nuhmeipun:* Kom shawl (women) (Bhadur, 2000)

Plate 7. *Saipikhup:* Koireng skirt (Bhadur, 2000)

Plate 8. *Ponthal:* Koireng shawl (men) (Bhadur, 2000)

Plate 9. *Saipikhup:* Thadou shawl (men

Plate 10. *Saipikhup:* Thadou shawl (women)

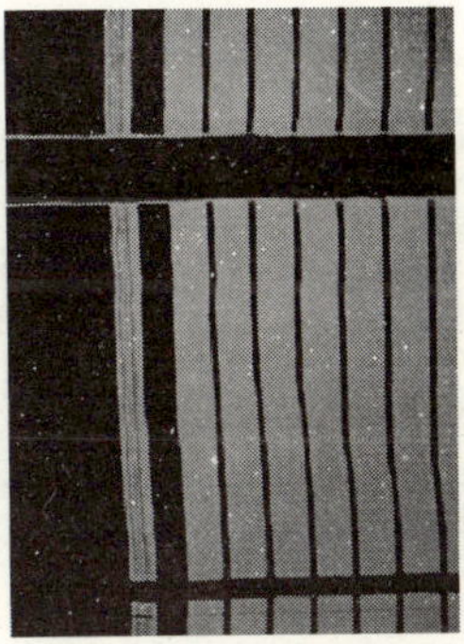

Plate 11. *Ngotekherh:* Mizo (men and women) (Bhadur, 2000)

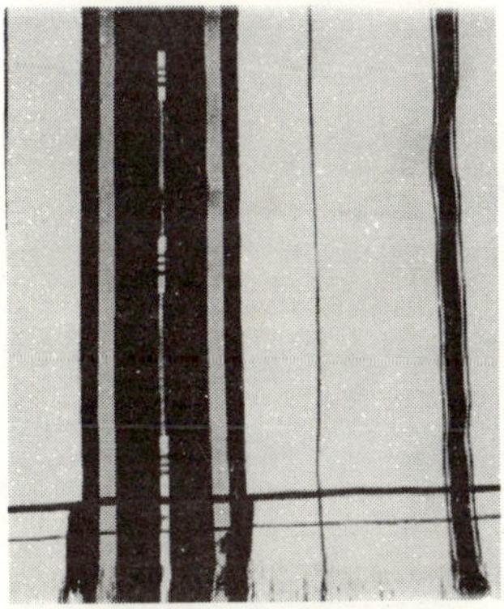

Plate 12. *Puanlaisen:* Simte shawl (men)

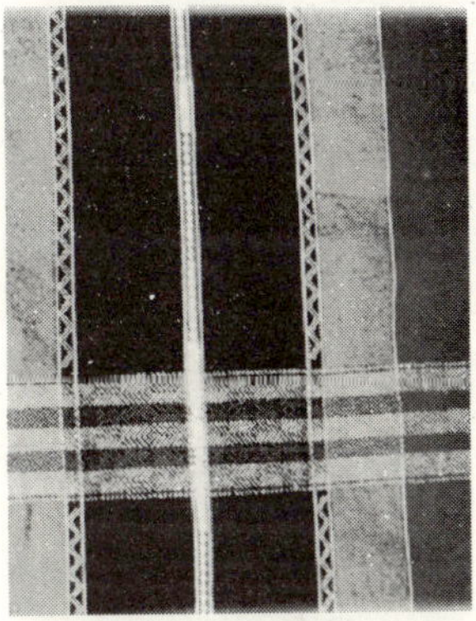

Plate 13. *Puandum:* Sukte shawl (men)

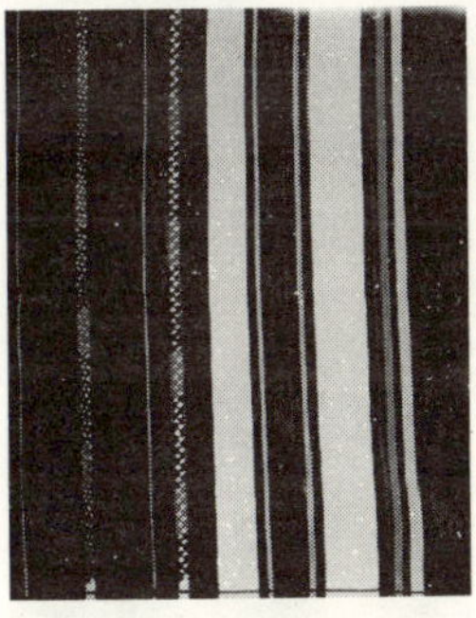

Plate 14. *Puanlaisen:* Gangte skirt (women)

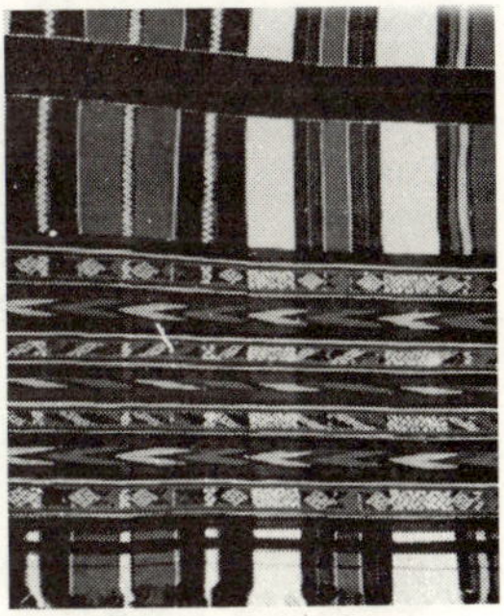

Plate 15. *Puanlaisen:* Paite skirt (women)

Plate 16. *Puanchei:* Mizo skirt (women) (Bhadur, 2000)

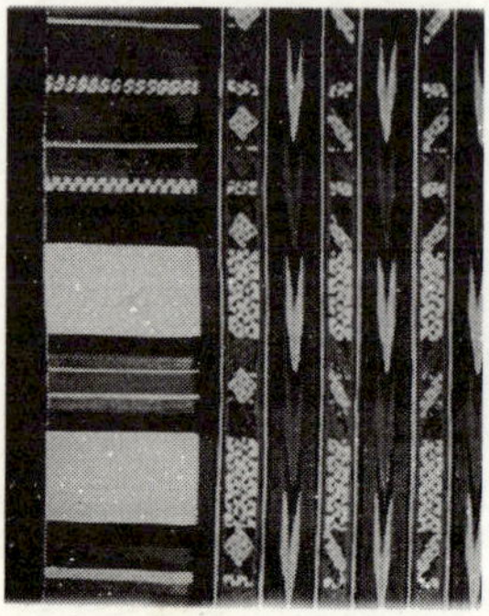

Plate 17. *Paunlaisen:* Hmar skirt (women) (Bhadur, 2000)

Plate 18. *Langphai:* Maring lower garment (Men) (Bhadur, 2000)

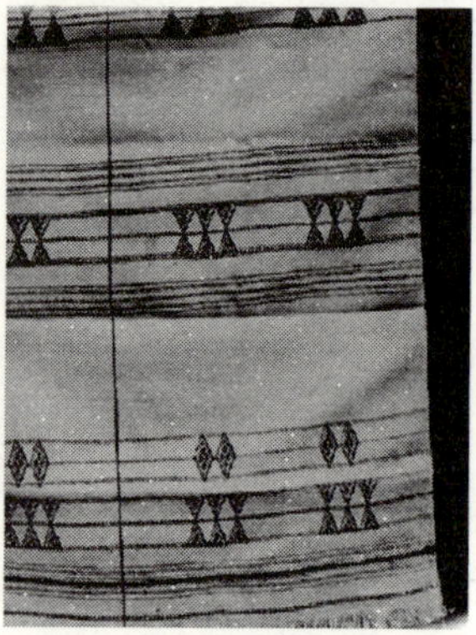

Plate 19. *Karkhop:* Maring skirt (Bhadur, 2000)

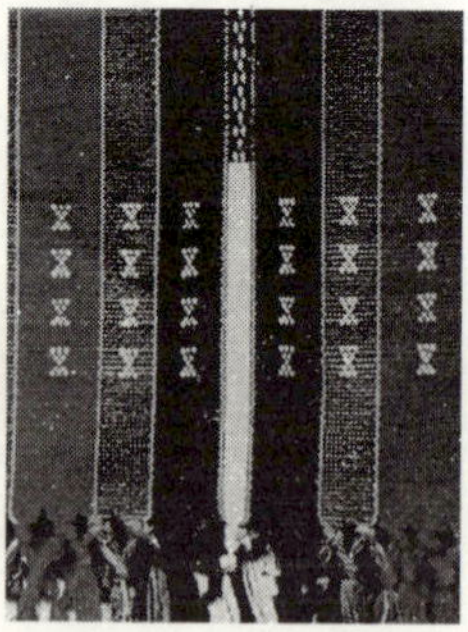

Plate 20. *Khangthahpuan:* Zou shawl (Men) (Bhadur, 2000)

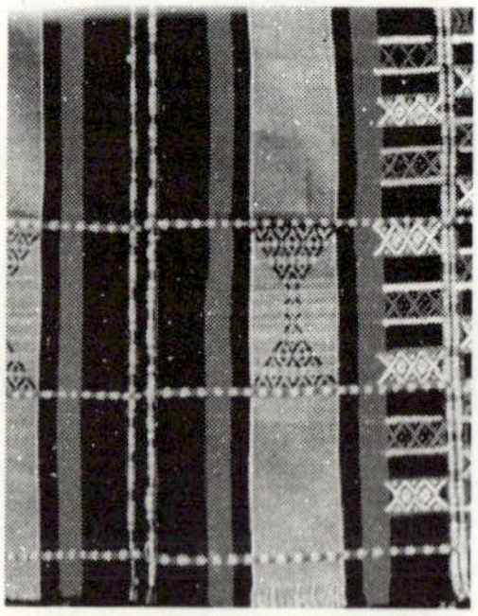

Plate 21. *Punsil:* Tarao skirt (Bhadur, 2000)

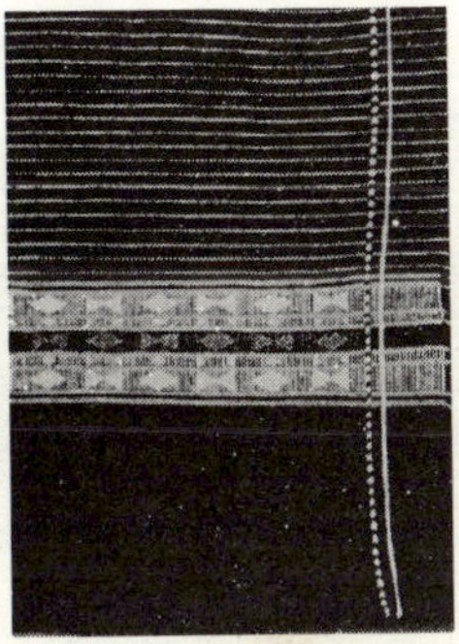

Plate 22. ***Senchal:*** **Aimol skirt (Bhadur, 2000)**

Plate 23. ***Lungakkhu:*** **Tarao skirt (virgin girl) (Bhadur, 2000)**

Plate 24. ***Pasepun/Thangnang:*** **Kom shawl (men) (Bhadur, 2000)**

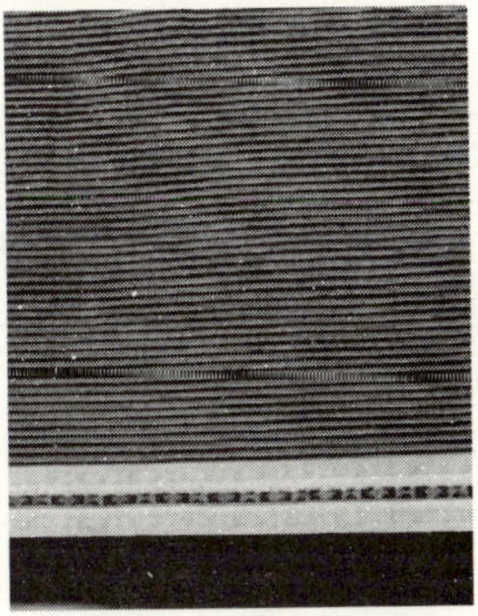

Plate 25. ***Chalakok:*** **Purum skirt (women) (Bhadur, 2000)**

Plate 26. ***Thangnang:*** **Thadou Shawl**

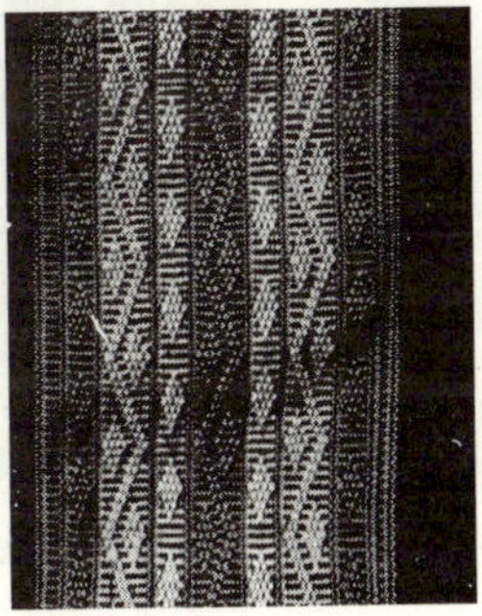

Plate 27. ***Khamtang:*** **Thadou skirt (women)**

Plate 28. *Ponchial Rulpuiyek:* Aimol shawl (Bhadur, 2000)

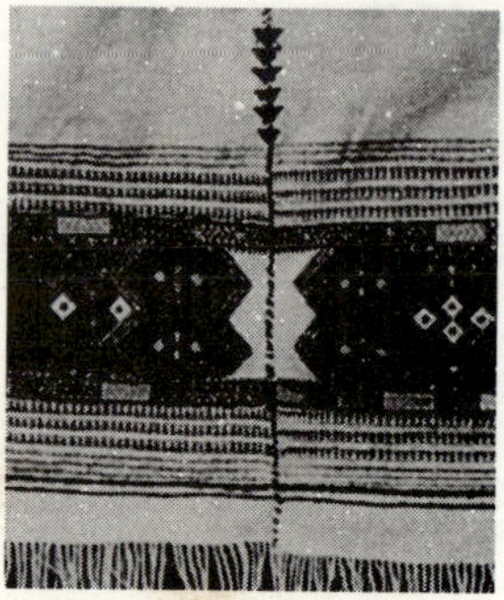

Plate 29. *Thompui Basal Ponsil:* Kharam shawl (Bhadur, 2000)

Plate 30. Weaving by Loin Loom

Plate 31. Weaving by Shuttle Loom

Plate 32. Spinning Wheel (IGNCA, 2010)

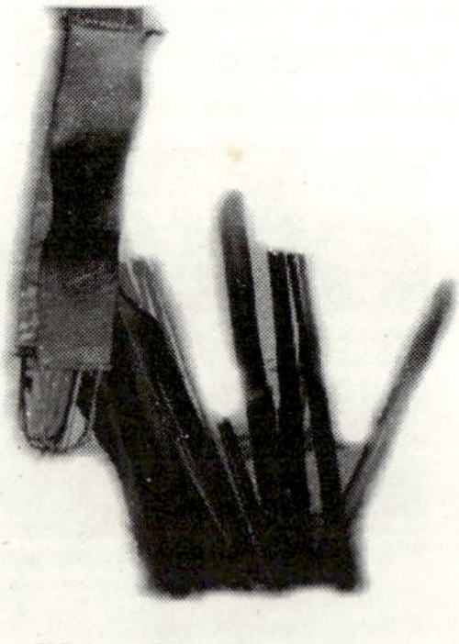

Plate 33. Weaving tools

Thadou woman attire

Loin Loom

Reference

1. Bhadur, M. (2000). Tribal Hand Woven Fabrics of Manipur. 9. Imphal: Mutua Museum.

2. IGNCA. Spinning Wheel. *Exihibition.* Indira Gandhi National Centre for Arts, New Delhi.

Chapter 4

Women in the Informal Economy: Unpacking realities of the Tribal Women Vendors of Manipur

Jaja Kipgen

"For most of history, Anonymous was a woman"- Virginia Woolf

"I am not educated, so all I can do is sit under the sun and sell vegetables, there is nothing much I can do otherwise to support my family. Life is not easy for a poor, uneducated village woman like me. It is a constant struggle for survival and earning my best".

-Hoizavung, 36 year old Kuki woman vendor (during data collection)

Women's participation in the economy still remains unrecognised and undervalued despite their contribution to the needs of the family, thereby indirectly adding to the national coffer. In a country like India, where most of its population are employed in the informal sector, it is the women folk who form more than 90 percent of the core labour force in this sector. However, their work remains ignored thus depriving them of recognition and monitory benefit. Therefore, it is quintessential to provide them with safe working conditions, access to essential facilities, social security and protection. These are imperative for the development and recognition of these women and hence cannot be denied or overlooked.

In this article, an attempt has been made to discuss the various aspects of women in the informal economy with a special focus on tribal women street vendors of Manipur. This article brings forth the plight of the tribal women street vendors in relation to their working conditions, needs, challenges faced, role within the family and society at large. A research study was conducted in the state of Manipur to understand and describe the ground realities of tribal women street vendors. However, this study is not a generalization for the country but there are studies conducted in other parts of the world by other scholars that support the contention. This article is an excerpt from a research study undertaken by the author.

Introduction

The existence and contribution of women has always been an untold and unheard story. It occasionally rings in the air only to die down after certain interesting debates and discussions. Women, for most of history and even till today have always remained at the backseat, invisible to the rest of the world.

There are hundreds and thousands of women like Hoizavung who struggle everyday of their lives to earn a living. Millions of women are in the unorganised sector, many are self employed while the rest work for meagre wages and salaries. The work of women has never been accounted or considered as contributing to the country's gross domestic product (GDP) or even to their individual families.

Similar is the condition of women in most of the third world countries. Women's work is taken for granted and hardly appreciated. Often assumed as only a 'pocket money' that women earn during their free time, interestingly this 'pocket money' goes into running the family and buying basic essential goods. Even during times of dire need and circumstances, it is the savings of these women which come in handy as life- savers in times of accidents and sickness.

It has been always assumed that self employed women carry out work at home during their leisure hours. This is not true at all, as women work because they feel the need of income to support their families. They spend almost 10- 15 hours a day working as contract employees in the *zari* business, rolling *beedis,* making *papads,* incense sticks and piece rate work. There are also those who work at construction sites or as vendors selling various items and goods.

This article on the informal sector focusing on the tribal women vendors of Manipur highlights the needs, constraints and opportunities of this particular group of women. The tribal women vendors of Manipur belong to different tribes. They come from one of the most marginalised and poorer sections of the community. Having no educational qualifications suitable for good government or private jobs, most women take up vending as their occupation.

Various reasons such as lack of skills, easy access to vending as an occupation, ability to start off with low investment have fostered in the increase of women who are vendors. These women come from different corners of the state and belong to other hill districts. The lack of sales in the nearby towns and villages has driven them to relocate to the capital city of Imphal.

Other factors which have contributed to the increased participation of tribal women in street vending over the years, in particular was the ethnic conflict between the Naga and Kuki tribes which led to loss of livelihood, land and villages, forcing people to migrate from rural to urban areas. This paved the way for the tribal women to be self employed to survive in the city and provide for their families. However, embarking on this journey has not been easy though many of the women interviewed have been vending for more than ten years, their problems and condition still remain the same. In some ways, problems have only multiplied leaving them with no solutions, at the mercy of the state government and the concerned departments.

For the purpose of this article, the terms informal economy, informal work, informal sector, unorganised sector are used interchangeably.

Women in Informal Economy- Global Scenario

What is informal economy?

Informal economy was first discovered in the 1970's when an employment mission was sent to Kenya in Africa by the

International Labour Organisation. Ever since, the informal economy is a topic of study for people from myriad fields. Academicians, policy makers, research scholars, activists and governments have undertaken and are still conducting research studies to analyse and understand the contribution of informal sector employment to the economy of many countries (Chen, 2004). According to Women in Informal Employment Globalizing and Organizing (WIEGO), the informal economy is described as a set of economic activities, enterprises, and workers that are not regulated or protected by the state (WIEGO, 2011).

Given its heterogeneity and its evolving nature, describing the informal economy in any meaningful ways is quite difficult. The term' informal economy' is invoked to refer to street vendors in Bogota; rickshaw pullers in Hanoi and Calcutta; garbage collectors in Cairo; home based garment workers in Manila, Madeira, Mexico city and Toronto; and home based electronic workers in Leeds, Istanbul, and Kuala Lampur (Chen, 2002; Jhabvala, 2002; Lund, 2002).

Women all over the world account for majority of those employed in the unorganised sector. Contrary to this, the number of women employed in the organised sector is negligible when compared to majority of them who are employed or self employed in the unorganised sector. Women form a vital part of the informal economy and most of them are self employed in this sector. According to Women in Informal Employment Globalizing and Organizing (WIEGO) large numbers of women worldwide work in the informal sector accounting for ninety percent of women working outside of agriculture in India and Indonesia, nearly three quarters in Zambia, four-fifths of those in Lima, Peru and more than two thirds of those in the Republic of Korea work in the informal sector (WIEGO, 2011).

In a way, women's status is directly related to the world of work. Work is currently understood as the 'expending labour in return for use-value (money).' In the world of work, women hold secondary position compared to men leading to a male- dominated society (Khandelwal, 2004). Women's work reality is low participation rate, low wages, crowding in low paid occupations, lack of access to means of production including credit, unfavourable climate for career development and so on (Stockyard and Johnson,1992).

Women's economic contribution is immensely significant, although most of their works remain unpaid, unrecognised and undervalued. But in the real sense, without the long hours of work that women put in both outside and inside home, many of the economic activities would have come to a halt. Women share at least half, if not more, the burden of most of the works (Kar, 2002). Women are seen as an invisible workforce. It is evident from the Human Development Report that women's economic contribution is undervalued to the tune of US$11 trillion a year internationally (Human Development Report, 1995).

According to the Human Development Report 1995, 'Development if not engendered is endangered', implying that women irrespective of their caste, class, culture, tradition and background need to be involved in the development process of the nation. Subsequently, according to Oxfam, women work 67% of the world's working hours. In terms of education, two out of three of the world's illiterate people are women and women's earnings range from 50-85% of men's earnings. Globally women make up just 10% of representatives in the national governments. The data is disheartening in comparison to the work done by women (Oxfam, 1995).

According to Prasad (2005), women's development may be viewed from two angles. Firstly, the individual development of women and secondly, women as a distinct social category, an important societal component and an essential part of human society. We may talk of women's development and development of her personality but for most women it is something that cannot be even dreamt of. Despite their enormous contribution women are pushed back and hardly given a chance to come forward and actively participate in all aspects of life.

National Scenario of women's work

In India the term informal sector or informal economy has not been used in the official statistics or in the National Accounts Statistics. The terms used in India are 'organised sector' and 'unorganised sector'. The unorganised sector refers to those enterprises whose activities are not regulated under any legal provision or do not maintain any regular accounts (Naik, 2009).

The Constitution of India clearly states down the Right to Work and profess an occupation in articles 39(a) and (b) of the Constitution which clearly state that the state shall in particular direct its policy so that-

a) *The citizens, men and women equally have the right to an adequate means of livelihood.*

b) *The ownership and control of the material resources of the community are so distributed as best to sub serve the common good.*

There are different occupational groups within the umbrella of informal employment. This sector comprises of different occupations such as domestic workers, home based workers, street vendors, waste pickers and other groups like construction workers, garment workers, small holder farmers and transport workers.

In India, more than 90 percent of women workers are engaged in the unorganised sector activities. Interestingly, the United Nations (2000) also states that unorganised sector is a large source of employment for women than men. In fact the proportion of women workers in the unorganised sector exceeds that of men in most developing countries, not only in India (ILO, 2002).

Street vendors form a very important segment of the unorganized sector in the country. It is estimated that in several cities street vendors account for 2 percent of the population. Women constitute a very large segment of these vendors in almost every city. Street vending is not only a source of self employment to the poor in cities and towns but also a means to provide 'affordable' as well as 'convenient' services to a majority of the urban population (National Policy on Urban Street Vendors, 2009).

Street vendors provide valuable services to the urban masses while eking out a living through their own enterprise, limited resources and labour. They facilitate convenient, efficient, cost effective distribution of goods and services to the public. They also contribute significantly to local economic growth and vitality of the urban economies.

According to the National Policy on Urban Street Vendors (2009), a street vendor is broadly defined as a person who offers goods or services for sale to the public without having a permanent built up structure in a street. Along with other occupations, street vending has been a major form of employment for a large chunk of population since ancient times. Despite claims of economic boon and growth, there are occupations such as these which have been accommodating any person willing to join it unlike the jobs offered only to qualified and educated sections of the society.

The vendors have also been divided into three basic categories namely: (a) stationary, (b) peripatetic and (c) mobile. The stationary vendors are those who carry out vending on a regular basis at a specific location, e.g. those occupying space on the pavements or other public places and/or private areas either open/ covered (with implicit or explicit consent) of the authorities. Peripatetic vendors are those who carry out vending on foot and sell their goods and services and include those who carry baskets on their head/ slung on their shoulders or those who sell their goods on pushcarts. Mobile street vendors are those who move from place to place vending their goods and services on bicycle or mobile units on wheels, whether motorized or not. They also include vendors selling their wares in moving buses, local trains etc (National Policy on Urban Street Vendors, 2009).

The inadequate employment of women in India in the formal sector is largely related to education. The literacy rate and educational levels of the majority women does not suit the purpose of formal sectors where technical knowledge and highly qualified degrees are a tool used to measure one's ability and capability and similar is the case globally.

Therefore, since changes or improvements cannot happen overnight for women to be employed majorly in the formal sector, what is important is to see that women's invisible 'paid work and unpaid housework should be recognised and counted as it would increase the share of women and informal workers in the workforce.

Women in India: Employment in the Informal Economy

In India women constitute 48.2 percent of the total population and the women workers constitute 25.68 per cent of the total workforce in the country (Census, 2001). Research on the impact of economic reforms on women's employment suggests that although women are getting more jobs, they are by and large employed in low skilled jobs, usually non-unionized, and experience adverse working conditions such as low wages and long working hours.

A study by Sastry (2004) has brought interesting insights on the informal economy. It was found that 92 percent of all workers were in informal employment, covering 90 percent of the total male workforce and 95 percent of the total female workforce. There is higher proportion of females engaged in informal employment visa-vis male workers (Sastry, 2004).

A study on women street vendors by Bhatt, Cohen and Pat Horn (2000) in different countries of Africa, Asia and Mexico show that despite their contribution, women are harassed by police and municipal authorities. The goods sold by them are confiscated and returned only after they pay fines. The study concludes by stating that women vendors want the government to recognize their rights to trade in streets and provide sufficient space for them. They also want supportive services like credit, training and so forth similar to those offered by other businesses. The women vendors want their legal rights to infrastructure and acknowledgement of their contribution to the economy.

A case study on Self Employed Women's Association (SEWA) and the women vendors of Ahmedabad revealed that women work as hawkers, petty traders selling fruits, vegetables, other food items, housewares, tools, clothes and a variety of self made goods. Inspite of their contribution to the society, the women vendors face a lot of challenges regarding space. They were accused of encroachment, creating chaos and obstructing transportation. To fight for their cause SEWA took a stand to ensure the rights of these women to vend at a prime location called Manek Chowk in Ahmedabad. This fight became a success thus ensuring the rights of both male and female vendors to ply their trade without any fear. They also took up the issue of securing more licenses for its members and a place to vend without police harassment (Bhatt, Cohen & Horn, 2000).

For example, in India the unorganised sector accounts for over 95 percent of women workers outside agriculture. The unorganised sector accounts for nine out of every ten women working outside agriculture. Secondly, the unorganised sector is a large source of employment for women than for men (UN, 2000). In fact the proportion of women workers in the unorganised sector exceeds that of men in most developing countries, not only in India. Third, women's share of the total unorganised workforce outside of agriculture is higher than men's.

The NSSO report of 2008 states that in terms of employment, women employed by the unorganised sector has gone up in Manipur and southern states of Andhra Pradesh and Karnataka taking the lead. The percentage of women workers in the unorganised sector increased from 34 per cent in 2000-01 to 38 per cent in 2005-06. The incidence of women employment was highest in Manipur and accounts for 74.4 per cent of the unorganised workers, as per the NSSO report on employment, assets and borrowings of the unorganised sector.

It is seen that the hill states like Arunachal Pradesh, Manipur, Meghalaya, Mizoram and Nagaland with significantly high proportion of tribal population have higher women work participation than that of the plain states like Assam and Tripura with predominantly non-tribal population. Among the tribal population again, the female work participation rates are found to be highest in Manipur (45.96 percent), followed by Arunachal Pradesh (44.08 percent) and the lowest in Tripura (25.30 percent) (Census, 1991 and NEC, 1980 and 1995).

Tribal Society: Tribal women and work

The tribals living in the Northeast India, Deccan plateau and some regions of south India all share a symbiotic relationship with the forests. Forests and tribals are inseparable and the ecological background of the tribes has much to do with the socio-cultural economic norms of the tribes. But with the advent of "development, "planning" and "industrialization", this close knit relationship is breaking down at an alarming rate disrupting and destroying the long bond of inter-dependency that has existed leaving the conditions of the tribal people at stake dragging them further below the levels of poverty (Fernandes, 1992).

Alam (2000) cites Fernandes (1992) who says the tribals suffer all the inequalities, and are economically backward, socially marginalised, politically powerless and culturally peripheral. Thus, to survive nowadays, they depend on more than one economic pursuit and various 'change agents' have transformed their life and culture to a complex whole.

The situation here is so different because females are not considered economic liabilities, and birth of a girl is not looked down upon. They are considered economic assets, instead. Forest based tribal economy, in most parts of the world, is women centred and the economic worth of work is reflected in the social position of the worker. Yet women have a subordinate status in community decisions, inheritance, rights and religious customs.

The tribal societies like most of the traditional societies have their own personal laws and customs around which the lives of women are governed. The customary laws and customs which include people's beliefs, customs, social mores, precepts, rites and usages practised since time immemorial are not always conducive to the interests of women. Most of the customary laws or personal laws, particularly those relating to property and marriage are highly oppressive to women except for only a few exceptions.

Although women shoulder heavy economic responsibilities, commensurate with men, the tribal customary laws like those of non- tribal societies deny them equal rights to property. The system of inheritance among most tribes is invariably in favour of men. In general, women are entitled only to maintenance rights and expenses for marriage while men inherit land and all other movable and immovable properties. Even in societies that follow matrilineal principle of descent and inheritance, where the woman is the focal point of the household organisation, when it comes to allocation of rights over land, a sharp distinction is maintained between 'ownership' and 'control'. While ownership of land is transmitted through women, control invariably lies with men (Nongbri, 2003).

According to a research study on the women vendors of the Khwairamband market of Manipur, the researcher concludes by stating that women vendors have contributed a lot in the maintenance and development of moral values and principles among the members of the family. The women vendors are also the preservers of the traditional social norms, values and beliefs of the society. They play a constructive role in resolving conflicts among the residents of localities and fight against social evils arising out of drugs, alcohol, sexual abuse and domestic violence. Nevertheless, their efforts and contribution are not recognized and they still face a lot of challenges everyday of their lives (Kshetrimayum, 2002).

A study conducted in the tribal state of Nagaland funded by the India- Canada Environment Facility (CIDA) and Government of Nagaland among women vendors in Kohima showed that 90-95 percent of the vendors were women. The women look after all the management, cultivation, harvesting and processing of the crops while men sometimes help in bringing the produce to the local market. Although some goods are sold in bulk to regular vendors, others are sold directly to consumers on a temporary site. Since the women are involved in trade, they achieve a certain control over household decision making and most of the income earned from vending is used to buy essential commodities (IDRC, 2011).

Another survey research carried out by a local NGO in Assam called North East Research & Social Work Networking (NERSWN) in the tribal areas of Kokrajhar and Gossaigaon under the Bodoland Territorial Council observed that there is proliferation of street vendors in the cities and towns because of poverty and unemployment. Despite the useful services they render to the society, they are looked upon as hindrance to the planned development of the towns and cities, both by the elite urbanites and the town -planners. These street vendors are subjected to constant mental torture by the local authorities and are harassed in different ways, which at times often lead to riotous situations (NERSWN, 2010).

Moreover, there is hardly any policy consistent with the needs of these vendors. In spite of their valuable contribution to the economy-rural and urban, and also in distributing system of goods and services, little attention has been paid to the services offered by them. Vendors are either overlooked or looked down as something to be controlled or as an eyesore to be removed.

In the city of Gauhati, a research carried out by an NGO called Society for Social Transformation and Environmental Protection (sSTEP) showed that there are 300 street vendors in the footpaths of the Ganeshguri area and about 50% of the vendors are women, out of whom almost 80% are tribal women, who travel long distances from far off places for 20 to 40 km to earn their livelihood. However, these women face a lot of problems daily in their activities due to lack of space for vending. They are also harassed by the police and municipal authorities and often, the poor have to run with their commodities to save it from the confiscation by the police. The poor vendors who eke out their living by selling vegetables with less return have to pay bribes in cash and kinds to these police to make their livelihood (The Assam Tribune, 2012).

Another research study by Laishram (2002) on the status of market women in Manipur reveals the problems surrounding the vending occupation and its impact on the women vendors. It is seen that women vendors are affected by the depletion of natural resources and degradation of the environment. Women vendors are also mainly responsible for providing basic necessities to their family and society and the destruction of the environment directly impacts their occupation. The findings also estimated that women in hill, semi arid and arid areas worked an average of 12 hours in a day.

The kind of work done involved a lot of health hazards and lack of facilities in the markets like inadequate water had a negative impact on women's health. It leads to high rate of urinary and reproductive infection in poor women. The other health hazards among the women vendors were obesity, hypertension, diabetes, arthritis, gall bladder diseases and coronary heart diseases increasing mortality rate. Women vendors also faced psychological hazards arising out of constant pressure and burden to earn leading to frustration, insecurity, poor human relationships and emotional tensions (Laishram, 2002).

A peep into reality: Life as tribal women street vendors

The tribal women vendors of Manipur belong to the economically weaker sections of the society. Majority of the women take up the vending occupation due to dire need and circumstances. In most cases, women sacrifice their entire lives, earning and slogging each day to be able to provide for their families. This is particularly when the income of the spouse does not meet the needs of the family. In other cases, death of the spouse or spouse's inability to earn due to illness and other health related problems were the main reasons.

Most street vending businesses are one-person operations that use unpaid family labour on as needed basis. Some sell from the comfort of covered stalls; others simply squat on the ground beside a basket or blanket displaying their merchandise. In the developing world, millions of poor people who cannot afford to buy from retail stored depend on the affordable goods that street vendors provide.

Compared to men, female street vendors are more likely to operate in insecure or illegal spaces, trade in less lucrative goods, generate a lower volume of trade, and work as commission agents or employees of other vendors. As a result, they tend to earn less than male vendors.

According to the 2001 census, the total population of Manipur is 23,88,634 out of which the tribal population of the hill districts of the state constitute 9,83,074 excluding those of many tribal villages located in the valley districts of Thoubal, Imphal East, Bishnupur and Imphal West, therefore, putting together the total tribal population of Manipur will be more than 11 lakhs. On the other hand there are non-tribal communities such Nepalese, Biharis, Muslims, Bengalis, Meiteis etc which constitute the population of Manipur. It has also added that the failure of the state government to allocate a single vendor seat at any of the three markets to the tribal women is nothing less than discrimination and segregation on the line of religion or caste besides it will amount to severing of ties with the tribal people.

The non-tribal vendors seem to possess more assertiveness to voice their opinions and demands as compared to the tribal women vendors. Till date, the tribal women vendors struggle to claim their rights to a proper vending space. Many a times, due to increasing competition and unfair means of allotment of vending spaces, it creates more problems for these women.

The state has constructed new market places for the women but none of it was allotted to the tribal women. Interestingly, in the markets constructed for tribal women vendors, one can also see even non-tribal women vending in the tribal market complex located at New Lambulane in Imphal, Manipur. On the contrary, tribal women vendors are not given a place to vend in the other markets located in Imphal. Even within the women vendors, for example in the state of Manipur, there is what one would call "internal discrimination" of the tribal women vendors.

The discrimination in employment and occupation affects indigenous men and women differently, and gender maybe an additional cause of discrimination against indigenous women. In the labour market, indigenous women are more discriminated against than both indigenous men and non-indigenous women. In addition, indigenous women may also be discriminated against within indigenous communities themselves.

Many indigenous women:

- Have less access to education and training at all levels;
- Are more effected by unemployment and underemployment;
- Are more often involved in non-remunerated work;
- Receive less pay for equal work;
- Have less access to administrative and leadership positions;
- Experience worse conditions of work, for example related to working hours and occupational safety and health;
- Are particularly vulnerable to sexual abuse and harassment and trafficking, as they often have to seek employment far away from their communities; and

- Are limited by discriminatory cultural practices which, for example inhibit the education of the girl child or prevent women from inheriting land or participating in decision making processes.

While often being subjected to discrimination, indigenous women have also been playing a leading role in the promotion of gender equality within their communities and also through mainstreaming gender perspective into advocacy for indigenous people's human rights (ILO, 2007).

However, though the state and the Indian Fiscal policies have given a hard blow to the women traders of Manipur and the other indigenous communities without having any thought of the specific needs of the women traders, the control of domestic market still continues despite numerous attempts to evict or destabilize the women's collective action (National Seminar on Women Vending in Urban Spaces, 2007).

Therefore, the tribal women vendors remain with no choice but to sell their produce at very reasonable prices to the non-tribal women vendors. If only, a mechanism is developed to help these women get storage places and vending spaces, their situation would improve considerably. According to the National Perspective Plan, only 14 per cent of women are in full employment. Nearly 90 percent of these are in unorganized sector, of these 83 percent are in agriculture and construction and below 8 percent are in organized sector (National Perspective Plan for Women, 2000).

More than sixty years of independence, the state of things with the women folk everywhere in the country has not met the desired results in terms of health, education, employment and securing better future. On the contrary with the venture into globalization, industrialisation and development, the conditions of women in general, and in particular those belonging to the working class from poor urban settlements and rural areas have been facing the brunt of the so called civilised society eking out a living in the most dehumanizing and difficult circumstances in their daily struggle to earn a livelihood. While the people enjoying the fruits of modern education and job opportunities thrive in the market driven economy, the poor are left to suffer and sacrifice everything.

Excerpts from the field: Account of tribal women vendors

Tribal Society: Status of tribal women in Manipur

It is often assumed that the tribal society is purely egalitarian in its outlook towards its women. Many previous studies have often mentioned about how tribal communities gave equal rights and opportunities to the women folk of their households or societies. It is no doubt that the tribal society does not regard the birth of a female child as a liability or burden. However, like in all patriarchal societies, the birth of a boy is considered as a great gift from god since the boy would grow up to continue the family lineage and take care of all the land and property owned by his parents. Though unacceptable, patriarchy rules the world in each and every society. In the same way, tribal society is also highly patriarchal and male dominated, women are expected to be mute spectators and agile listeners even in community discussions and meeting.

In order to study the status of women among the tribal women vendors, the context of the study was considered. The interview schedules were designed in a way so that information regarding such aspects pertaining to women's rights and status would be obtained. Though questions regarding property, inheritance and family dynamics were not directly asked in the questions. The present situations and circumstances shared and narrated by the respondents confirms the existing patriarchal notions that are still part of the society.

Since time immemorial, the customs and traditions which are highly biased towards women have not changed. No attempt has been made to amend or discard the old prejudiced beliefs and customs. Be it in matters of child birth, marriage, divorce, property, inheritance etc even with the adoption of

Christianity, the preconceived notion remain the same. Even in church, though women have their own women's society like the men. It is rare to find a woman pastor heading a congregation. Hence, it is also not encouraged by the society too.

Some customs benefit the women but many are a setback to her as an individual as it curtails her rights and snatches essential and important opportunities from her. In every tribal setting, one does not see the existence of *purdah.* Women are not confined to the four walls of their houses. They have the freedom to venture outside according to their will and work hard in the fields or employ themselves to run their respective families. Their lives are difficult economically especially if they belong to the lower economic strata. Most of their time is spent in eking out a living for their families livelihood.

Even if the woman is the sole provider or breadwinner for her family, her status in comparison to her husband or male members of the family is always lower. Economic independence solely does not improve her status in the family; it comes with age and acceptance from the part of the respective family of the position of the woman in the household and the surrounding community that she is a part of. For example, a woman will never disregard or deny her husband from taking her earnings. If he asks for it, she usually readily gives or has no other choice but to give.

Many customary laws relating to marriage and divorce deprive the women folk of their rights. Though the custom of bride price unlike dowry emphasises on the worth and importance of a daughter, for which bride price is sought from the groom's family. A girl is not considered worthless or liable to the family. In a traditional setting, a girl contributes to her family even before her marriage since her childhood by helping the mother in the kitchen, fetching water and usually taking care of the younger siblings. That is why bride price is a compensation usually taken and given to bride's parents.

However, in matters of divorce, like in all other societies, the woman is looked down upon and stigmatized. Nevertheless, with changing times such preconceived notions are slowly fading away as one can see many women headed households doing well. It is usually the women who take up all the responsibilities for their children's upbringing and interestingly many are successful despite being separated or divorced.

Many remarkable discussion regarding the women vendors families came up during the data collection. Male supremacy surfaced from all sides of the corner as it was evident from the conversations that women consider their spouses or male relatives as their superiors. The presence of a man/male relative in the household makes the women feel secure even if he is burden to her or even ill-treats her. Most women accept it as part of their fate and continue to work hard by slogging everyday of their lives.

In a typical tribal village setting, women do not participate in discussions and affairs of the village. Though they are part of the village assemblies, a woman being outspoken is not considered as good behaviour. Women are usually more involved in preparing tea for the people assembled in meetings. Those are part of the meeting, rarely voice their opinions or take part in discussions.

In tribal societies like the Kukis, where the traditional form of chieftainship is still prevalent the right of women to become successors is not granted. The chieftainship is passed down only to men. Therefore, being a daughter in the household of the chief does not give the right to her to succeed her father's position. Usually, it is the male relatives who take over as chief in case of old age or death. Inheritance and distribution of property is also biased and in most cases women are not given immovable property. The only things she receives are gifts given by her parents in terms of household goods, traditional clothes and some other things.

The ways we are nurtured and cultured affects our approach, way of thinking and are products of the outlook one has too. Since childhood, a girl child is taught to be gentle, kind and obedient. To be an understanding person and self-sacrificing are essential qualities expected of a girl/woman. As for a boy child being strong, independent and bold are considered pre-requisites of being a male. If any of the sexes deviated from the conventional norms, they were not considered inappropriate as an individual.

Nevertheless, summing up the above findings, it was also visible that changes are taking place in the tribal society. These days, many parents equally divide property among all their children. Though male child is preferred, many parents have realised that it was usually the daughters who took care of them even after getting married. They were many cases of how men did not bother much about their parents after getting married.

Though women are discriminated against and preferential treatment is given to men, it is clearly seen that tribal women are active members in their churches. They are the ones who run their households and take up all the responsibilities. While the men dominate the social sphere thus establishing control and male supremacy. Hence, one can say that the status of women in tribal societies is much better than their Indian counterparts residing in various parts of the country.

Street Vending Occupation and tribal women vendors

The tribal women have always been active economically in contributing some income to their families. They are hard working, tough and enthusiastic about earning their own livelihood and being independent in their own right. One usually does not see a woman sitting idle in their homes. There is zeal to be economically independent individuals and this can be seen through their lived experiences and daily struggle.

From the data obtained about the educational level of the respondents, it was seen that majority of the women had not completed even their primary education. The low level of education was a setback for them as they had no means of employment to secure jobs which pay well. The women belonged to rural areas where the means of livelihood is primarily agriculture.

Many of the villages have a high drop-out rate of girls and boys due to poverty and lack of interest in studies arising out of improper teaching and guidance. Usually the elder children, mostly girls are left to take care of the younger siblings while the boys find odd jobs in small mechanic shops, as handymen in trucks that carry heavy loads like timber and construction materials. Since they start earning at a very early age during their teenage years, young boys and girls tend to have early marriages. The consequence of rampant mushrooming of several militant outfits have also created more problems to find better means of livelihood as the state is in a constant turmoil.

It is evident that even middle aged women vendors in their late thirties also had grandchildren. The cycle of early marriage is also a problem because most of the people do not go in for family planning therefore leading to big families. For a relatively well off family who can provide basic needs, health facilities and good education it does not make much a difference. However, for the poor who struggle day in and out, it is very difficult. Owing to such problems also, women venture out of their homes and come to the city to sell their home-grown vegetables and other forest products.

Even in small villages women form groups of their own and whatever little money they are able to earn in a day are put together as part of *Sumlom*[1]*(Marup)* The term *Sumlom (Marup)* is a Manipuri word which means a village socio-economic organization. It is a type of a co-operative saving and credit institution. It originated as one of the most important institutions for mutual help at the time of death, marriage, child birth and other personal crisis. It stands as an institution for socio-economic security in every stage of one's life. However, people usually view the system broadly as social, whose main purpose is to strengthen social solidarity.

But over time it has expanded its activity much more than the social sphere and covers most of the economic sphere of the individual (Oinam, 2005).

The operational part of *Sumlom (Marup)* is that collection is done on a weekly, bi- weekly or monthly basis. Each member of the organization contributes a fixed amount which they have agreed to pay. The sum collected each time is given to a member on a rotation basis. Usually a draw of lots takes place to ascertain the winner. Unlike the lottery system, the best part of the *Marup* is that each member gets the money. Once a member receives her money, she has to continue giving the fixed amount for the others too.

The study conducted among the tribal women vendors show that majority of them who take up this occupation are married women who are self employed. Having no other means of livelihood apart from agriculture, the women come to Imphal, the commercial hub of the state to earn some money as street vendors.

It is not an easy life or occupation as it requires them to be away from home for many hours. Moreover, they not only work outside their homes but do all the household chores too. The kinds of life they lead are stressful and many of them have health problems but continue to work in spite of all their ailments.

There are also stark evidences of rural- urban migration for the means of livelihood. Many of the respondents had left their native villages located at different hill districts and settled in Imphal. The distance and daily travelling required is cumbersome so women took up rented accommodations at localities close to the markets where they vend.

The previous ethnic cleansing drive carried out by the Naga insurgents in the 90's is also another contributor to migration of especially the Kuki people from their villages to the city. This conflict lasted for about 5 years, where thousands of innocent people were killed. It was the issue of land and identity that led to a massacre of many women and children rendering thousands of people internally displaced, homeless and poor. Many of the villages were burnt down and destroyed, forcing people to run away. This has further increased poverty and intra-state migration. Amongst all those who suffered, it was the women who faced the brunt losing their families, children, their villages and their means of livelihood. Thus, entering the city meant starting off from scratch by doing the most viable occupation.

The data on the number of income earners also showed that there were many women who were sole breadwinners of their families. Besides, the women are also not aware about the National Policy for Urban Street Vendors Act (2009) which lays down the roles and responsibilities of each entity be it the government, the municipal corporations, vendors etc. It is the utmost duty of the government and street vending associations to make the vendors informed of important things related to their occupation. To have a well informed citizen creates awareness and people are then able to make informed choices and secure their rights without being made fool hardy. However, the responses received from the women showed that they were very perseverant and positive in their outlook towards life.

Though the government has not been of much help for this section of the society even after repeated demands for a well functioning vending area, the women vendors are not those who slide back but they are keen to get what they consider is their esteemed right. The responsibility of the government to be of welfare to the people is only farcical because it is the same government machineries that evict and trouble the women vendors.

The need of the hour is to have a strong cohesion between people in the government, NGOs and the women vendors. To ignore them of a protected vending area and basic facilities is to deny them their right to profess their occupation. Time the government steps forward to provide them the essential needs of the women vendors and solve the problems and confusion of allotment of individual spaces for each woman.

Role of Street Vending Associations, Municipal Corporations and Police

The previous literature available on women vendors mostly focussed on the Meitei or mainstream Manipuri women vendors who traditionally since the time of the Manipuri kings had been vending in the city markets of Imphal namely the Khwariamband market popularly known as the Ima market.

The Meitei women vendors of Manipur have different street vending associations which are lead by well informed and empowered persons. These street vending associations are also part of the National Alliance of Street Vendors in India (NASVI). This has helped the Meitei vendors to be more aware and come together to fight for their causes.

The picture is unfortunately different for the tribal women vendors and minority of the Muslim women vendors. These women are hardly aware of what is happening and majority of them have no knowledge of street vending associations working for vendors in Manipur. The women vendors belonging to these communities are usually those who vend at the peripheries of main markets, roadsides, pavements and make shift markets constructed by the government. They face more discrimination for being tribal women and one cannot blame them for their ignorance on how to go about with application of licenses and other important documents because it is obvious that the street vending associations have not reached them till today.

From what could be understood through discussion with the tribal women, it is clear that they go through daily struggles at two levels- personal consisting of their home and family and the professional which includes their occupation. None of the women vendors have a license which invariably makes them illegal to vend. Thus, making it easier for the municipal corporations and police to evict and harass them.

The women also shared about submitting their passport photographs and some amount of money to some people in order to get licenses. However, it has been months they have still not received it. The women are in a dilemma whether they have been fooled by those people or it is the slow procedure and lackadaisical attitude of the government that is causing a delay in getting the licenses.

Majority of the women are not part of any street vending associations, but almost all of them are a part of *marup* groups and women society in their respective churches. They have been part of protests and sit-in demonstrations called my street vending associations where majority membership is of the Manipuri women vendors. The tribal women mentioned that it did not benefit them at all since those protests they were part of did not include their needs or problems.

There is a need for street vending associations to reach out to even the minority groups of Muslim women and the tribal women too as they are also street vendors. The women do not have very positive things to say about the municipal corporation and the state government because in the name of beautification and development they are always being pushed around. On the other hand, the police resort to petty extortion by taking the little amount that these women earn as bribery. However, this is quite rare unlike in other cities and states around the country.

The state government needs to fulfil its promises and ensure that the minority Muslim vendors and the tribal women also get seats in the vending areas. The responsible departments like the municipal corporations need to be more proactive and conduct surveys to ensure that all the vendors are included when new vending areas are constructed in the future. This would check unnecessary problems that crop up every time allocation of vending spaces is done.

From the study, one can conclude by stating that tribal women vendors whether belonging to one of the Kuki or Naga tribes face problems of similar nature but with varying degrees. The main reasons cited by women vendors for taking up the vending occupation are as follows: easy access or entry, lack of skills for better jobs, mere survival strategy to support self and family income, small size of business, less investments, no labour costs and easy labour arrangements usually coming from friends and families. However, the problems and issues faced are innumerable right from lack of access to vending space, poor availability of resources, limited finance and credit facilities due to which they mostly rely on their own or family's meagre savings. Women vendors usually end up borrowing money from individuals or money lenders at a high rate of interest. Moreover, there is a lot of burden on these women to take care of family needs and there is total absence of any support from the side of the government. At this juncture, the needs of the women are essential for them to run their business successfully. Some of the needs are basic provision of vending space, clean and protected vending zones, vocational training, accounting skills, business ideas, facilities for hygienic sanitation, clean drinking water, proper waste disposal, electrification of vending places, childcare facilities, access to finance and credit and social protection in terms of affordable health care, pensions and safe working conditions.

Conclusion

Hence, there is of utmost importance to extend social protection to the informal sector workers like the tribal women vendors of Manipur. Though facilities like micro finance in terms of micro credit are important for them, it is not sufficient to ensure success of these women vendors. It is crucial to provide for better infrastructure, social services and assistance to ease caring burdens entrusted upon them. Though, Manipur is one of the pioneer states that has its own state vending policy, there has not been commendable constructive efforts by the government to resolve and regulate the problems of the tribal women vendors. Those responsible at the policy level should ensure that the street vending policy intervenes the lives of the tribal women vendors in a positive way.

There is an indispensable necessity to conduct more studies on the particularly marginalized, invisible, hidden and vulnerable groups in the society so that their contributions and conditions are visible to national, local policy makers and practitioners. It is imperative to take steps towards promoting and enabling their representation and make their voice heard through a process of collective bargaining and social movements and also to distinguish between different groups of women in the informal economy so as to understand where they are situated differently on the basis of their class, race, occupation, gender and geo-political locations.

Note

1. Sumlom is a Thadou Kuki word for Marup, which means collection of money by the members of the respective group.

References

1. WIEGO (2011) Available from: http://www.wiego.org/occupational_groups/streetVendors/index.php [Accessed: 21st May 2011].
2. CHEN, M, A. JHABVALA, R. & LUND, F. (2002) Supporting Workers in the Informal Economy: A Policy Framework. *Paper prepared for ILO Task Force on the Informal Economy.*
3. KHANDELWAL, P. (2004) Employment in Organised Sector in 1990's: An Analysis from Gender Perspective. *Indian Journal of Industrial Relations.* 40 (1). p 17-38.
4. STOCKYARD, J and MIRIAM, M, JOHNSON. (1992) *Sex and Gender in Society.* New Jersey: Prentice Hall.
5. OXFAM. (1995) Women and Culture, Gender and Development. *Oxfam Journal.* 3 (1) Oxford: Oxfam.
6. PRASAD, R (2005). Women's Development: The Rhetoric and the Reality. *IASSI Quaterly.* 24 (2).
7. NAIK, A, K. (2009) Informal Sector and Informal Workers in India. Available from: http://www.iariw.org/papers/2009/5a%20naik.pdf [Accessed 7/06/2012].
8. UN. (2000) Available from: http://www.unescap.org/stat/isie/reference-materials/Definitions/Informal-Employment/

Defining-measuring-Informal-Employment-ILO.pdf [Accessed: 03/07/2011].

9. The Constitution of India.

10. NATIONAL STREET VENDORS POLICY. (2009) Ministry of Housing and Urban Poverty Alleviation. Available from: http://mhupa.gov.in/policies/natpol.htm [Accessed 15/04/2011].

11. CENSUS (2001) Government of India. Available from: http://censusindia.gov.in/Census_And_You/economic_activity.aspx [Accessed 22/09/2011].

12. SASTRY, N, S. (2004) Estimating Informal Employment and Poverty in India. *Discussion paper series 7, Human Development Resource Centre.* India: UNDP.

13. India- Canada Environment Facility and Government of Nagaland: Strengthening market linkages for women vegetable vendors: Experiences from Kohima, Nagaland, India. Available from: http://www.idrc.ca/en/ev-93076-201-1-DO_TOPIC.html [Accessed 17/06/2011].

14. OUTLOOK. (2008) Step-motherly treatment for women workers in wages: NSSO. Available from: http://news.outlookindia.com/items.aspx?artid=3550 [Accessed: 20th September 2011].

15. Census 1991, Government of India

16. NONGBRI, T. (2003) *Development, Ethnicity and Gender. Select Essays on Tribes in India.* Jaipur and New Delhi: Rawat Publications

17. KSHETRIMAYUM, U. (2002) *Women Vendors of Khwairamband Market, Manipur.* Doctoral dissertation, Department of Political Sciences. Manipur University.

18. HMAR, S. and TONSING, T. (2010) Empowerment of Women Vendors: A Right Based Approach. Available from: http://mungdoc.weebly.com/research-for-nerswn.html

[Accessed: 23/09/2011]

19. CENSUS 2001, Government of India. Available from: http://censusindia.gov.in/Census_And_You/economic_activity.aspx [Accessed: 07/06/2011].

20. CHEN, M. (2004) Rethinking the Informal Economy: Linkages with the Formal Economy and the Formal Regulatory Environment. *Paper presented at EGDI and UNU/WIDER Conference, Unlocking Human Potential Linking the Informal and the Formal Sectors.* Helsinki.

21. UGC-DSA-ASIHSS Programme. (2007). National Seminar on Women Vending In Urban Spaces.

22. ILO. (2007) Eliminating discrimination against indigenous and tribal peoples in employment and occupation. 111. Available from: http://www.ilo.org/wcmsp5/groups/public/—ed_norm/--normes/documents/publication/wcms_097727.pdf [Accessed: 05/06/2011].
23. KAR, B, K. (2002) *Women Population of North East India: A Study in Gender Geography.* Delhi: Daya Publishing House.
24. COHEN,. BHATT,. HORN. (2000) *Women Street Vendors: The Road to Recognition.* New York: The Population Council Inc.
25. JHABVALA, R. and SINHA, S. (2002) Liberalisation and the Woman Worker. *Economic and Political Weekly,* May 25, p.2037.
26. DEVI, L. S. (2002) *Status of Market Women and their Role in the Socio-Economic Life of Manipur.* Doctoral dissertation, Department of History. Manipur University.
27. CENSUS 2011, Government of India. Available from: http://www.census2011.co.in/census/state/manipur.html [Accessed: 10th July, 2012].
28. THE ASSAM TRIBUNE (2012) City Street vendors make a living against odds. Availablefrom:http://www.assamtribune.com/scripts/detailsnew.asp?id=jun2211/city07 [Accessed:17th July 2012].
29. MURAYAMA, M., INOUE, K. & HAZARIKA, S. (2005) Sub-Regional Relations in the Eastern South-Asia: With Special Focus on India's North Eastern Region.

Chapter 5

Women Organisations and Collective Protest: Nature, Scope and Challenges

Hoineilhing Sitlhou and Lamtinthang Haokip

Introduction

On 16th of August in the year 2011, a group of women belonging to the Kuki community began their fast unto death to assist in the ongoing demand for the up-gradation of Sadar Hills Autonomous District Council into a full-fledged district in Manipur. A day before, on August 15, the people of Sadar Hills observed India's Independence Day in mourning by wearing black dresses to protest the government's inaction. Though, this is the first time that the contributions of Kuki women and their collective protest have been acknowledged within and outside the society, it does not necessarily mean that the Kuki women have been passive observers to the problems confronting the society. Women have always stood up for their men-folk even in terrains which are considered dangerous for the men, like negotiating with insurgents and armed personnel in Manipur (India) or militancy in Myanmar. Women and men experience the social realities differently and often have differential experiences and play distinctive roles in a social situation.

I. Locating the Subject of Study

In the writing of James Johnstone, the Kukis were present in the hill tracts of Manipur as early as the year 1830 and 1940 (Johnstone, 1987, p. 25). Colonel McCulloch, the British political agent of that time settled the fierce tribes along exposed frontiers to act as buffers against other recalcitrant tribes (ibid, p. 26). Since McCulloch's "buffer policy" planted Kuki settlements at strategic places to act as barriers, the Kukis have been found settled in scattered pattern all over the Manipur hills. Kukis constitute an overwhelming preponderance in Churachandpur district, Sadar Hills subdivision of Senapati district and Chandel district. Elsewhere, they are found mingling with Tangkhul (Naga) tribes in Ukhrul district, Mao-Maram-Paomai (Naga) tribes in Senapati district, and Zeliangrong (Naga) tribes in Tamenglong district (Gangte, 2007, p. 95). The British ethnographers' like Lt. Colonel J. Shakespear divided them into two broad groups – (a) old and (b) new (Shakespear, 1975). The new Kukis of Manipur in the year 1981 comprises of the tribes like Gangte, Hmar, Lushai, Paite, Simte, Thadou, Vaiphei, Zou, Ralte and Moyon under the same Classification, whereas Old Kuki comprises of the tribes like Aimol, Chiru, Koireng, Kom, Anal, Chothe, Lamkang, Koirao/Thangal, Purum and Monsang.[1]

II. Gendered Space in the Society

a. As defined by Customary Laws

To understand the feasibility of gender relation among the Kukis, it would be helpful to look into the structural arrangement of the society. Legitimately, the Kukis follow the patriarchal system of family structure. As a result, the line of descent, law of inheritance and law of residence is appointed to the male line only and the children follow the clan name of the father. Therefore, a male child is always preferred to a female child to continue the line of descent. In the case of 'Chapagam' (barren fatherhood), the law of inheritance is passed on through the next closest or nearest male relative of the family, which is the reason why a male child is preferred (Gangte, 1993). It is unfortunate to note that in spite of their tremendous contribution to the family income, they have no right of inheritance. At present also, this is still the general trend though a few thoughtful parents do divide their property among daughters and sons (ibid).

b. As explained in existing Literatures

Women were assigned an altogether subordinate position in the society. They were honoured, but in separate domains.

According to T.S. Gangte, great importance is given to the relationship of the mother's brother and the sister's son in the Kuki society. This has significance in view of the practice of preferential marriage to maternal uncle's daughter (or cross-cousin marriage.) The "tucha-sunggao[2] relationship", of the Kukis is also reckoned from a female line. *'Luongman'* or Corpse Price[3] is another peculiar *(customary)* system of the Kukis. This is the price for a woman paid after death by her husband or her husband's brothers and her sons, if her husband predeceased her. Her father or her father's sons (in case her father predeceased her) claim the *'loungman'* as a token of love and affection between the uterine relatives. This also reveals the important position held by a woman in a family life, and the weightage given to propagation of the descent through male line. In the system of *'Lom'* or *'Lawm[4]'* that was functional in villages in the past, there was also a female *'Lom Upanu'*. The Kuki women do not hold any priestly office but there are instances of unofficial priestess or sorcerers. Among the many ceremonies and festivals that they celebrate, *Chang-Ai*[5] is the only one where the Kuki women play the leading role (Gangte, 1993).

The women folk's at all crucial times would unduly be behind all major issues and events. While the role of men in human capital formation have been stressed and studied, women's roles have been ignored though their roles are as substantial. The economic role played by women in traditional rural society particularly in the field of agricultural and cottage industry is magnanimous, but their contribution has been devalued and ignored most of the time. Even in the past, the role of women, especially in the economic sphere was inevitable. The women did most of the work of the village both in the agricultural field and in the household. In the writings of Mangjel Paokai Sitlhou, we find how women in the past were busy in weaving after the harvesting is over (Sitlhou, 1995). A Thadou woman who has exceptional knowledge of embroidery technique has a very high reputation in the community (ibid). The women in the house were responsible for clothing the whole family. In the process of shifting cultivation, most men were content to perform the more honorary task of slash and burning to clear the area for cultivation, whereas the women were attributed the more monotonous and laborious task of planting, weeding, nurturing and harvesting the crops.[6] Captain T.H. Lewin in 1870 wrote about the barbarous customary war practice of the Cucis (Kukis) in which they kill all women of the adversary party. The idea was that "if the women did not take care of the house and prepare their husbands' food when going on a war-path, there would be considerable inconvenience accruing" (Lewin, 1870, p. 144).

Within the household domain it has always been the women: who did the burdensome chores, carried the heaviest loads, rose earliest in the morning and if they had any opinions, those were never regarded as important. Every husband was afraid of being dubbed as 'hen-pecked' and so would not lift his finger to help his wife in any domestic work. Traditional saying give popular expression to this attitude: "a woman's mind does not reach across the stream"; "neither Crabs nor women have any religion; "a fence can be changed; so can a wife" (Lloyed, 1991, p. 109). A woman had no rights at all. Body, mind and spirit, she belonged from her birth to her death to her father, her brother, her husband. Her men folk could treat her as they like; and a man who did not beat his wife was scorned as a coward (ibid, p. 13).

According to Mangkhosat Kipgen, in the social organisation and village administration, women had no place - except under special circumstances where the widow of a deceased chief might rule over the village on behalf of her minor son until his maturity. The society was male dominated. In community matters, women were not consulted - and if they volunteered their opinions were not given weight. However, within the four walls of her room, she exercised more influenced if not more important than the men folks than the later were prepared to admit (Kipgen, 1997).

The mission schools changed the participation of the women in public sphere of community life through church and mission activities. It was true that even Christian parents preferred that the girls should be at home to tend to household chores and to work in the field, but the organisation of Christianity gave them a space, which was not provided to them by the traditional and customary village administration. Nevertheless, there is a hierarchy inside the church in which the women are not allowed in certain areas considered the strict domains of the men (Sitlhou, 2011). Education changes the very structure of the society by changing the status of women. It was a role that saw them as the centre of domestic life, but not as active participants in the kinds of decision-making positions and processes that education encourages of those who receive it. These factors, contributed to the status pattern and concept of world views of the Kukis towards the issue of gender equality. This concept also became the basis for other arrangements at the level of the family, the community and the society as a whole. With the acceptance of Christianity, the gender hierarchy debate has been further justified by the Creation Theory in the Bible.[7]

c. As defined by the Family

Another issue that needs our consideration is the unequal education meted out to sons and daughters. Women's educational opportunities have expanded substantially today in our society, including opportunities for all forms of academic as well as professional training. However, significant gender differences persist in the relative importance attached to the education of girls and boys, and in its perceived purpose. Women's position is still defined primarily by marriage, home and hearth, and only secondarily by the need for economic independence. This is reflected in gender differences in school enrolment, dropout rates (villages), levels of completed education, entry into university, and the subjects chosen. Even where parents send girls to school, most do so mainly to improve their marriage prospects. Investment on the education of women beyond a point is considered a waste of money as they were going to another family anyway. The girl membership in the family is deemed as only temporary. Even if the family is broad minded enough to encourage the ambitions and academic excellence of their daughters, men feel insecure and threatened at the prospects of having a spouse who would be more outgoing than they would.[8] The domestic ideology of European societies that was formed among the middle class between 1780 and 1830 applies among the Kukis. The ideology maintained that the world was divided into two separate spheres, the public and the private. Men should be involved in the public sphere of work and politics, making money and supporting their families. Women should stay at home in the domestic sphere, caring for their children and husbands and dependent on their husbands for financial support.[9]

III. Nature of Women Organisations and Collective Protest

a. Sadar Hills Women Union

It is difficult to precisely define the nature of women movements operating amongst the Kukis. In many villages falling within the Sadar Hills region of Manipur, there are two types of women leadership operational. One is the religious grouping within the church called the 'women society' or 'women fellowship' and the other is the more secular yet *(socio-political)* welfare related association called the 'women union'. They are not conscious effort at liberating the status of women in the society, but an important beginning to challenge the age-old status quo of power relationships in both rural and urban settings of the Kuki society (Sitlhou, 2011, p. 251-252). In a village Tujang Vaichong, in Sadar Hills region, the role of the women union includes maintaining peace and solving issues related to insurgency problems and negotiating with the army personnel. They are able to solve problems which means danger if men are involved. Within the villages, they deal with deviance that obstruct normalcy like disputes and disturbances caused by vices like drinking and gambling.

They put a ban on selling liquor, which they call *(khamna thei gahna)*, popularly known as *'nisa ban'* taken from Meitei language of the valley people in Manipur (ibid, 254).

In order to understand Kuki women participation in issues confronting the society, the paper will discuss their involvement in the demand for a separate district in Manipur. The state of Manipur has nine districts, namely Bishnupur, Chandel, Churachandpur, Imphal East, Imphal West, Senapati, Tamenglong, Thoubal and Ukhrul, based on the hill district reorganisation after Independence. The demand for the Sadar Hills as a separate state started back in 1974. Tengnoupal as Chandel district was the first to undergo bifurcation. This was followed by Bishnupur, Imphal East, Imphal West and Thoubal in 1997 (Sitlhou, 2011, p. 211). The first leaders to lead a separatist movement were the leaders of the organisation called the Kuki National Assembly.[10] The Kuki National Assembly (established in 1946) had submitted a memorandum to the then Indian Prime Minister Pandit Jawaharlal Nehru on 24 March 1960, demanding the 'immediate' creation of a Kuki state comprising all the Kuki inhabited areas of Manipur.[11] The proposal for a separate state yielded no response from the Government (Haokip, 2011, 223). "The original root of the KNA can be traced back to the formation of the Kuki Chiefs' Association in about the year 1935-36. The Association was pressing the government for the abolition of '*pothang*' and '*beggar*' systems which were prevailing in the hills of Manipur in the British days (Ray, 1990, p. 112)."

After an agitation organised by Kuki National Assembly turned violent on 22nd November of 1981, the demand was entrusted to another organisation by the name Sadar Hills Youth Organisation. It took the name Sadar Hills District Demand Committee in 1995. The movement was started with the support of different sub-tribes under the Kukis/*(Kuki nomenclature)*. The constituent members of the then Kuki National Assembly were Thadou, Paite, Vaiphei, Gangte, Simte, Zou, Anal, Kom, Hmar, Chiru, Monsang, Koireng, etc.[12]

The methods adopted by the Sadar Hills District Demand Committee in bargaining with the government were protest and dialogue. Since, land is the cause of disagreement, the Kukis in their demand have faced stiffed resistance from the Nagas.[13] The Kukis and the Nagas have had a history of inter-ethnic unrest, which reappears again, whenever there are contesting claims for land and resources in the state. In 1992, ethnic conflict erupted between the two communities that escalated into a violent conflict. The violence resulted in the loss of hundreds of lives, destruction of hundreds of villages, and displacement of thousands of people. Although the violent conflict had ended in 1997, the conflict continues to remain in different forms of embodiments (Kipgen, 2011).

All Manipur Naga Social Organisation led by United Naga Council (UNC) called an indefinite economic blockade on National Highways 39 and 53. The motive of the economic blockade was against the creation of full-fledged Sadar Hills

District that was tabled by SHDDC during Chief Ministership of Nipamacha in 1998. This blockade lasted for about 58 days. It severely affected the state economy. A memorandum of understanding signed between the government and the UNC ended the protest. It states, "no Sadar Hills districts will be created without the consent of leaders of United Naga Council, All Naga Student Union Manipur, Zeliangrong-Student Union, Thangkhul Long, Naga Women Union etc."[14] The strong resistance was against the deadline or ultimatum given to the state government dated 30th June of 1998 by Sadar Hills District Demand Committee. The state responses as per the record of the district demand committee made delusive and false promises to pacify the movement (Sitlhou, 2011). In 1996, the boundary committee was formed with Shri Dr. Chandramani, Minister I.F.C.D as Chairman with four other members. Letter from Ch. Birendra Singh, the then Commissioner (Revenue), Government of Manipur to Shri K.R. Prasad, Secretary Election Commission of India, New Delhi on the subject of 'Inauguration of Sadar Hills District,' Dated 11-1-2000, Office order no. 6/1/ 73-R records:

> The State Cabinet had taken a decision on 14th July of 1982 for the creation of three districts including Sadar Hills in Manipur to be inaugurated after the boundary adjustment on 10-1-2000. The State cabinet had re-affirmed the decision taken in 1982 for creation of Sadar Hills District with the existing three sub-divisions namely Kangpokpi, Saikul and Saitu Gamphazol. Inauguration as decided by the cabinet may be done with the approval of the Election Commission of India (as recorded in Sitlhou, 2011).

There was a strong indefinite bandh by Sadar Hills District Demand Committee, during the tenure of Shri Rishang Keishing in which 87 agitators were imprisoned and beaten up by security personnel. The bandh was suspended on the seventh day with the promise by the government to grant a district. On the 12th September 1996, the then Revenue Minister Shri Hellalludin had declared in the state assembly during Shri Rishang Keishing's Chief Ministership "the state government is committed to grant sadar hills as a full-fledged district with the bifurcation of Imphal Districts." On March 7th 1997, the then Governor of Manipur

Shri Outh Narain Shrivastava, in his address stated "my government is firmly committed for creation of Sadar Hills as a full-fledged district" (Sitlhou, 2011, p. 214). However, despite the unfold promises made by the government, no development was happening and turns to be a mockery of state governance. Thoubal, Bishnupur, Imphal East and Imphal West were created in 1997. A memorandum was submitted to the two Prime Minister Shri H.D. Dewa Gowda and I.K. Gujral. They gave their commitment to give direction to the state authority concern to initiate necessary action on the issue. During the W. Nipamacha government in 1998, memorandum submitted had no meaning. This was yet another futile attempt. He blamed the boundary controversy as being the obstacle to their demand. A sub-committee was formed with Shri Loken Singh (then Finance Minister) as Chairman and four other members. Subsequently, the Sadar Hills District Demand Committee issued an ultimatum that the district must be created by 30th June, 1998 (Sitlhou, 2011, p. 214).

In 1998 four Kuki Ministers submitted their resignation from their ministership in protest against the inaction of state government in creating Sadar Hill District. They were[15]:Pu Thangminlien Kipgen, Pu Ngamthang Haokip, T. N. Haokip and T.T. Haokip. On 6th November, they withdraw their resignation after a Memorandum of Understanding was signed between District Demand Committee and the State Government. The government agreed to the following terms:—

1. Full DC[16] power to ADC Kangpokpi
2. Full SP[17] power to additional SP Kangpokpi

Opening the following department branch office—

- District Industry Centre
- E.E.[18] Electricity
- E.E. PWD[19]
- Dy. Director, T. D.
- Divisional Office, horticulture and soil conservation

- District transport officer/ motor vehicle
- Taxation office
    - o Additional Deputy Commissioner (ADC) Kangpokpi,
    - o Necessary action for implementation of District Rural Development Agency (DRDA), shall operate all funds of these two blocks (Senapati and Sadar Hills)
    - o Deputy Commissioner and Superintendent of Police Powers to Additional Deputy Commissioner & Additional Superintendent of Police were not fulfilled (Sitlhou, 2011, p. 215-216).

The Government of Manipur was supposed to expedite its decision on the creation of Sadar Hills (Kangpokpi) district latest by 31st of March in 1999. In 1999 new executive members of SHDDC was formed. The then Nipamacha government have consistently rejected all pleas for the creation of the district due to the reasons best known to his government.

A retaliatory move was the response by boycott of MSCP[20] in the recent election by the people who constitute the Sadar Hills vote-banks (ibid, p. 216).

A new government under O. Ibobi Singh, a Congress candidate, took over in 2002. On 29th October 2003, a public meeting of the whole Sadar Hills' chiefs, MLAs, Ex-MLAs, all leaders of social/civil organisations, NGOs etc. was held at Kangpokpi Thomas ground to resort to any means to achieve Sadar Hills District. On 29th and 30th July 2007, the members of the demand committee and the MLAs of Sadar Hills unit had a meeting. The Ministers present in the meeting were Shri T.N. Haokip, Shri Biren, Shri Jayenta and the present Chief Minister Shri O. Ibobi Singh. The process has been underway for converting the ADC mini secretariat into a DC Mini Secretariat though it still needs the approval from the election commission (ibid).

The present controversy regarding the committee is its opposition to the implementation of Panchayati Raj Act in the jurisdiction of hill area district council. On September 17 in 2007, a forty-eight hours total bandh in Sadar Hills area including National Highway 39 and 53 was called to protest against the failure of the State Government to upgrade Sadar Hills to a full-fledged district and the move being made to hold Panchayat election in the Sadar Hills area (ibid).

The President of Sadar Hills District Demand Committee Haokholen Guite said that the reason for calling the bandh is due to the imposition of two types of administrations, saying 'we already have District Council and we don't need another administration under Panchayati Raj'. Expressing regret over the alleged failure of the non-Kuki community to respect the agreement signed with the Kuki community settling in mutual harmony in Sadar Hills area in 1974-75, Guite said that the attempt being made by the Government to impose two types of administration in Sadar Hills area is not the right step. This proposed bandh had a great impact in the whole state as the lifeline of Manipur passes through this Sadar Hills area[21] (ibid). No further development or plans towards the demand for full-fledged Sadar Hills district comes forward in public domain from SHDDC then.

The SHDDC has been ongoing for years without any concrete result. Talks were held between public leaders of different civil and philanthropic organisation on how to move the movement forward towards achieving its goal. With the input made by civil bodies and the concerned public, there was revival of SHDDC with the election of new leaders on 21st June of 2011. Mr. Ngamkhohao Haokip and Mr. Tonghen Kipgen were unanimously appointed as the new Chairman and General Secretary respectively. With the change of guard, the organisation was re-christened as Sadar Hills District-hood Demand Committee on 16th July 2011.

Though they made a very late appearance, their cooperation to the effectiveness of the movement was gigantic as well as historic. The tactics adopted by them in the protest were initially non-violent protest, agitation, and negotiation with the government. Not satisfied with the response from the state and central government, the Kuki Women adopted more violent ways of protest by blocking the roads, preventing vehicle movement during the protest and heightening their protest with burning trucks, tempos, light vehicles who deficed their strike and bandh. When the women folk joined the movement, other avenues of domestic life in the Sadar hills region came to a standstill.

Finding no other option in order to attain their goal of a separate district, the women folk resorted to fast unto death if their plea is not met by the Government. The idea of fasting was started by 12 women and was later joined by more women in different venues of the Kuki dominated area. On August 16th of 2011, more than 40 women belonging to the Kuki community began their fast unto death in their demand for a full-fledged Sadar Hills district in Manipur. A day before, on August 15, the people of Sadar Hills observed India's Independence Day in mourning by wearing black dresses to protest the government's inaction. On August 28 of 2011, three hunger strikers were arrested by the state police on charges of attempting to commit suicide, after they refused medical aid and on August 20, seven hunger strikers were hospitalized because of deteriorating health condition.[22] As part of their agitation, elected representatives of Sadar Hills met both the state and central governments. While the central government advised the state government to look into the agitators' demand, the state government fails to implement it thus far. The agitation was initially planned for a seven-day strike starting July 31(2011), but it escalated to an indefinite strike with the death of three women on August 2, 2011. They were mowed down by a tanker, whose driver lost control.[23]

After the incident, the movement took a violent turn. On September 6, 2011, at least fifty-six women protestors of Sadar Hills were injured and eleven protestors were reportedly arrested by forty-three Assam Rifles while nine trucks were set on fire by women protestors in an urban town called kangpokpi. The incident happened shortly after the Sadar Hills Districthood Demand Committee made its announcement for the suspension of general strike from Sadar Hills area. Women protestors at Kangpokpi set ablaze at least nine trucks escorted by a convoy of forty-three Assam Rifles. At least four trucks were completely destroyed during the arson. Following the attack, the Assam Rifles personnel carried out a baton charge on the protestors wherein at least fifty-six women protestors were injured. Of the fifty-six injured victims twenty were reportedly hospitalized in serious condition at Kangpokpi Mission Hostel while thirty-six were hospitalized in a less critical condition. At the same time, at least eleven protestors both men and women, were reportedly taken into custody by the AR personnel.[24]

On the other hand, the Sadar hills districthood demand committee (SHDDC) alleged the forty-three Assam Rifles under the command of its commanding officer of conducting business of escorting civilian vehicles. The women protestors at Kangpokpi stopped the vehicle and conducted verification wherein they found out only five vehicles were genuinely, on army duty, while the rest were civilian trucks escorted for money. A commotion broke out on the issue from both side (AR and protestors) and the enraged protestors set ablaze some of the trucks. The AR then indiscriminately baton charged the women protestors injuring at least fifty-six women. The SHDDC had been seriously considering withdrawal of its general strike, blockade and other forms of agitation phase wise however the activities of the forty-three AR under the command of its Commanding Officer hurt the sentiment of the people. The state police department then sent four vehicles of woman police; however they were chased by the protestors and they had to take shelter at Gamnom Sapermeina police station in Manipur.[25]

The Sadar Hills Women Union also negotiated with the Government on many issues. One of them is on the allegation of two majors of the Assam rifles who molested and abused some women protesters who were enforcing the highway blockade at *Gam-giphai* on August 31, 2011. The Sadar Hills Women Union forwarded a petition to the Union Defence Minister seeking an Army Court of Inquiry against the two Majors of the unit. In the petition forwarded to the Defence Minister, the women body alleged that Major Bhavish of forty-three Assam Rifles and Major Ashish Dubey of Kangpokpi post of the same unit abused and molested the chastity of the womenfolk and rained blows on them. Infuriated over the rude behaviour of the Assam Rifles troops, the womenfolk retaliated and managed to overpower them. They were then asked to explain their action. The womenfolk of Sadar Hills viewed the incident seriously.[26]

In showing solidarity to the peoples' (SHDDC) demand and concern over the fate of the Kuki women, the Kukis' residing in Delhi submitted a letter to the Union Home Minister, Government of India for rendering equal justice to the people of Sadar Hills and befitting action against the Assam Rifles. A copy was also send to National Commission for Women, National Commission for Human Right, and Commission for Minority Affairs. (Kuki Student Organisation (Delhi) Official File record). The memorandum was submitted to the Union Home Minister, Government of India under the header, 'Press Statement against Atrocities committed by Assam Rifles personnel upon peaceful women agitators in Manipur, dated 12th september of the year 2011'.

Though, the demand for a full-fledged Sadar Hills district is still not met today, it can be said that the Sadar Hills Women Union played a crucial role in the whole process.

b. KWHROs

The Burmese military regime dealt with the democratic uprising of the 8th august, 1988 in a brutal massacre of protesters and civilians. The regime's responses to these demonstrations became increasingly violent, escalating from curfews and closing of universities, to opening fire on protesters and rape.[27] This brutality of the junta upon civilians forced many of them to take refuge in neighbouring countries such as Thailand, India and Bangladesh where they continue to carry out activities aimed at ending military rule and restoring democracy in the country. One of the peoples severely affected by military rule are the Kukis, who inhabit the Indo-Burma border area, along the Upper Chindwin, in Sagaing division. Kuki civilians have thus suffered intolerable harassment under the military junta. Their men have been forcibly conscripted, and their women sexually abused by the military. These abuses have forced many Kukis to take refuge in India, where they have gained active support for the cause of democracy. Realizing the need for an organized effort towards these goals, and to promote awareness and activism among Kuki women, a meeting of Kuki women leaders was held first at Moreh and later at Imphal to establish a Forum.[28] The Kuki Women's Human Rights Organisation (KWHROs) was formed on the 1st of January, 2000.

The KWHROs has the following aims: 1) To bring to the world's attention the rampant violation of the basic human rights of the Kukis of Burma by the military junta and to seek an end to it. 2) To work towards the dissolution of the military regime and the restoration of democracy in Burma. 3) To enhance the participation of women in all areas of socio-political activity and to promote human rights awareness among the masses.[29] The main head quarter is at Moreh district in Manipur state of India. KWHRO have their own organizational structure in which the central committee has the highest authority and power and the president is the head of the entire organization. A general conference and election is held every two years.[30]

Ever since its inception, the organisation has been involved both in empowering and engaging women to come to the forefront and join the men as equal partners in handling the issues confronting the Kuki society. During 2001-2002, KWHRO organized a basic and advanced vocational tailoring training course at Moreh town on the Indian side of the Indo-Burma border. KWHRO has taken part in various political activities with other pro-democratic organizations to restore human rights and democracy in Burma, especially in Manipur and New Delhi. They have organized the Kukis in Burma to unite and fight the military government to establish democracy in Burma.

On 8th December,, 2011, they organised a peace protest rally at Jantar Mantar in New Delhi over the issue of the Tamanthi dam. The Tamanthi dam is a hydroeclectric project on the Chindwin River in Burma's Sagaing division. It is a hydroelectric project undertaken by National Hydroelectric Power Corporation in India. They wanted the project to be stopped. In its press release, the Moreh based Kuki Women Human Rights Organization (KWHRO) stated that the said Tamanthi dam had displaced over 2,400 villages and will further displace 45,000 more people in future if the construction continues. The displaced Kuki communities were forcefully bulldozed by the Burmese

Army. The KWHRO said "our demand is for the villagers to be repatriated back to their original villages". They further informed that the villagers who were relocated in the new site were not given any basic amenities and were facing hardships. The women spokesperson asserted that such mega hydro projects benefit will definitely go elsewhere and not to poor villagers.[31]

Since its inception, KWHRO has been working to promote social, educational and health rights of women, and gender equality among Kuki society and other communities both inside and outside Burma .They have often organized the Kukis in Burma to unite and fight the military government to establish democracy in Burma. The organization has been working for not only women but also for the entire Kuki community to get equal rights and status within a future federal democracy in Burma.[32]

The movement looks to the Burmese leader Aung San Sukyi as a role model for the Kuki Women. The Kuki Women's Human Rights Organization (KWHRO) believes that the role of Kuki women should be improved within Kuki society as stated under: "History and tradition might have denied us (women) any positive role in society and women might have been confined within the four walls of the kitchen, but with the changing times and the progress of civilization, the time has come where women have to play an important role in society and politics that is equal to that played by men. In fact there are areas where women even excel men. Therefore, KWHRO (B) appeal to all Kuki women to shake off their shackles and emerge out of the kitchen to play an active and positive role in shaping the future of the Kuki nation. It is time we realize that unless we go forth and play the roles expected of us during the times we are in, the struggle of the Kuki nation will be that much weaker".[33]

IV. Theorising the Kuki Women Organisations and Collective Protest

a. Nature of Unrest

For Herbert Blumer, Social Movements are collective enterprises to establish a new order of life (Blumer, 1995, p. 60). "They have their inception in a condition of unrest, and derive their motive power on the other hand from dissatisfaction with the current form of life, and on the other hand, from wishes and hopes for a new schemes or system of living" (ibid). "In its beginning, a social movement is amorphous, poorly organised, and without form; collective behaviour is primitive and the mechanisms of interaction are elementary and spontaneous. As a social movement develops, it takes on the character of a society. It acquires organization and form, a body of customs and traditions, established leadership, an enduring division of labour, social rules and social values—in short, a culture, a social organization, and a new scheme of life" (ibid).

Both the Kuki women organisations, Sadar Hills Women Union and Kuki Women Human Rights Organisations were started in a condition of unrest and dissatisfaction with the current social systems as also unequal distribution of power in the society. The people had no other means to get the attention of the government to take into consideration their demands for justice other than to resort to protest. It starts as collective anguish against a system that treated them unjustly. Different villages in Sadar Hills region as also all Kuki women from different parts of Manipur and even outside joined in solidarity with the Sadar Hills Women Union during the demand for a separate Sadar Hills district for the Kukis in Manipur. The agitation of the women roused the sentiment and interest of people. They resort to tactics like fast unto death, negotiations and violent protest when necessary. According to M.S.A. Rao, the social mobility and change that are brought about by social movements are based on challenge, protest, confrontation, aggression and revolt as opposed to acquiescence, request, obedience and loyalty. It perpetuates the established order and changed the traditional balance of power (Rao, 2006).

The movement interestingly had more active participation from village women with urban educated women taking the leadership though in minority. The various 'women society' groups of the church and 'women union' groups in many villages became the meeting points where discussions were held on what could be done for the success of the movement. These meetings enabled the development of Esprit de Corps or the organization of feelings on behalf of the movement. This helped to develop a condition of rapport, feelings of intimacy and closeness and the sense of sharing a common experience (Blumer, 1995). The esprit de corps developed in a social movement in three ways: the development of an in-group and out-group relation, the formation of an informal fellowship association and the participation in formal ceremonial behaviour (ibid, p. 67-70).

b. Comparative Analysis with other Women Movement in India: Chipko Movement and Nupilan Movement

Mahatma Gandhi, the father of Indian Nation encouraged women to participate in the freedom struggle in such events as the Satyagraha Movement. Kuumba in her book, 'Gender and Social Movements', tried to view the liberation struggles through the lens of women and brings to our understanding how gender affects women's mobilization, strategies and outcomes in social movement organizations (Kuumba, 2003). Ramachandra Guha in, "The Unquiet Woods: Ecological Change and Peasant Resistance in the Himalaya", studied the Kumaun and Garhwal region of Uttarakhand in India (Guha, 2006). An important question asked by the book is—whether it is possible to relate the subordinate position of women in Uttarakhand to the enthusiastic support given by them to the Chipko Andolan (ibid, p. 109). The popular conception of Chipko is that of a romantic reunion of humans, especially women, with nature (ibid, p. 173). "The dramatic act—often threatened but rarely brought into play—of hugging the tree to save it from the contractor's axe is the chief characteristic with which the movement is identified (ibid)." The hill women traditionally bore an extremely high share of family labour. They collect fodder, firewood and carry water, which form their main chores besides farming (p. 169). Their participation in Chipko (movement) according to Guha could be due to an outcome of the increasing difficulty with which the tasks was accomplished in the deteriorating environment caused by deforestation (ibid, p. 175). The movement also shows the local people attachment to and dependence on the forest for their livelihood.

Manipur has three ethnic populations: the Meities in the valley and the Kukis and the Nagas in the surrounding hills. The *Nupilan* movement took place in valley areas of Manipur in which

Vaisnavite Hinduism was the dominant religion. The *Nupilan* movement which means women's war or agitation is one of the important movements in the history of Manipur. While the original demands of the women were confined to the banning of rice export, their later demands also included changes in the administrative set-up (Yambem, 1976, p. 331). It sowed the new seeds of economic and political reforms for a new Manipur in the early 40s. The first *Nupilan* was in 1904 and the second was in 1939. They were protest made against the oppressive economic and administrative politics ruled by the Manipur maharaja and the political agent Mr. Gimson of the British Government (1933-45) and later on, evolved into a movement for the constitutional and administrative reform in Manipur (ibid, p. 325).

How was collective mobilization amongst women possible in a conservative society like the Manipuri society? The role of the Manipuri women in the agrarian economy is a crucial one. They are involved in the production to the marketing of food grains (ibid). The movement interestingly centralised around a women's bazaar in Manipur. In Imphal, the capital of Manipur, there is a market which is believed to have been founded by a king by the name Khagemba in the year 1580. The market is known as 'Khwairamband Bazar' or 'Ima Keithel', and has over 2000 women occupying regular stalls while an even larger number are seated outside. The whole market has always been managed by the women and this practice is still continuing today (ibid).

Apart from the economic activities, the market is also an important avenue of social and political interaction. It was this aspect of Khwairamband bazaar which played a crucial role in the outbreak of the Nupilan in 1939 (ibid). In fact it was this market which gave the space for women to come together and share their experiences and ideas on the issues confronting their society. Discussion and debates happened everyday and they eventually decided they should do something about the political situation of Manipur. Later on, the market became not only the venue for collective mobilization but it became the very object by which they negotiate with the government as it constitutes the life line of the economy. Their tactic was to boycott or stop business in the market and the Khwairamband Bazar remained devastated for three years.[34] According to Sanamani Yambem, Manipuri women were more vocal and volatile than the male section of the Manipuri society (Yambem, 1976, p. 331). The boycott of the market for more than one and a half year convinced the state authorities that the women of Manipur could take up any form of agitation once they were convinced of their purpose. The women of Manipur in the process became the vanguard of change (ibid).

c. Culture and Protest Movement

Culture also plays a central role in explaining protest movements and their development. The beliefs, values, mentalities, social representations, habitus, specific norms of behaviour, attitudes and ideologies that influenced social movements are often determined by the culture of the society. The Latin root of the word 'culture' is *colere,* which can mean anything from cultivating and inhabiting, to worshipping and protecting. Culture can be summarized as the complex of values, customs, beliefs and practices, which constitute the way of life of a specific group. E.B. Taylor in *'Primitive culture (1871)'*, puts it as "that complex whole which includes knowledge, belief, art, morals, law, custom and any other capabilities and habits acquired by man as a member of society".

According to Hank Johnston, "when we refer to culture in everyday parlance, we recognize that different groups of people make different assumptions about the world, categorize it in different ways, and adhere to different values and beliefs, all of which significantly shape behaviours and ways of thinking. The commonsense notion of culture can be applied readily to social movements insofar as participants often hold values, attitudes, beliefs and ideological orientations that are often quite distinct from the broader culture and that shifts in beliefs causes social change" (Johnston, 2009).

Cultural factors are central elements in shaping trajectories, organizational forms, recruitment, protest strategies and ideologies of social movements (ibid). The Sadar Hills Women Union and Kuki Women Human Rights Organisations were movements that were both bounded and directed by the culture of the society. They are both movements against an external force, the Indian government in the case of the former and the Burmese militant group in case of the later. The Sadar Hills Women Union started with a peaceful means of agitation, but became violent due to the oppressive attitude of some state representatives. The Kuki Women Human Rights Organisation is more deep seated in its attempt. It not only tries to protect the interest of the Kuki community but also aims at an overall empowerment of the Kuki women.

The Aftermath

The advent of Christianity and modernity has enabled Kuki women to evolve into a stronger personality. In the present decade, there is a paradigm shift from women subordination to tremendous involvement in socio-political welfare of the Kuki society. The Bijang Kuki women welfare association was formed on 3rd June 2013 to check against the use and selling of drugs in the Bijang area of Churachandpur district of Manipur. This added another number to the multifaceted role of women in the Kuki society. Since, the inception of the association, it has dismantled eighteen houses of drugs peddlers. The opening of a branch for Kuki Women Human Right Organisation (KWHRO) in Churachandpur on 15th August 2013 and the seminars organised on issues like Human Right and Current Political Issues on 6th September 2013 at Churachandpur district envisaged new initiatives by Kuki women to create awareness and empowerment to fight for themselves and for the cause of the society.

Notes

1. Official Classification of Tribes in Manipur by the Directorate of Tribal Welfare & Backward Classes, 1981
2. Relationship with one's maternal uncle is considered very important in the traditional Thadou society. The practice has lessened in importance, yet still prevalent. The maternal uncle is responsible to the welfare of his sister's children, so much so that his responsibility sometimes supercede those of the father of the children. He is also given due honour and respect in the sister's household.

3 . When bride price is paid, it is customary for the father to take only (not half but 2/3 or two-third) half of the demanded amount at the time of marriage. The balance one-third is to be paid to the bride's family on the decease of bride. This is called 'luongman' (corpse price).

4. The traditional labour corps in the villages that is common in any Thadou-Kuki villages. The purpose of the grouping is mainly for agricultural activities.

5 . Chang-Ai is a festival performed by a person who harvests paddy much above his requirements for more than a decade and expresses thanks to God for the bountiful harvest.

6. Sitlhou, Hoineilhing. 13th August, 2008. 'Women's Role in the Community: In the Context of Kuki Society,' *Kuki International Forum* in http://kukiforum.com/2008/08/women-role-in-community-in-the-context-of-kuki-society/ (accessed 31st May, 2011)

7. Sitlhou, Hoineilhing. 13th August, 2008. 'Women's Role in the Community: In the Context of Kuki Society,' *Kuki International Forum* in http://kukiforum.com/2008/08/women-role-in-community-in-the-context-of-kuki-society/ (accessed 31st May, 2011)

8. ibid

9. ibid

10. The leaders were— Pu Z. F. Routhanglien (Pres.), Retd. Major Pagin Kipgen and Pu Paokai Haokip Gen. Secy K.N.A

11.. Gangte, T.S. 2007. "Struggle for Identity and Land among the Hill Peoples of Manipur." *Manipur Research Forum*. http://www.manipurresearchforum.org/struggleidentityhillpeoples.htm (accessed 28 May, 2011).

12. Nabakumar, W. "Ethnic relationship of different communities in Manipur." *Kukiforum*. http://kukiforum.com/2007/08/ethnic-relationship-of-different-communities-in-manipur-2/ (accessed 28 May, 2011)

13. Manipur population has three major ethnic groups: the Meiteis of the valley, the Nagas and Kukis of the surrounding hills.

14. Meeting of the SHDDC with UNC (United Naga Council), ANSAM and Manipur Government on 23rd June 1998 on the demand of Sadar Hills as a full-fledged district

15. Records in the Documents of the SHDDC, 1998

16. Deputy Commissioner
17. Superintendent of Police
18. Executive Engineer
19. Executive Engineer Public Work Department
20. The Manipur State Congress Party (MSCP) is a splinter group of the Congress (I), which formed the government in coalition with the Federal Party of Manipur in 2000.
21. The materials are based on the records, documents and proceedings of the Sadar Hills District Demand Committee. Interview was also conducted with–

1. The President–Mr. Haokholen Guite, interviewed on 5th December, 2008
2. Misao, Thangkam, General Secretary of SHDDC, Interviewed on 5th December 2008

22. Kipgen, Nehginpao, Hunger Strikes in India the needs world's attention, 8th September, 2011, http://ifp.co.in/imphal-free-press-full-story.php?newsid=1354&catid=3, accessed date 5th May, 2013
23. Ibid
24 Tension runs high at Sadar Hills 56 women injured, nine trucks burnt down, 11 protestors arrested by AR, 7th September, 2011, http://www.ifp.co.in/imphal-free-press-full-story.php?newsid= 1346 &catid=1, accessed on 5th may, 2013
25. Ibid
26. Sadar Hills women petition DM, September 2, 2011, http://tse.manipur.us/2011/09/03/sangai-express-news.php%3Fnewsid=8559.html, accessed date 5th May, 2013.
27. Burma Partnership, 2010, http://www.burmapartnership.org/photo-petition-background/, accessed date 5th May, 2013
28. Ngulminthang, http://www.bombiel.com/zaila/lunglen-audio/item/106-kuki-womens-human-rights-organization-kwhro.html, accessed date 2nd May, 2012.
29. Ibid
30. Ibid

31. Hanghal, Ninglun, Kuki Women Protest Against Tamanthi Dam, The Sangai Express, http://www.e-pao.net/GP.asp?src= 11..091211.dec11, accessed date 5th May, 2013
32. Ngulminthang, http://www.bombiel.com/zaila/lunglen-audio/item/106-kuki-womens-human-rights-organization-kwhro.html, accessed date 2nd May, 2012.
33. Ibid
34. Kshetrimayum, Otojit, Rethinking Women's Power in Manipur, http://e-pao.net/epSubPageExtractor.asp?src=news_ section. opinions.Rethinking_Women_Power_in_Manipur, accessed date: 5th May, 2013

References

1. BLUMER, HERBERT. (1995) Social Movements. In Stanford M. Lyman (Ed.) *Social Movements: Critiques, Concepts, Case-Studies*. London: Macmillan Press Ltd..
2. GANGTE, T.S. (1993) *The Kukis of Manipur – A historical analysis*. New Delhi: Gyan publishing house.
3. GANGTE, T.S. (2007) Struggle for Identity and Land among the Hill Peoples of Manipur. *Eastern Quarterly Journal.* 4(II) (July-September).
4. GUHA, RAMACHANDRA. (2006) *The Unquiet Woods: Ecological Change and Peasant Resistance in the Himalaya (The Ramachandra Guha Omnibus)*. Delhi: Oxford University Press.
5. ZELIANG, ELUNGKIEBE. (Ed.) (2005) History of Christianity in Manipur, source materials, 2005 (ed.) Guwahati: Christian Literature Centre/ Imphal: Manipur Baptist Convention
6. JOHNSTON, HANK (Ed.) (2009) *Culture, Social Movements and Protest*. USA: Ashgate publishing company.
7. JOHNSTON, JAMES. (1987) *Manipur and the Naga Hills*. Delhi: Gian Publishing House.
8. KIPGEN, MANGKHOSAT (1997) *Christianity and Mizo Culture: The Encounter between Christianity and Zo Culture in Mizoram*. Aizawl: Mizo Theological Conference.

9. KUUMBA, M. BAHATI (2003) *Gender and Social Movements.* New Delhi: Rawat Publications.

10. LEWIN, CAPT. T.H. (Deputy Commissioner of Hill Tracts). (1870) *Wild Races of South-Eastern India.* Aizawl: Firma KLM Private Limited for Tribal Research Institute.

11. LLOYED, J. MEIRON. (1991) *History of the church in Mizoram: Harvest in the hills.* Mizoram: Synod Publication Board.

12. RAO, M.S.A. (2006) *Social Movements in India.* New Delhi: Manohar.

13. RAY, ASOK KUMAR. (1990/1951). *Authority and Legitimacy: A Study of the Thadou-Kukis in Manipur.* Delhi: Renaissance Publishing House.

14. SHAKESPEAR, LT. COLONEL J. (1975 /1912) *The Lushai Kuki Clans.* Mizoram: Tribal Research Institute.

15. SITLHOU, HOINEILHING. (2011) Land and Identity: A Sociological Study of the Thadou Kuki Tribes of Manipur (Thesis submitted to Jawaharlal Nehru University). New Delhi: Centre for Study of Social Systems/ School of Social Sciences.

16. SITLHOU, MANGJEL PAOKAI. (Ed.) (1995) A Brief Account of the Thadous. In Naorem Sanajaoba. *Manipur Past and Present: The Ordeals and Heritage of a Civilisation,* Volume III (Nagas & Kuki-Chins). New Delhi: Mittal Publications.

17. TAYLOR, EDWARD. (Ed.) 1871 *Primitive Culture.* (4th Ed.). London: John Murray.

18. YAMBEM, SANAMANI. (1939) Nupi lan: Manipur Women's Agitation. *Economic and Political Weekly.* Vol.11, No. 8 (Feb. 21, 1976), pp. 325-331

Chapter 6

Customary Laws of the Chikims with Special Reference to the Thadous

Priyadarshni M. Gangte

Introduction

Bekker[1] in his work on "Customary Law in Southern Africa" observed that when lawyers write about Customary Laws, they have professional concern to reduce the typically undifferentiated repertoire of principles, adages, maxims and folk proverbs of an oral tradition to a systemic code of rules. For this he exemplified court precedents, statutes, ethnographies and colonial commissions of enquiry so as to make use of them in the Courts and legal practitioners. Such approach suffers because of defects in the rules which are abstracted from social context, and are frozen in precedents and other formal legal sources~ their function is obscured as is their standing in relation to the reality of current social practice.

Customary Law is the term most commonly used to describe the largely unwritten indigenous laws of the indigenous people especially the tribes recognized by European powers in their colonial territories. The basis of validity for these laws, which are similar to the "custom" of the western legal systems, lies in social practices accepted as obligatory[2].

It must, however, be kept in mind that from an early date, the task of writing about customary law was mainly the task of anthropologists. In doing so, they took care to place law in its social context by developing a separate scholarly tradition. Schapera[3] was one such a distinguished scholar as could be evidenced from his account of the Customary Laws of the various peoples of the Bechuanaland Protectorate (now Botswana) which is considered a model of the gentry. He described Tswana law against a background of Tswana Social and political institutions and the tensions between tradition and the influence of modern world. His work had been commissioned for use in the Colonial courts.

Following closely the approach of Schapera, Holleman[4] sought to avoid pitfalls in his work on Shona Customary Law with reference to kinship, marriage, the family and the Estate. As an anthropologist, Holleman, explained the institutions of marriage and succession of a Shona people in Southern Rhodesia (now Zimbabwe) primarily with reference to their system of kinship. The works of both Halleman and Schapera are best considered as representatives of a high point in functionalist anthropology despite the fact that law and societies they described have long since succumbed to the forces of capitalism, under-development, urbanization etc. not to mention such post-colonial concerns as national unity and gender equality.

Among the third group of scholars who undertook such studies on Customary Law, Simons[5] may be mentioned. He tried to show in his work on African Women: Their Legal Status in South Africa as to how social, economic and political policies regulated the status of women in South Africa. In doing so, he placed the law, be it customary, statute or precedent, in the historical framework of South African politics in the then existing social context when colonial authorities were highly conscious of their "civilizing mission", they sought to suppress bride wealth and polygamy on the ground that these practices degraded the position of women. When policies of segregation and apartheid came into force, the courts and the government revive African culture and with it the tradition of patriarchy[6].-

A leading anthropologist, Gluckman,[7] stands in a class on his own and acquired a reputation as "the father of African jurisprudence". His main interest was primarily to reveal the universality of legal concepts, such as ownership, contract, delict, crime, and his argument was based on a study of Lozi in Zambia comparing it with early English and Roman laws. Many have criticized Gluckman for imposing English terms and concepts on his materials, but his works are still fruitful sources of ideas about the effect of Social Structure on legal institutions.

Since the second half of eighteenth century, "legal pluralism" had been adopted which contended that law should be seen to be derived from social practice, not state authority. Thus, a valid study of customary law has three versions[8] -

i. Used by the legal profession~

ii. Academic variety (found in scholarly texts on the subject)~ and

iii. The "living" law (rules actually observed in social practice).

Yet customs are not customary laws. There may be various customs without any legal authority whereas the customary laws have the sanction of the bulk of the society and if not obeyed, such violator is liable to be punished. Custom, like law, in its widest connotation, is a body of rules which regulates the conduct of human beings with each other and vis-à-vis the individual and the society as well, said Paras Diwan[9] in his work on Customary Law of Punjab and Haryana.

Indeed, custom is coeval with the very birth of community itself. The moment man started leading some organized life, whether in small nomadic groups or in small settled or semi-settled ways, the stage was set for the evolution of customs[10]. Today, this merits reiteration for understanding of the origin and growth of customs. As human beings engaged themselves in multifarious activities, there emerged certain uniform patterns of human behaviour. These patterns are perpetuated either on account of belief in their propriety or on account of sheer necessity of living together. As men gained experience in group life, they learnt that a particular mode or behaviour or conduct was conducive to collective living. Universal recognition made modes of human behaviour well established and accepted. Simultaneously, as new individual and complex social needs arose, new patterns of human behaviour emerged[11].

This dialectics gave endless impetus to the behaviour patterns, probably, this process continued in all human societies till they evolved a conscious law making machinery. But subsequently the need for codifying the Customary Laws was strongly felt and many societies formulated the codified laws. Manu's Dharmasastra illustrates codification of laws or for that matter the cultic codification of laws all reveal the need for a social change and social regulations through laws[12].

As a matter of fact, Paton[13], an eminent jurist, in his attempt to define, origin, nature, growth of customary law has said that 'custom in any early society was not only the main but also the only vehicle of legal development'. When man first started to live together constituting a society among themselves, they adjusted among themselves of their different individuals nature so that they might live in harmony. This was the beginning of creating social behaviour with various activities conducive to their diverse nature. Such nature, which has the greatest possibility of acceptability by most of them gradually, became accepted law, which duly became customary laws on account of being practised repeatedly within and without that particular society or social group. In this connection, it may be of relevance to note that Maine[14] in his celebrated work, Ancient Law, propounded the theory that in the evolution, the judgments of inspired Kings preceded the customs. But it is now well established that it is the other way round. There is not much scope to doubt that the first stage of evolution of law was custom.

It has been proved that the group habits collectively lead human beings to get accustomed to doing certain things in a certain regulated manner. The adherence of the group or of the individuals to these modes of behaviors, gives rise to customary laws which command obedience since disregard of them will involve some kind of penalty whether imposed in the realm of conscience or by the collective will of the group or the community[15].

Now, before we proceed further, it is incumbent that historical and traditional background of the Chikim's need to be understood in its right perspective. The Chin-Kuki-Mizo comprised of several ethnic tribal groups who are closely allied to one another. They have a common culture, tradition language, custom, mode of cultivation, form of government, etc. They inhabit entire Chin Hill state of Myanmar and are known as 'Kuki'. These same groups of people are known as 'Chin' when they are in Manipur, Nagaland, Tripura, Assam etc. in India and also in Chittagong Hill Tracts of Bangladesh. Similarly in recent times these people inhabiting erstwhile Lushai Hill District of Assam, preferred to abandon the term 'Kuki' which is recognized by the Government of India and granted the State of Mizoram as belonging to the Mizo people. Therefore, the terms, Chin-Kuki-Mizo would clubbed together and called them in the acronym, CHIKIM, which is literally speaking a word that conveys "all nationalities". Moreover, the term 'Thadou' is the majority and dominant group of the Kukis in Manipur.

They are classified Shakespear[16] as given below in his work on LUSHAI KUKI CLANS of which we are concerned with the Thadou Clans under Group 5(five) as given below are:

(i) Doungel, (ii) Sitlhou, (iii) Singson, (iv) Kipgen, (v) Haokip, (vi) Chongloi, (vii)Hangshing (viii) Touthang and some non-Thadou groups who have been absorbed among the above mentioned Thadous having for all practical purposes embraced all customs, culture, language, religious beliefs, rites, rituals, etc. except that they do not claim to be the descendants of Chongthu with a tradition of Khul or Khur origin, instead, posing as descended from 'Celestial origin'. These groups are - Lianthang and his brother Thlangum (Lhangum), Lunkim and Changsan who also claimed to have survived the 'Thimzin' trauma.

Social Institutions

In the study of customary laws versions in their practices and usages of social institutions have to be indispensably referred to for better understanding of the same. Hence, social institutions and customary laws which have been adopted by the Thadous, such as, marriage, marriage payment or bride price, inheritance, divorce, birth - rite, death - rite, would therefore be dealt with for consideration.

Marriage

Marriage as an institution is a social arrangement by which a couple is legitimized, said Radcliffe-brown[17], in their physical relationship and their child is given a legitimate position in the society which is often determined by parenthood in the social sense. This concept of marriage is comparable to the early English and African marriage form that existed in the 19th Century as a standard form of civilized marriage.

There are different kinds of marriage of which the following are common among the Thadous –

i. Mother's Brother's Daughter marriage or Neilah or Cross-Cousin marriage or preferential marriage~

ii. Mutual consent or love marriage~

iii. Marriage by elopement,

iv. Levirate marriage, and

v. Konglo marriage. (author's own)

Marriage payment or Bride-Price

Marriage payment or bride-price or marriage price is the most important factor in Thadou marriage. No marriage can be performed unless part of the marriage payment is made in advance by the bridegroom to the bride's family. It is a sacred institution prevalent in Thadou society. It is, however, not to be understood as a sale-price, said Parry[18]. It is not a commercial transaction either. This practice of marriage payment is made in kind and Mithun necessarily. In this connection, Gangte has conteded that it has an interesting mythology[19] behind it which runs as given below:

Chongthu was the younger brother of Noimangpa, the Chief of the underworld. As per Thadou custom, in the presence of the elder brother called *'Upa'*, the younger brother called *'Naopa'* cannot become a chief. So, Noimangpa, being the elder, was the chief, Chongthu also intended to become the Chief. Therefore, he went out in search of a suitable land where he could establish himself separately as a Chief. He found one. On his plan to become a chief, he wanted to go with his own closed friends whom he could trust. Thus, he arranged for the marriage of each of his selected men. In doing so, he made the marriage payments of each bride to their parents. In those days, no valuable property or cash was available. All the valuable items that one could think of was a *'Paigen'*. This was a belt made of leather and decorated with a kind of beads, called *'Longchang'*, in seven lines. This was then considered to be a very rare and valuable item of property. This could only be afforded by the chief alone. So, traditionally it became associated with the sole property, the right of which was vested only in the chief and was venerated very much being associated with a certain amount of superstition.

Chongthu being the younger brother of *Noimangpa*, the chief, had access to it and when he arranged for the brides of his friends with whom he planned to go to his newly found land, he paid the *'Paigen'* to the parents of the girls as marriage payment. It so happened that though the commoners dared not refuse to accept the *'Paigen'* when offered to them as marriage payment subsequently, they could neither dare keep it with them owing to their superstitions attached to it nor could they dare refuse the bride in marriage. Thus, along with the bride, the parents returned the 'Paigen' to Chongthu saying that being a valuable property associated with the Chief exclusively, they dare not keep it or else, the wrath of the unseen supernatural power visit them and bring misfortune to them. This process went on and on until *Chongthu* was able to arrange 30 of his best and closest friends with the payment of *'Paigen'* as the marriage payment. (see the ref as shown at pp.92-93)

Hereafter, marriage payment of every clan was paid in terms of seven mithuns based on the seven lines of *'Longchung'* on the *'Paigen'*. This however needs further investigation and confirmation, the prevailing different versions on the matter among the Thadou tribes needs specific enquiries. Ethnicity and folk-lores reveal that since then marriage payment came to exist though in actual practice there are variations among the clans in terms of kind and number of mithuns. However, assuming that the following structure is the broad base for marriage payment as propounded by Crawford.[20]

Bride -Price Structure of Thadous

Clan		Price
1. Doungel	i.	selsom (10 mithuns)
	ii.	dahpi ni (2 big copper gongs)
	iii.	dahbu ni (2 sets of three different small sizes of copper gongs)
2. Sitlhou	iv.	Khichang ni (2 ear beads)
	v.	Khichong ni (2 bead necklaces)
3. Singson	i.	Selsomlanga (15 mithuns)
4. Kipgen	i.	selsom (10 mithuns)
5. Haokip	ii.	dahpi ni (2 big copper gongs)

	iii.	Khichong ni (2 bead necklaces)
	iv.	Khichang ni (2 ear beads)
6. Chongloi	i.	Selsagee (7 mithuns)
7. Hangshing	ii.	dahpi khat (1 big copper gong)
	iii.	dahbu khat (1 set of three different small sizes of copper gongs)
	iv.	Khichang khat (1 ear bead)
	v.	Khichong khat (1 bead necklace)

Crawford is the first and only person so far to work on the customary laws of the Thadou ever-undertaken by an authority. The work did not pretend to be exhaustive and was printed in such a form as to enable officers to make their own additions. Examples of then existing court practice in the matter of loans and oaths were inserted even though they were not strictly speaking customs. Therefore, the book is not intended to be a legal code. He was sincerely assisted in his enquiries by William Shaw, B.C. Gasper, L.L. Peter, the Sub-Divisional Officers of Tamenglong, Churachandpur and Ukhrul respectively and by J. H. Hutton, Director of Ethnology and J.C. Higgins, Political Agent in Manipur. In his work he rendered valuable suggestions and advice. Today in high sight we feel though the work is not comprehensive as it could have been, it is however, worthwhile to be used as the basis on which Thadou customary law could be built up for more detailed study. It provides the base for analyzing the customary laws of the Thadous.[21]

Shaw[22] in his study on the Thadou observed several deviations from what Crawford had specified in his work. He contended that the question of amount of marriage payment among the Thadous was not definite and commented that the chiefs and wealthy persons usually claimed and paid the equivalent of ten mithuns, Rs. 200/- in cash, 23 dahpi (large gongs), 2 dahpu (set of two gongs), 2 khichang (ear beads), 2 khichong (necklaces). He did not name any specific clan of the Thadous. He further opined that ordinary person often actually pay a couple of mithun, khichang and khichong. As in an instance, he said that a pig in some cases may be taken as one mithun and that as per his personal experience he had come across cases where Rs. 40 had stood for 4 mithuns, a jar of 'ju' for a khichang or khichong. Thus in actual practice the parent of the bride hardly ever received the marriage-payment in full but in the form of more or less fictitious substitutes. He was emphatic in this regard to the effect that the parents loved to name large amounts as the 'man' not with any idea of getting it, but to be able to boast that their daughter was married for so much. Often when enquired as to what precisely they had received, it was found that actually a much smaller amount had been accepted in full satisfaction by a system of fictitious values. This is very similar to the practices among the Lushais, Zous, etc. Fictitious values have more often created false pretensions of wealth and richness, which became bones of contentions later and led to unhappy marriages.

It must also be mentioned that Hutton[23] was convinced to have observed the fact that the first and last number of the marriage payment by mithun must necessarily be paid in mithun (selkeng-liding*) by this it means that marriage payment has to be by live-mithun). The first and the last marriage payment must in no case be substituted in any form of cash or kind. *(It is liding- mithun's four leg condition i.e a standing mithun)

Gangte[24] another authority working on the marriage payment of the Thadous maintains that the marriage payment of the Singson Thadou is 30 mithuns without any other items added to it unlike the other Thadou clans. The higher rate of marriage payment among the Singsons has no origin according to him. It is said, the Singsons are the direct junior collaterals of the Sitlhous. So when their senior collateral (Sitlhous) increased the marriag payment the junior also deemed it proper to follow suit.[25]

In this regard it is found that one common conspicuous missing fact is that of '*Lutom Laisui*', a very important and compulsory item in the marriage payment. It signifies the importance of father and mother of the bride. *'Lutom'* is given to the father of the bride in token expression of gratitude. Likewise, *'Laisui'* is an exclusive item to be given to the mother of the bride for having given birth to her daughter and son from her naval. Here, it must be said that, while the father is shown respect for his paternal masculinity, the mother too is highly respected for giving birth to the child.

It is interesting to state that there cropped up differences between William Shaw and J.H. Hutton, who out of confusion literally dealt with the two terms out of ignorance of the language and meaning provided to the two items. Shaw[26] attributed *'Lutom'* as a gift given to the mother and *'Laisui'* to the father. Hutton[27] contended otherwise and explained that Shaw got it the wrong way round. In doing so, he explained saying that *Laisui* means a woman's waist-band, while *Lutom* is a man's loincloth. They were cloths for bride's parent and further contended that it could be accounted for a money payment of Re. 1/- and Rs. 2/- respectively, that a woman can claim for property and that a Thadou woman can make in her own account.

Similarly, another feature that has not been dealt with by the several authorities in regard to Manpi which stands for principal marriage-payment that consists of one mithun on the tail of which one piece of big bead 'khichang' through the ear of which the tail of the mithun can be made to pass as a decorative piece[28]. This bead is counted as equivalent to one mithun. Therefore, the Manpi or the principal mithun is counted as to bear the price of two mithuns. The principal mithun is expected to have given birth to as many calves as possible. It is believed that with such principal mithun included in the marriage payment similar number of many children is in return given birth by the bride[29] as we have noticed in the Meitei society "cow" gifted in their daughter's marriage. Therefore it is insisted that such principal mithun should necessarily reveal calf bearing.

It is also observed that the broad based marriage payment as shown above is not totally followed by different clans. As for an instance, the Haokips of Chassad lineage known as the seniormost (piba) of the Haokip take ten mithuns inclusive of the principal mithun.[30] However, as for other junior lineages of the Haokip clan of the Thadou, the marriage payment is fixed at eight mithuns.

Another pertinent point I have observed i.e. the fact that though the marriage -payments of different clans are fixed it is customarily not paid in full throughout the life time of the bride.[31] The practice of marriage payment is that provided the principal mithun accompanied by one or more subsidiary mithun can be paid, the remaining marriage payment be not necessarily in terms of mithuns.[32] They can be substituted in kind. Symbolically the counting could represent mithun depending on the agreement between the groom's and bride's parties.

It is also observed that in some societies such as that of Sumatra and Malay Archipelago, marriage payment in full[33] had to be made compulsorily so as to be eligible for father-right. By this, it implies that the children of father-right marriage payment system, the children are of exclusive possession of the father. Similarly if no payment is made at all, the children belong to mother and her kin. These South East Asian social trait's could have entered the Thadou social customs during their period of origination and intermingling of their culture with tribes in Manipur[34].

Inheritance

Inheritance is a kinship institution the dominant pattern in family organizations in any society.[35] Natural as this may seem it nevertheless creates a troublesome social environment as a source of conflicts. Each individual in a family can procreate several offsprings, and thereby a problem of inheritance created. This necessity constantly arises because of 'dividing the property' of the family among the members History tells us that no scheme of division has ever done full justice to all the parties concerned. Morgan[36] defined 'inheritance' as the distribution of property among the cognate kindred. With descent in the male line, the children of a deceased person would stand at the head of the cognates and very naturally receive the portion of the heritance. To Lowie[37], rule of inheritance is like the whole of property law reflects the total ideology of a society. 'Laws of inheritance indeed give an unprecedented insight into the socio-economic and political formulations of any society'.

Real or personal property, which is inherited by heirs according to law the process of succession to a property~ the devolution of the property to the heir on the death of an owner is precisely opined by Hari Mohan Sinha and Dheeraj Narula[38] as the right to succeed to the state of an intestate. Sometimes it is loosely applied to the right of devises or legates in a 'will' made in their favour if the persons who might have taken on intestacy. The estate goes itself to which the right attaches.

Some interesting but contradictory laws of inheritance also prevail~ e.g. some of the old Kuki tribes such as Anal, Purum and Lamgang, divide the deceased father's property into shares according to the number of sons. The youngest son inherits the ancestral house and supports the widow~ thus it is akin to the Lushai custom[39].

The laws of inheritance of the Thadous from father to eldest son exclusively irrespective of the number of sons born to the family persist. To share, or otherwise, of his ancestral inheritance with his younger brothers is entirely left at the discretion of the eldest son. Even his father cannot stop inheritance of his eldest son over his property under normal circumstances.

In case a deceased man does not have male issue, the property cannot be inherited by daughter. It has to go necessarily to his male senior lineage closed to him by relationship. Herein, the contention of Crawford[40] may be mentioned in that if a Thadou has no male issue of his own, his property including his right to claim marriage price, dead-price (*longman*) etc. and his debts go to his eldest brother or his eldest brother's son, if the eldest brother is dead or a failing brother, to the eldest of the nearest male line. A younger branch cannot do so until all the senior branches are extinct '*ingam*' in Thadou male line[41]

Divorce

A study of divorce could not be undertaken in isolation. It has to be necessarily linked with marriage. In fact it is the outcome of negative aspect of marriage. For this it will be in the fitness of things that the concept of marriage and the certain religious beliefs need to be given as the background as to how divorce is looked upon by societies. For this purpose the concept of marriage as an institution according to Christianity and Hinduism was briefly looked in to understand the issue of divorce. According to Christian concept of marriage, it is accepted as sacramental and indissoluble except through special dispensation or for the grievous causes for it is said, the Gospel according to Saint Mathew[42],

"... But I say unto you, that whosoever shall put away his wife, saving for the cause of fornication (Chaste), causeth her to commit adultery and whosoever shall marry her that is divorced committed adultery" Similarly, the Gospel according to Saint Mark[43] says, "And he said unto them whosoever shall put away his wife and marry another, committeth adultery against her and if a woman shall put away her husband, and be married to another she committed adultery".

According to Bhushan and Sachdeva[44], the Hindu Shastra regarded marriage a bond of indissoluble in life, the wife was to worship her husband as a god and that there was no such thing as divorce in the Hindu law. However, there existed the custom of divorce among the lower castes. Soppitt[45] in his work on the Kuki Lushai tribes in 1893, observed that the traditional system of divorce practiced among the Thadous since eighteenth century till the period he undertook the study was definite to say, "Once married, no divorce is allowed except for adultery and even in these cases, if there be children, it is resorted to. The adulterer is heavily fined but he/she does not otherwise suffer punishment.

It is a masterpiece of contention, which can be observed as being prevalent even today. Yet, Grawford[46] observed that when a married woman did not behave as a virtuous woman should, the entire *mankat* (marriage payment) plus one mithun as a fine for causing disgrace (*maithi*) or *migepman* as adultery price by the adulterer to the aggrieved husband has to be paid.

In case a widow living in her deceased husband's house has a liaison with a stranger *maithi* is payable even if no pregnancy follows[47]. This is exactly similar to the *Lushai* system called *Uire*. Divorce may also occur due to cruelty of husband toward his wife. Under such atmosphere in the family, the wife not being able to stand cruelty of her husband may ultimately ask for divorce. The Thadous belonging to strong patrilineal society give no right whatsoever to women to who may be attributed the main cause of cruelty of husband rather than to the wife[48].

In such kind of divorce the initiative often comes from the side of the wife leaving her husband's place. The guilt presumed to have originated from the wife due to her inability to bear or to encounter her husband. Therefore, though, in point of fact, husband is the root cause of divorce the wife is implicitly alleged to have taken the step towards divorce for which she was found with fault. The husband, therefore, is exempted from any fine imposed under the normal dispute cases. Hence, the wife is penalized to return to the aggrieved husband the entire marriage-payments except the *sumtansha*[49](a pig killed by the girl's parents for fixation of the girl marriage-payment).

Birth Rite

We are aware of the fact that in any society, modern or primitive, the birth of a child is welcome. It is an addition of a living human soul that adds to the population of the society in which the child is born. It is considered that birth of a child ensures perpetuation of the family lineage. This act of procreation is considered indispensable for a living society lest it becomes extinct.

Similar tothe Lakher belief in the ceremonies of birth and naming of a child the Thadou also has an interesting legend. On such legendary belief the practice of the Thadou at the childbirth is that a provisional name is immediately given to the new born child as soon as the child comes out of the mother's womb simultaneously with the cutting of naval cord by a split of bamboo[50]. This provisional name is associated with the superstitious belief that unless it is done so, the '*Thilhas*' (evil spirit) may overtake the person attending to the mother and the child. It is believed that if the *Thilhas* give name of the child ahead of the attending mid wives the life span of the child is under the discretion of the *Thilhas*. It is faith among the Thadous.

One interesting thing is the traditional process of delivery of the child among the Thadou group. A jar of *ju* is kept prepared with full maturity of fermentation for eight to nine months. It is distilled to be offered to the mother of the child as medicinal potion. It is a fact that with the offer of the *ju* to the mother her entire bowel contaminated by pregnancy and child-birth health is ensured. In this regard there appears slight difference from the contention of Shaw who maintained that the naval cord was cut with a knife or bamboo split[51]. However, Hutton[52] differed from this contention and his views have been convincingly proved. He maintained that the use of knife or any metal on occasions, such as, child birth is considered as taboo among the Thadous. He gave similar belief prevalent among Nagas as well as many other tribes e.g. the Moi of Annan, the Kayan of Barneo and Tinguian of Luzon[53].

After delivery of the child and immediate offer of *ju* to the mother, the real name of the child is given by elders and closed relatives of the family. At this stage though provisionally the name of a boy is selected after his grandfather and grandmother lends her part name in the case of girl child. Thus, in most cases this provisional name is confirmed on this occasion.

The restriction to the mothers not to leave the house for some days among the Lakhers is also prevalent among the Thadous which is called *Naolaichan*. It is done after three days after birth in the case of girl baby and five days for the boy child. On this very day commences feeding of the child. The mother gives food to the child from her own mouth as birds feed their young. It is called *Nao-an-mop*[54].

This is followed by another rite called *Kilhalho*[55]. It is performed after the birth and naming of the child. In the process, the part of '*Thempu*' (priest) comes into the picture. A twisted cotton thread is prepared in the middle of which feathers of a cock are tied. Holding the two ends of the twisted thread around the neck of the child the *Thempu* will perform propitiation, which includes begging for the health and future prosperity of the child to God. After doing so the *Thempu* will tie the thread around the neck of the child with his blessings spraying a mouthful of *ju* around the child symbolizing purification of the child including the surroundings.

The next stage of birth rite is '*Naopui*' (Christening of the child) performed at the residence of the maternal grandparents or uncle. According to Gangte[56], on this occasion the parents of the child take the following items with them.

i. One jar of rice-beer called '*jubel*' and

ii. One cloth called *puondum* (a black coloured with two lines of white colour on the border, lengthwise).

The christening party[57] comprises '*Tuchas*' (representatives drawn from female relatives of the family such as aunts, sisters, etc.) and *Bechas* (representatives and closed friends of the family such as uncles, brother, good friends, etc.) leave for the maternal grandparents or uncle of the child early in the morning. On their arrival at the maternal grandparents or uncle's house, the party is not allowed to enter instantly. They are stopped at the '*Haungcha*' (verandah). The *Becha* of the maternal side cuts ginger into pieces and '*Thempu*' (priest) performs purification rite on completion of which they are allowed in the house. This signifies that the child is spotless and is not impure when they take him or her to the house of the maternal grandparent or uncle. All kinds of evil influences and bad things that may befall the child are then warded off by the performance of the purifying rite at the door with ginger. This ritual has only changed forms but is found in every ethnic community. Among the Meiteis, it is by burning fires.

This follows all the ritual formalities on completion of which the visiting individuals are given a feast together with some presentation including the half portion of the sacrificial meat. Thereafter, they leave the maternal grandparents or uncle of the child's residence with the blessings from the 'Thempu' of maternal side.

Death Rites

Like birth of child every society has its own funeral rites[58]as well. When a member of a society dies, a group of people usually including close kinsfolk of the dead, assemble round the corpse, mourn for it, and arrange for its disposal[59]. The assembly is not merely a matter of choice, but it is dictated by obligation of a strong sanction. Likewise, the mourning is also usually not left to the discretion of the mourner's own emotions[60]. He is expected to mourn in prescribed forms, the intensity of his grief is almost codified according to the kinship status and not infrequently he receives some material acknowledgement of these services. It may be thought that the funeral rites would be concerned primarily with the fate of the soul of the dead man to facilitate his continuity and well-being in the next world. This is often the case, but frequently this aspect receives only small attention. There may be a little talk about the afterworld and of the soul, which has departed and few rites to ensure its safe passage and preservation. Most of the time may be occupied with feasting and exchange of goods and future arrangement for the members of his family. There is much truth in the view that the essential function of the ritual is to deal with the survivors rather than with the dead. As Radcliff-Brown has shown for the 'Andaman Islander' the death of an individual leaves a gap in the social group and disturbs the emotions of those who still live. The funeral ritual provides a channel for the expression of these emotions, and enforces consideration of the role that the individual has played in the social life.

Dalton[61] found the Thadous and their cognate tribes bury their dead but even amongst the poor the bodies are first allowed to lie in estate for several days. And the corpse of great men are placed before slow fire till the flesh is effectively smoke dried and then laid out dressed and equipped for a month or two. Before the process is started, the corpse is washed and is wrapped in a cloth[62]. If the death occurs in the morning or during the night, the corpse is buried in the (next day's) evening. The burial takes place outside the house.

According to Gangte[63], deaths are divided into three broad divisions, namely:

i. *'Thi-pha'* (Natural death)~

ii. *'Senhut'* (child-hood death upto the age of three)~ and

iii. *'Thi-sie'* (unnatural death).

(i) *'Thi-pha'* (Natural Death): As soon as the death takes place, it is informed to all the relatives of the deceased by sending messengers to their respective places. It is believed that the messengers, on their return and after they have reached the deceased's house, *'Kitom'* (brandishing whatever in the hands as a weapon, either scythe, gun, axe, etc.) is performed and who does not do *kitom* he will be sick or any misfortune may happen to him[64]. In the meantime, the dead body is kept for burial and the people await the works of digging of grave, funeral ceremony, etc. to be completed. As for the location for the grave, the village '*Thempu*' (priest) selects the same accompanied by *Tubul* (highest *Tucha*) female relatives. The digging work is first started by the *Tubul*, by digging at least one or two strokes with a spade symbolizing the commencement of the work, then the others follow[65]. Right from this work gets started, the *Tubul* is not allowed to go to the spot nor is he allowed to enter the house till the corpse is buried. This is called *Lhan chan*. A separate *jubel* is arranged for him to be sipped exclusively by him. However he may invite others to join him. When all necessary formalities including the *Phui Sam*[66], are done with and a dedication rite by torching the well- framed corners of the grave is completed, the *Tuchabul* announces that 'the grave is ready'. The *Thempu* leads the funeral party, followed by others crying and *kitom* proceeding towards the graveyard[67]. The *Thempu* also performs *kitom* at intervals on way to the burial ground in the midst of others. Gunshot or blank fire is done in case the man is of fame or status. Then the corpse is laid down in the grave.

Immediately after burial service, a large pot or brass with beads and silver dipped in water is arranged for the Lhan Chan party[68], the Tubul and all the concerned persons who took part in the burial proceedings take bath, wash their hands and other parts of the body, similar with that of Meiteis, Lakhar, etc, signifying purification of defilements.

A feast called '*Kosana*' is normally hosted by killing a mithun, or pig or a cow whatever is available and an animal that can be easily afforded as soon as possible by the deceased's relatives. Actually, '*Kosana*' is to be performed on the day of the burial itself. However, some people arrange on other day as is convenient to them. The '*Sangong*'(neck) of the sacrificial animal in this regard is given to the '*apu*' (maternal uncle).

(ii) **'Sen hut Thi' (infant death)**: The Thadous bury an infant's corpse as soon as possible under the floor within the café of the roof at the outer wall of the house parallel to the hearth of the family without any publicity and ceremonial rites[69].

(iii) **'Thi Sie' (unnatural death):** Any type of unnatural death called *'Thi Sie'*, such as by accidental fall from tree, drowning, killed or murdered etc. irrespective of their social status including the chief does receive the least possible death rite. Such death is also considered as defiled, thereby prohibiting the dead to be brought to the village not beyond the village gate called, *'Khomol'*, which is the entrance gate located before reaching the actual village site[70].

The death of a person with fame, including the chief, received utmost possible elaborate death rites for a normal death. The brief death rites are such that the body is buried with food and drink, and with the skulls of animals, slaughtered for the funeral feast. It is particularly worth mentioning that at one time it was considered essential that a fresh skull of human victim sacrificed for the occasion, should adore the grave of a chief[71]. It is amazingly true that a man-hunt is deliberately organized so as to complete the rituals for the purpose. This has persisted throughout history in different communities with some regional variations. At the time of erecting a dam or a house a human sacrifice was performed clandestinely. It was considered to be auspicious, as doubt, but loss of life could be recompensated. So it was a negative practice not to be encouraged.

The death rite of Thadous is observed that the general principles of the rites are based upon the belief that the soul of a man continues to exist and it therefore transmigrates in some form or the other. In this connection it may be of interest to refer to the findings of Soppitt[72] wherein he stated that on the death of a man his spirit is believed to remain for a period of one full moon in the house he occupied when living, at the lapse of that time the soul departs to a village termed "the village of the dead", where it stays until it returns to earth (at the lapse of an uncertain number of years) in the body of a new born child.

Conclusion

With the passage of time, contacts with outside of their own homogeneous communities entered into the fibre of their social life. People who observed such customary laws became aware of the world beyond their own small community. Gradually, western education began to hold its roots followed by Christianity that propagated to dispense with hitherto known 'culture and tradition. Ultimately, when increasing number of people started embracing Christianity, observance of customary laws became less and less important and ignored, culminating into gradual abandonment of some elements of customary laws. People have almost forgotten even the existence of such a 'cultural heritage' as customary laws.

Identity of a community is known by its rich cultural heritage and perpetuation thereof. Rapid vanishing of the age-old tradition and direction placed the resurgent generation at a loss, and became aware of the vacuum that had been created by such abandonment of the customary laws due mainly to Christianity. It was dreaded that with such relegation of the rich cultural heritage into oblivion, posterity would be at the cross-road of life is of course, the creation of new aspects in the form of new tradition or redefinition of an old one.

It was found that there was no conflict whatsoever between Christianity on the one hand and culture, custom, tradition, in particular~ Customary laws on the other. The two could go hand in hand without being encroached upon each other. As for instance, while the part of 'village priest' can be appropriately substituted by the role of Christian Pastor, the glamour of '*Ju*' and its resultant pleasantries can be replaced by tea and snacks, fund and frolics of all kinds, etc. More innovative can be incorporated into the system retaining the intrinsic social values, such changes are that have been fed into the new fibres of customary laws.

Likewise, with a view to harmonizing with modernity and new way of life which are completely divorced from the traditional homogeneous village life, the many innovative changes have been brought about to strengthen customary laws as observed in the days of yore have been moduled in the faces of modernism, growth, development all around, which in fact resulted in direct conflicts with governmental schemes to improve their lots. This phenomenon is particularly made rather fest with the attempted abolition of Chieftainship which has all through their tradition been the perennial source of customary laws among the Thadous.

Of all empowerment with their importance, political empowerment may be considered more important one. It is meant for participating in political decision - making processes which will normally affects society. The reason is that process has to do with power or influences which can make others behave in line with other wishes. Moreover, what has largely inhibited Thadou women in their empowerment efforts is that majority of them like their Chikims sister is not aware of the opportunity of equal access to political structures provided in the Indian Constitution. Lack of awareness, owing to unsensitisation and exclusive traditional practice dependency abided by customary laws since many centuries.

To bring a change in its mindset of masses certainly, education is the only weapon, by which social trend is made to a twist steadily or suddenly. And in accomplishing its materialization, males participation is also highly needed, we cannot depend on women alone. Moreover the specific constraints and restraints that prevent women's access to education and reduce the possibilities of their completing it have to be counteracted, so that they may have all forms of human securities that have to be provided and whatever due shares apt to. The syllabus and curriculum must be incorporated the presence of women to break through feminine stereotype through texts rights from the grassroots level.

Customary Laws reflect the uniqueness and identity of this group of people, however in this contemporary world the concepts of equality, democracy, women empowerment and human rights are the most special inter-alia and as a matter of fact the contextualization of the same to access at the utmost is perhaps found to the need of the hour. Whatever, said and done, the traditional systems, never recognized the rights of women as primary decision makers in matter of community is due like inter-ethnic conflict crisis management, social sanction, etc. Their customary laws prevalent among this ethnic group, though portray an egalitarian socio-economy structure, is discriminatory when it comes to women's right specifically in traditional governance due to the absence of women representative in their body of village council. Thus, the customary laws of Chikims in general Thadous in particular while despensiating is not justicefically manifested at all, of course inhumane and deprived women in right to property or inheritance, succession etc.

References

1. Bekker, J.C., Seymour's *Customary Law in Southern Africa*, 5th Edition, Cape Town, Juta, 1989
2. P.M. Gangte, *Customary Laws of Meitei And Mizos Societies*, Akansha Publishing House, Delhi-2 2008
3. Schapera, I: A Handbook of Tswana Law and Custom, 2nd Edition, London and New York, Oxford University Press, 1955.
4. Halleman, J.F. : Shona *Customary Law with reference to Kinship marriage, the family and the Estate*, Cape Town and New York, Oxford University Press, 1952.
5. Simon, H.J : *African Women : Their Legal Status in South Africa*, London~ Hurst, and Evanston, Illinois North-Western University Press, 1968.
6. Ibid
7. Gluckman, Max : *The Ideas in Borotse Juresprudence*, New Haven, Connecticut : Yale University Press, 1965.
8. Ibid
9. Paras Diwan : *Customary of Law of Punjab and Haryana*, Publication Bureau, Punjab University, 1978~ p.8
10. P.M. Gangte, op. cit .23
11. Ibid p.24

12. Ibid
13. G.W.Paton : *Jurisprudence* (4th Edition), OUP, London~ p.191.
14. Henry Sumner Maine : *Ancient Law*, 1907, Chapter 1, London (John, Murray : 1897, 1st edition).
15. P.M. Gangte, op. cit .26
16. Lt. Col. J. Shakespear : *The Lushai Kuki Clans*, London~ 1912, Part -I~ p.3
17. A.R. Radcliffe-Brown and Daryll Ford: *African System Of Kinship And Marriage*: OUP, London,1950~ p.5
18. N. E. Parry: *A Monograph on Lushai customs and Ceremonies*, Firma, KLM Pvt. Ltd., Calcutta~ 1928~ p.24
19. T.S. Gangte : *The Kukis of Manipur*, Gyan Publishing House, New Delhi~ 1993~ pp.92-93.
20. C.G. Crawford, *Hand Book of Kuki Custom:*, Directorate of Printing and Stationery, 1984, (reprint), pp.2-3.
21. *It is also observed that the Gauhati High Court has undertaken a project on the customary laws of the Thadou-Kukis with special reference to the land holding systems, sponsored by the North Eastern Council, Shillong under the Directorship of Dr. J.Barooah, Law Research Institute Gauhati High Court, assisted by Mayonmi Shimray as Research Officer and Apem K.H. as Assistant Research Officer. It is found that the Research Institute has given a blanket acceptance to see the above marriage payment structure without slightest analysis on comment on the same.*
22. William Shaw : *The Thadou Kuki*, Shillong, 1928, pp.58-59.
23. J.H. Hutton : *Notes on the Thadou Kukis : Journal of the Asiatic Society of Bengal*, N.S. XXIV 1929 ~ p.59.
24. T.S. Gangte, op. cit., p.95
25. *The contention of Gangte in regard to marriage payment of the Singson was confirmed from S.L. Singson, aged 70+, interviewed on 3.5.2004~ Dr. Seikho Singsit, aged 58+ interviewed on 18-7-2006~ Reverend Kaikhosei, aged 60+ interviewed on 7-4-2005 as informants.In order to further ascertain or otherwise Mrs. Lunkhoneng, aged 80+ was also interviewed on 30-9-2006 to share her personal experience as daughter of the chief of Lungthulien Village. She belongs to a Singson clan of the Thadou, Tipaimukh, Churachandpur District who married Thangkhopao in 1947 belonging to Kipgen of the Thadou claimed that she vividly remembered her marriage payment was 30 mihtuns.*
26. William Shaw: op. cit, p. 63.
27. J. H. Hutton: Ibid.

28. Information provided by the Letkhojam Haokip a close cousin of Chief Chassad on 19.7.2005
29. Ibid
30. ibid
31. Thangkhonieng, aged 94 years, Old Lambulane, interviewed on 4.2.2000.
32. Ibid.
33. A. R. Radcliff - Brown: Op. cit, p. 51
34. P.M. Gangte, op. cit .169
35. Kingsley Davis : *Changing Concepts of Marriage and Family*, Havard Basker and Penkenfill, 1981 (Reprint), p. 409
36. Lewis Henry Morgan : *Ancient Society*, Bharati Library, Calcutta~ 1958, p. 548
37. Robert H. Lowie : Social Organisation: Routledge and Kagan Paul, London, 1950, p.146
38. Hari Mohan Sinha and Dheeraj Narula : *Legal Dictionary*, Allahabad Laws Agency~ 1993~ p.101
39. J. Shakespeare, *The Lushai Kuki Clans, Part.II*, London :1912, p. 154.
40. C.G. Crawford, Op. cit ~ p. 1
41. William Shaw : op. cit~ p. 67
42. Mathew Chapter V, Verses 32 of the *Holy Bible.*
43. Mark Chapter X, Verses 11 & 12 of the *Holy Bible.*
44. Vidya Bhushan and R. Sachdeva, *'An Introduction to Sociology'* Kitab Mahal, Allahabad:1993~ pp. 343-345.
45. C.A. Soppitt, *A Short Account of Kuki Lushai Tribes*, Firma, KLM Pvt. Ltd., Calcutta:1893, p. 15
46. C.G. Crawford, Hand Book of Kuki Custom(Reprint in) : 1984, p. 8
47. Ibid.
48. P.C. Misao: *History and Customs of The Thadou Kuki*, Imphal :1970, p. 38
49. Ibid.
50. T.S. Gangte, op. cit, p. 89
51. William Shaw, op. cit, p. 51
52. J.H. Hutton, op. cit, p. 51

53. E. T. Dalton, Descriptive Ethnology of Bengal - *Tribal History of Eastern India* Originally published by the Office of the Superintendent of Govt. Printing, Calcutta:1872, p. 47
54. T.S. Gangte, op. cit, p. 105
55. Thangkhoneing, op.cit
56. T. S. Gangte, op. cit, p. 107
57. P.M. Gangte, Ibid, p.209
58. Raymond Firth, *Human Types : The New American Library of World Literature,* Inez, New York, U.S.A., 1958, p. 145.
59. Ibid.
60. *Hindu Dharmashastras. Especially Manu's Dharmashastra and the provisions made therein have been codified in the Hindu Funerary rites.*
61. E. T. Dalton, Ibid.
62. William Shaw, op. cit, p. 53
63. Ibid.
64. Ibid.
65. P.M. Gangte, op.cit.p2.21
66. T.S. Gangte, Ibid .Its meaning is utterance of words of magic
67. Ibid
68. P.M. Gangte, op. cit. p.222
69. Ibid
70. Ibid
71. E. T. Dalton, Ibid
72. C.A. Soppitt, op. cit, p. 12.

Chapter 7

The Socio-Cultural Lives of Vaiphei Women as Defined by the Vaiphei Customary Laws

Mary Nengneichong Baite

A custom is defined as the socially sanctioned behavior of the members of a particular community which has been transmitted from generation to generation. There is no universally accepted definition of customary law. It can be described as a set of rules through which a tribe lives its culture and expresses its worldview. Most of the customary laws have traditionally been unwritten and maintained by oral traditions. They include moral, legal, religious and other principles through which a society is controlled. They govern a person's marriage, family, dowry, maintenance, divorce, inheritance and succession, adoption, minority and guardianship as well as community relations such as tenurial rights over forests, lands, water bodies and other natural resources.[1]

They are believed to have been followed from time immemorial and can be rigid as any written codes could be. Vaipheis are one of the tribes belonging to the Tibeto-Burman race and they are one among the 29 recognized tribes in Manipur according to the Constitution of India with regard to Scheduled Caste and Scheduled Tribes Lists (modification) Orders 1956, Part X Manipur. For a historical period where written documents are not available, epigraphic evidence is indispensable. But no such dependable inscription has been discovered for an early history of the Vaipheis or for any tribe of the *Chin-Kuki-Mizo-Zomi* group of tribes. Monographs and travelogues of colonial administrators will be used as primary data. However, they are neither prolific nor accurate as the colonial writers' experiences were limited. Under the situation, oral traditions are the only and indispensable sources for which the essay in this regard will be placed to the minimum possible limit. Lastly, secondary sources will consist of scholarly books and articles which have been written from the late 1950s.

Vaiphei society is patriarchal and patronymic and the state of living is regulated in strict conformity with customary laws. The family is often a joint family and the head of the family is the sole authority in so far as the family and its relations with other families are concerned. The tribe is divided into a number of clans and sub clans. The clan is a continuation of the family unit on the paternal side, commonly bearing the same surname and supposed to have a common ancestor. Central to the body of customary law is the institution of a traditional chief called *Khaw-Hausa,* who hereditarily occupies this position and the entire land belongs to him. Every Vaiphei village has a traditional chief and he is assisted by a council of elders known as *Siamang-Upa* or *Siamang-Pachong* (ministers, nobles or elders) who are nominated by the chief. As the customary practices were deeply embroiled in their socio-cultural lives that the continuity of the past can be seen till today in Vaiphei society though some changes have occurred due to the influence of modernization and westernization.

The objective of this essay is to create a space for the Vaiphei's women within the larger socio-cultural framework of the Vaiphei patriarchal society; and to analyze how far the presence of women plays a role in changing the socio-cultural lives of the Vaiphei society as a whole. The experience of colonial rule was one of the most important formative influences on the feminist movement of the late nineteenth and early twentieth century.[2] As a consequence of changes in the economy and administration of India, introduced by the British, there were large numbers of women who were educated, articulate, mobile and increasingly involved in public activities.[3] Parallel to this change was the establishment of new educational, religious and social institutions. Moreover, throughout the nineteenth and twentieth century, important maneuvers in thought and ideology such as westernization, modernization, reforms, revivalism and nationalism stirred important aspects concerning the women of India.

MARRIAGE

Marriage is the most important social institution among the Vaipheis. In the pre-colonial period, clans were endogamous though inter clan marriage was not uncommon and arranged marriage was the most popular method. Such an arrangement was made according to the customarily preferential form or the selection of one's mother's brother's daughter. A woman had the right to claim the daughter of her brother in marriage for her son. When the parents of the boy were determined that their son should marry no other than the daughter of his maternal uncle called *Neinu*, the marriage negotiation was initiated by the parents of the boy during the childhood of the boy and the girl.[4] This negotiation should not be confused with child marriages. The practice of child marriage was unknown and there was no prescribed age for marriage. In some extreme cases, when a daughter was born in a family, her father's sister and husband could claim that the baby girl, being the *Neinu* of their son (he is the *Neipa* of the girl), should not be given in marriage to anyone else. Such a claim or set aside was called *Kikhau-Khi* (reserved or earmarked).[5] In case both the families agreed and then either one of them failed to marry the other person, then he or she was liable to pay one mithun to the other person as a manifestation of breaching the promise. This manifested the pattern of relationship of giver-receiver called *Pu-Tu* (the boy's maternal uncle was usually addressed as *Pu* and the boy as *Tu* by the former). As a matter of fact, the initiative taken by the parents of the boy establishes that a man was at liberty to take whatsoever he or she had wished from the maternal uncle if the demand was deemed to be reasonable. Nevertheless, a marriage by mutual consent or love also prevailed and children could breach the arrangement made by their parents if they so not wished. The mechanism of forced marriage was rarely applied in Vaiphei society.

Vaiphei marriages can be categorized into four forms:

1) CHAWNG-MOU: It is an arranged or love marriage but done with the prior consent of both the families. Every girl is entitled to be married under this ethical order which is done with acknowledged solemnization and celebration. It gives respect and honour to the girl and her parents. This is the most common and accepted form of marriages followed by the Vaipheis since time immemorial.

2) SAINAPUA OR KIJAAMPI: This form of secret marriage is done through elopement without the consent and knowledge of their parents. This form of marriage is not a common practice though it is accepted socially.

3) THEPTHAAK: A girl is persuaded or convinced by a representative of the boy without the knowledge of her parents. It could also be that the girl is forcibly abducted against her will without prior agreement. In the cases of *Kijaampi* and *Thepthaak,* the marriage is considered socially legal because a woman is earmarked as impure once she is taken by a man.

4) KIPUI: This kind of marriage happens only when she is impregnated by the boy. The situation is a matter of compulsion rather than of her acceptance. It is often viewed as dishonourable to their parents as well as an immoral act to the Vaiphei society. If the boy

> refuses to take the girl, then he is penalized with Sialpi-Salam according to the Vaiphei tradition though this type of circumstance rarely occurred.[6] The social penalization in the form of *Sialpi-Salam* is still practiced among the Vaipheis and other hill tribes in Manipur.

In the standardized pattern of marriage, like *Chawng-Mou*, the customary procedure is as follow: The first stage of visit started with the ritual of seeking the bride. This is called *Mou-Don*. In the past, the parents and relatives of the boy approached the parents of the girl with a pot of rice-beer called *Zu-Bel*.[7] After appraising the main purpose of their visit by the Bechabul, the Tuchabul of the boy's family inserted the stem of a thatch into the Zu in order to measure the quantity each person presented in the house had to take. Firstly, the Tuchabul took a sip and then he requested the eldest female member of the girl's family to take a sip of the rice-beer. Thereafter, he offered it to those men present in the house in sequence of their importance: the eldest member of the groom's circle (*Akuanlam*), *Inncilam* (the girl's family)-*Bechabul, Akuanlam* (the boy's family)-*Bechabul, Inneilam-Inneipa* (the girl's father), *Akuanlam-Inneipa* (the groom's father), *Inneilam Tuchabul, Akuanlam-Tuchabul,* and then to men and women according to their seniority and relations to both the families.[8] Meanwhile, the father of the girl or the *Inneilam-Bechabul* ordinarily expressed family opinion about the proposal, which could be certain or diffident. If the proposal was not accepted, the Becha of the girl in return offered the Zu to the boy's family, which was a sign of refusal.[9]

In the event of acceptance of the proposal, a second visit was agreed upon and a date was fixed. On this second visit, both parties feasted on a swine, which was usually three feet in width and below, at the girl's abode in honour of the agreement they had to negotiate; and the swine in this occasion was provided by the parents of the girl. In the presence of the Bechabul of the boy's party, the swine was pierced by the Bechabul of the girl's party with a shaft and muttered "*Sial zia zat hitawh kasun khawm e"* (I pierced the swine with the number of mithuns necessitated for the bride price).[10] Only after the meat was cooked, negotiation started. First, the priest opened a jar of rice-beer bought by the boy's party, sipped and spat out and sanctified it by uttering *"ka mimpi Zu, ka changpi zu, pathian nang kahun tai hi"*.[11] The customarily intake of rice-beer then commenced following the same procedure as that was done for the *Mou-Don* stage. Subsequently, negotiations were held between the two parties where they discussed the details of the bridal price as well as decided on and fixed a date for the marriage. This stage was called *Sumtan-Sa* (literally *Sum* means money or price, *Tan* refers to fixed or cut and *Sa* signifies a meat or feast).[12] As it was mentioned earlier, the cooked meat was customarily distributed to various sets of relatives of the two groups as deemed necessary. The neck portion of the meat was fractioned into eight pieces and was allocated particularly for each Bechabul, Tuchabul, parents and village chief of the two parties simultaneously. This practice is customarily defined as *Sangawng-Pe.*[13]

Significantly, on this occasion, the exact price of the bride was manifested through small blocks of the cooked meat and intestine and were fastened in a rope and been given to the boy's party. This tradition is called *Sumphalsa.*[14] Similarly, the Tucha relatives who were responsible for cooking, cleaning, fetching water, etc. for the occasion were each acknowledged and redeemed with two or three pieces of cooked meat tightened in a bamboo rope known as *Sabaak*. One of the front legs and hind legs of the swine were allocated to the Tuchabul and Bechabul of the boy's party respectively.[15] This stage of *Sumtan-Sa* was also apparently referred to as *Sialkhau-Thung,* i.e., earmarking the mithun's rope or an engagement. However, the social standardized distribution of meat to different categories in a layer of relationship was not complied as a swine usually of three feet in width and below was not allocated for which the reason is obscured. In case of a death in either of the two families before the day of the wedding, the engagement was postponed for several months or a year;

and was renewed later following the same customary procedures. This sort of befalling before the wedding day is called *Luangin-Akhen*[16] and it is followed till today. In case of another man running off with the betrothed girl, he was fined with a mithun and a pig, which were given to the boy's family as a sign of exculpation. The girl then belonged to him and he was thus depicted as *Sialkhau-Sattan* (breaking the mithun's rope).[17]

The third stage of negotiation took place on the *Sawng* ceremony, which was also known as *Sawng-Satha*, i.e., a farewell feast held in honour of their daughter by her parents. This *Sawng-Satha* was usually done three times in her life time depending on the convenience of both the families.[18] The boy's party which included many young boys and girls reached the house of the girl on the eve of the *Sawng- Satha* by placing a jar of rice-beer at the girl's house as a mark of their arrival; and in reception of the groom's party, rice-beer was offered to them. They were at liberty to feast with the hens and roosters of the latter or of other people if the bride to be did not own any.[19] Besides, they were intercepted by the young boys of the bride's village to participate in an event called *Buantual-Khaw*. It was a friendly wrestling game between the two parties. Before the wrestling commenced, a circle was drawn which served as the wrestling arena. Conventionally, the boy's party gave way to the girl's group of wrestlers and allowed themselves to be defeated. This was done in the belief that if the girl's party won, then she would be blessed with many children.[20] It was also considered that the boy's party had already won the competition by winning the hands of the bride, and therefore, they should be equalized in wrestling as a consolation.

Moreover, on the day of *Sawng-Satha*, the boy's parents with their kindred, *Bechas* and *Tuchas* went to the girl's house taking along the bride's price.[21] A meeting was convened between the two parties where the discussion over the bride price was resolved. Again the rite of sipping rice-beer took place as similar to the sequences followed in the *Mou-Don* and *Sumtan-Sa*. Mostly, the price of a girl varied from seven to fifteen mithuns and was fixed depending on the clan she belonged to. Each clan had a fixed number of mithuns as the price of a girl though the differences were minimal. To a certain extent the price of the girl was also taken as an indication of relative importance of the clan.[22] As a tradition, some men from the boy's party were sent to the forest to catch the required numbers of mithun needed for the bridal price. The group of men were referred to as *Aiilam*.

Besides, the payment being made in terms of mithuns, the other articles usually consisted of *Khipi* (Onyx bead), *Khival* (Cornelian bead), *Puandum* (a traditional shawl), *Dakcha* (a set of small gongs) and *Dakpi* (a big gong). They were placed on a Gawdal (a large plaited plate made of bamboo) as bridal price.[23] These were counted and considered as *Man-mala*, i.e., bridal price paid in advanced. Once accepted, the father of the girl and clan elders finalized and fixed the rest of the girl's bride price called *Manpi*. A unique feature of the Vaiphei customary law of marriage was that it did not allow the full payment of the bride price which was forbidden during her life time. Her parents fixed some amount in the form of a mithun as a due which could be paid only after her death by her eldest son to her maternal grandparents or maternal uncles.[24] For instance, in case of ten mithuns as a bridal price, the payment of only nine mithuns was accepted. It was done as a sign of healthy relationship between the two families.

Also, if the girl had an unmarried elder sister at the time of her marriage, then the boy's parents were to pay one mithun to the girl's parents for *Ukhel-Man* (breaching the age pattern) as a mark of consolation though every family wished their daughters to get married according to seniority.[25] However, *Ukhel-Man* could not be accepted in a case when the sister of the girl was a divorcee. Further, if the girl happened to be the younger of the two daughters or the youngest daughter, tradition held that the boy's parents had to give her mother a traditional shawl as a mark of consolidation which is known as *Lai-Sui*. In the old tradition, it is said that whenever a mother gave birth to a child, her abdomen was tightened up with a soft cloth after the delivery in order to lessen the flow of the blood from the mother's womb.[26] Recalling that, a traditional shawl was given to her mother denoting the girl being the last person her mother had tightened up her abdomen for. Similarly, if the girl happened to be the eldest daughter, again one mithun as a mark of *Lutuam* was given to her mother. However, the other daughters were not bounded with this custom. The traditional practice of *Lutuam* and *Lai-Sui* is followed till date in Vaiphei society.

On this occasion of *Sawng-Satha*, the girl's parents killed two swines in honour of their daughter's leaving her natal home. One of the swine was cut into two halves and one half known as *Sa-Haap* or *Chanu-Sa* (meat share of the daughter) was given to the boy's parents; and this share of meat accompanied the bride to be on her departure to the boy's place.[27] The boy's party gave a jar of rice-beer to the parents of the girl before they left as a mark of consoling their tears. This practice is called *Zu-Ngawng*. Once again, the customary distribution of meat to various sets of relatives from the cooked meat of the other swine was the same as that of the *Sumtan-Sa* observation. In case of a girl who had remarried, her parents could not kill two swines at the time of the marriage and she was considered as *Lamthang Chuantha* (literally it means slipping on the sidelines of a road) and widow remarriage was practiced.[28]

The gifts of the girl from her parents consisted one *Tuthaw* (a small hoe), one *Puanpi* (a large woven shawl), one *Senzing* (bamboo basket), one *Nam* (braided brow band), *Haak le Chau* (an armlet and a bangle), one *Sumbel* (a silver pot), *Sathau* (a bottle of hair oil), *Samthi* (a comb), *Kawng-Gaw* (a small bamboo container-like bag for carrying seeds) and *Dial* (a thin sheet of cloth) for covering the *Sa-Hap*.[29] These goods were articles given to her by her parents and relatives as a token of their love and concern. Besides, a number of household articles called *Mou-kham* were arranged but only to be distributed among the female relatives of the groom side. However, these articles should not be confused with dowry. The Vaipheis do not have a dowry system. The girl in the meantime prepared a jar of rice beer called *Zu* and organized a farewell party called *Nugual* with her friends in her house. These days, the practice of *Nugual* has been discontinued in Vaiphei society.

After a day or two, the groom family left for their home with the bride-to-be taking along the *Sa-Hap*. Before they departed, the *Thiempu* (priest) muttered his charms and spewed out wine from his mouth as a mark of blessing for the girl.[30] All these meetings took place before the marriage. The boy and the girl did meet in between the negotiation stages. However, pre-marital sex was socially discouraged. Marriage solemnization was performed on the day the girl arrived at the boy's village. The bride and the groom were made to sit together with the *Thiempu* who would be seated before them holding a fowl by its neck and intonating:

> *La tha ten thil phalou le vangsiat nate a mau apat jap dawk hen la; amalam uh vansiatna ten a don ding ahichun la ek hung than.*[31]
>
> *Free translation: May your wings blow away all the ominous things from them; if any adversary comes their way, let your dung comes forth.*

Besides, the *Thiempu* also examined the liver of the fowl and pronounced that the spirit had either approved or disapproved of the marriage and the omen and the decision were usually favourable.[32] A newly married woman was forbidden to go to her natal home as and when she pleased unless and until some formalities were performed. In order to enable the girl to visit and have food at her parent's house, the boy's parents and the married couple along with their *Tucha* carried a pot of rice-beer and sought a customary acceptance of bridging the relationship with the girl's family called *Kisulle.*[33] The formalized visit was conjoined with the customary implementation of *Sawng-Satha Niveina* (second *Sawng-Satha*) for their married daughter. The parents of the girl then formally allowed their daughter to enter the house after the priest performed certain rites. There was no exact period being demarcated for any married girl before she could officially visit her parents though it was said that unless the girl could see herself as one of the members of her husband's family she should not go.[34] Unless this rite was performed, the parents and relatives of the girl took it as an insult to them, for it implied that the boy's family did not wish to establish a good relationship with the family of their bride.

On this particular day of observing Kisulle, some of the bridal price which was kept apart only to be given on the second *Sawng-Satha* was paid to her parents. In contrast to the previous *Sawng-Satha*, only one swine was killed and the half body of the killed animal was given out to the groom's family as *Sa-Haap*. The rest of the customary rituals and social distribution of meat were the same as that of the first *Sawng-Satha*. Mostly, the third *Sawng-Satha* was ordinarily unaccomplished in contrast to the decree of the Vaiphei customary laws.[35] As the third feast signified the last relationship and bonding a daughter had as part of the natal family, her parents ceased to complete the custom as it was not initiated during the life time of the daughter. This was performed by her eldest son at the time of her death. He give his maternal family one mithun as the final bridal price called *Man Chai Na*.[36]

In the case of *Kijaampi* (elopement) or *Thepthak* (persuasion), the boy's parents immediately conceded to the girl's parents carrying a pot of rice-beer and apologized with a request to condone the misdeed committed by their son for taking their daughter as his wife without the knowledge of the girl's parents and approached them for the hands of their daughter. This formality was called *Luang Kaidaw Man*. If the girl's parents were not convinced, they had the right to take back the girl.[37] But if they agreed, then the manner of seeking a bride was the same as that of the normal course of marriage procedure discussed above. Meanwhile, the boy's parents gave a mithun to the girl's parents as fine or penalty for the misdeed of their son. In these cases, marriage celebrations rarely occurred though the marriage was accepted as legal.

In all these types of marriage, the details of social obligations, rituals and other social etiquettes indicated a preference to marrying the *Neinu*, the mother's brother's daughter.

These customary rules and practices in a marriage are still followed in Vaiphei society. The mode of seeking a bride for a son, the different stages of visits and advances, the feasts, the social distribution of meat to various sets of relatives, etc., are still the same as what the Vaipheis had followed in the past. Since olden days, the bridal price is paid by the eldest brother of the groom-to-be (younger brother); and when the eldest daughter of the latter gets married, he receives one mithun as his share from the bridal price of his niece. Customs and traditions can be discontinued or continued according to their necessity and adaptability in the post-colonial period. But there are also some changes with time that could be noticed. The game of *Buantual-Khaw*, the *Nugual* farewell party, sipping of rice-beer, and the role of the *Thiampu* are discontinued in the marriage tradition. The feast of *Sumtan-Sa* seen in the second stage of negotiation is optional and mostly people at present times do not comply with it any longer. The second Sawng-Satha does not necessarily need to be accomplished at the time of the *Kisulle*, but can be done anytime depending upon the conveniences of both parties. At present day, some of the articles given to their daughter by her parents at the time of marriage are optional and the articles rather consist of necessary moveable goods mainly for home appliances. Sometimes, immovable property is also given to her depending on the good will of her father.

At present time, a mithun, due to the less accessibility, is replaced by a cow, pig or buffalo. The consolidation made in terms of mithuns given to the girl's mother in the cases of *Lutuam* and *Lai-Sui* is replaced by a particular Vaiphei traditional shawl called *Puandum*. The gifts given to a daughter do not consist only of the prescribed articles discussed earlier, but also articles ranging from household needs to immoveable properties depending on the capacities of the girl's parents though they are not under compulsion. Also, the mode of payment made in terms of mithuns does not prevail any longer. Similarly, a man has the right to marry anyone and not necessarily his mother's brother's daughter called *Neinu*. The preference thus given to this daughter of mother's brother marriage seems to dwindle or forgotten the more as the tradition of Neinu is rarely in vogue at present. Such cross cousin marriages are declining in numbers and are not considered as a serious offence in the society. One of the reasons for the changes is due to the influence of westernization and modernization. However, the discontinuity does not necessarily represent a total departure of the people from their age-old traditions and customs.

CHILD'S BIRTH

In the past, customary ritual formalities were observed during the birth of a child. The mother was asked by the family to sip rice-beer to her heart's content as a sign of gratitude. It was believed that the rice-beer would regenerate her veins and nerves. She had to rest and was forbidden from doing household chores or work at least for a week after the child birth. There were some taboos to be observed by the mother during the rest period. For instance, if she fed the pigs, the soul of the child would be mixed with the pigs' food and be eaten by the pigs; and if she ate something she should not give the left over to the animals but throw it away. Also before the child's birth, the mother was forbidden to expose her waist to the fire for a heat-treatment as it was believed that the womb would be pasted to the waist and that the child would face difficulty in birth.[38] The priest felicitated the mother with a fowl and garlanded her with a wreath called *Aak-Nel* made from the feathers from around the pelvic of the fowl. At present, the ritual formalities observed at the time of child's birth are discontinued.

RE-MARRIAGE

The Vaiphei customary laws allow the remarriages of married or widowed woman as long as she wishes to after an official divorce or the death of a spouse. A widow marrying before the lapse of one year of her husband's death is regarded as dishonourable and detested. Similarly, men do have the right to remarry if they so wish after a lawful divorce settlement or the death of a spouse. However, the customary laws of the Vaiphei do not permit the practice of polygamy. A widow still belongs to her husband's family if she has children and wishes to stay back. She is seldom asked to go back to her natal house if she has only daughters or no children. In case of remarriage, the children are adopted by the nearest male relatives of her deceased husband because a woman has no right to inherit property after remarriage.[39] In a case when her husband dies at an early age and has an unmarried younger or elder brother, then the young man is usually bound to marry the widow of his deceased elder brother though it is not a compulsion.[40] However, this sort of union seldom happens in the society and this is improper to be considered as polygamy. However, though the customary laws of the Vaiphei do not license the practice of polygamy, there are cases where a man having more than one wife is known.

Also, the widow has the right to reject the proposal to marry her brother in-law. Unconventionally, in a case when a widow remarries while living in her husband's house, the bridal price given by her deceased husband is reimbursed to her in-laws by her second husband; and she is not permitted to take her children. The bridal price of a widow with children who returns to her natal house is less by five mithuns than the normal value of a new bride.[41] Similarly, widower also has the legal rights to remarry after the death of his wife. Remarriages happened in this way in the pre-Colonial period and it is followed till date in the Vaiphei society.

INHERITANCE

Inheritances are transfers of the unconsumed material accumulations of previous generations. The Vaiphei law of inheritance is patrilineal. It gives the eldest son the legal right to inherit property and entrusts him with the responsibility to look after his parents. Even so, property seldom leads to disputes among themselves. Besides, the Vaiphei law of inheritance also allows a woman to inherit property under specific circumstances. If a widow remains childless but stays permanently with her late husband's clan, then the property which her husband possessed cannot be taken away by her in-laws.[42] These advantages also belong to a widow who does not remarry and has only daughters. However, if she remarries the person closest to the matrimonial family or clan, she is entrusted with property rights. He is termed as *Gamngak*.[43] Nevertheless, she does not have the right to sell off the property and after the marriage of her daughter, the inheritance passes on to the nearest male relatives of the deceased and the daughter receives nothing.[44]

Though there is no law of inheritance related to daughter, in present days, the right to inherit property is also subjected particularly to the good will of the father. A daughter gets a share of her father's property in the form of land, commodities or entitlements to business transactions if the latter wishes it to be so. Due to modernity, the younger generation has become more liberal and has started to incorporate the idea of equality. This has affected the traditional patriarchal family. However, the majority of the people still adhere to the traditional customary laws and because of the continuity it gives to the community, customary law becomes intrinsic and basic to their identity till today.

LUANGMAN

Vaiphei customary law gives the *Songgau* relative another social right called *Luangman*, which he can claim from his *Tucha* or *Tute* relatives.[45] Luangman is literally defined as 'the price of the corpse' and is given to the Songgau relative in the event of death of a *Tute* relative. Just as every woman has a bridal price at the time of her marriage, so does a man at the time of his death. When a man dies, it is customary and compulsory to give some portion of the killed animal as Luangman to the deceased maternal grandfather or maternal uncle. This allocation share known as *Pu-Sa-Awm* given to the Songgau relative is a recognition of the latter as the life-giver of a man through his mother. This customary practice is followed even today and it shows the continued relationship or bonding both the families have shared even after the death of the person. Nevertheless, a man with no male offspring and a woman in a Vaiphei society do not have a corpse price.[46]

Dissimilar to the Vaiphei tradition, a Thadou woman owns the price of the corpse when she dies. In recognition of the contribution of a Thadou woman in the propagation of the male line of the family of her husband, her father or brother or brother's son has the right to claim and is entitled to charge a corpse-price called *Luongman* (Luangman in Vaiphei) on the death of the woman. The husband or son of the woman has to pay one mithun as the price of the corpse to the Songgau relative. Had the woman not given birth to a son or sons, no *Luongman* is to be charged on her death.[47] However, the Hmars of the Chin-Kuki-Mizo-Zomi[48] group of tribes do not hold the culture of practicing *Luangman*. Over all, every Chin-Kuki-Mizo-Zomi group of tribes has more or less the same culture of paying the *Luangman* as stated above.

CRIME, OFFENCES AND ADJUDICATION

The degree of penalization in Vaiphei society differs depending on the nature of offences a person committed. In the case of a wife divorcing her husband with or without a sufficient reason, the entire bridal price has to be returned to her in-laws.[49] She is also compelled to pay *Salam*[50] and arranges a feast for the Chief and his *Siamang-Pachong* (council of ministers) by offering a pot of rice-beer and a female swine. However, if matters are still not settled at this level, then the final decision is adjudicated by the Vaiphei Peoples' Council court. In 2005, the Vaiphei Peoples' Council (the highest apex body of the Vaipheis) established a traditional court known as VPC Court for its people. The court adjudicates cases in all matters on the basis of the customary laws of the Vaipheis. Its members are selected from the standing official members of the Vaiphei Peoples' Council. People can directly approach the VPC Court if they do not wish to settle matters at the clan's or chief's level. A person is penalized depending on the nature of his crime or offences; and the judgment is considered as the final plight to the solution. However, sometimes, matters are also settled among individuals.

Strangely, there are no complicated laws regarding the guardianship of children in case of divorce. All weaned infants, both boys and girls, belong to the husband as his heirs. A woman keeps the unweaned child but has to give it back to the legal father when the child reaches the age of three. However, the legal father could claim his child only after giving a swine, a traditional shawl called *Puandum,* a jar of rice-beer and a sum of one thousand rupees as an apology and consolidation to his parents' in-law. This is also known as *Nau-Vakman* (price for nourishment).[51] In case of dissatisfaction with the offer, his in-laws have the right to demand a rite called *Inn-Thiansua* (sanctifying the in-laws house by killing a swine and feasting with them as a sign of apology).[52] After fulfilling the rite, the father can have his child. Similarly, if a pregnant woman delivers a baby at her parental home after the divorce, then the husband has to arrange a feast of apology called *Naulai-Dom* for his wife and her parents. In this situation, the in-laws are again entitled to claim *Inn-Thiansua* at their own discretion. If the husband fails to accomplish it, he is subjected to a heavy fine of only *Salam* or *Sialpi-Salam* in addition to the mandatory performing of Inn-Thiansua.[53] *Sialpi-Salam* is the highest form of penalization a person could be given under the Vaiphei customary laws. A person who is tried under this penalty is looked upon as a disgrace.

Also, if a man kidnaps a woman or a young girl for speculative purposes other than to marry her the crime committed by him is considered equivalent to homicide. These penalties are still enforced in Vaiphei society. Also, in case of a man or a woman committing adultery, he or she is also penalized with *Sialpi-Salam* and the divorce proceeding is confirmed if one is not willing to forgive the other.[54] In case of a married woman, her husband does not give *Nawlman* (the price paid for divorce penalty) to her and the bridal price given at the time of the marriage is repaid by her parents; and the articles she brought are all unreturned.[55]

For the Vaipheis, custom is the life-blood in their society and they cannot be disjointed from their customary laws. The tribe regulates their community and social affairs according to the customary law and treats it as integral to their culture and basic to their identity. It is so ingrained in their life and culture that any invasion on their customary laws may lead to serious consequences. Any breach of customary law is a subject matter of dispute in the society for which the violator is punishable.

CONCLUSION

Scholars have explained the low status of Vaiphei women along with other women of the hill people are dictated by many social obligations as the consequence of the patriarchal nature of their society. However, deeper analytical study of the Vaiphei women shows that they were rather the central actors due to their participation and the role they had played as a mother, wife or sister in the socio and cultural domains of the society. Regardless of the role women played they did not get recognition and appreciation proportionate to their politico-economic and social contribution to the society. As a result, they remained an important group, nevertheless undermined group, in the Vaiphei society.

In the context of India as a whole, British writers condemned Indian religions, culture, and society for their rules and customs regarding women. They reckoned the position and status of women as one of the indices to assess the extent of modernization and traditionalism of a nation. Women, in fact, became a group on whom tradition was debated and reformulated. Historically, the construction of the veiled and enslaved woman has fuelled the colonial imagination and allowed it to conceive outright exploitation as a "civilizing mission".[56] The British pronounced the disunity of the country as a consequence of the low status of women, and thus concluded that domination of India was natural and inevitable.[57]

As such, due to the impact of education, modernization and westernization, the younger generation of the Vaipheis has become more liberal and has started to incorporate the idea of equality and modernity. No doubt, slight changes are also seen in its usages and functions of the customary practices through the time but they are generally done by people at their own discretion outside the legal framework of the Vaiphei customary laws. Nowadays, the right to inherit property is also subjected particularly to the good will of the father and a daughter gets a share of her father's property if the latter wish it to be so. In the same manner, a widow enjoys the property of her husband and shares it among her children for their welfare.

END NOTES

1. K. S. Singh (Ed), *Tribal Ethnography, Customary Law and Change*, Concept Publishing Company, New Delhi: 1993, p.14.
2. Radha Kumar, *The history of Doing: An Illustrated Account of Movements for Women's Rights and Feminism in India (1800-1990)*, New Delhi: Kali For Women, 2002. p.1
3. Geraldine Forbes, *op. cit.*, p.28
4. Vumson, *Zo History: With an introduction to Zo Culture, Economy, Religion- and their status as an ethnic minority in India, Burma and Bangladesh.* Aizawl: 1986, p.14. Also see, S. Prim Vaiphei, *Op.cit*, p.8.
5. T.S. Gangte, *The Kukis of Manipur*, Gyan Publishing House, New Delhi: 1993, p.79.
6. Sialpi-Salam is the highest punishment or penalty a person can incur with regard to committing a crime or an offence. As tradition demands, the fine consists of a mithun called *Sial*, a swine and a jar of rice-beer in order to appease the victim's family and to cleanse himself from the act of immorality.

7. Kamkhanpau (ed.), *Vaiphei Customary Practice Book*, Hilltown, Churachandpur: 2000, p.12. Also see, S. Prim Vaiphei, *The Vaiphei Tribe*, Chekon, Imphal: 1975, p.9.
8. Dr. Lalkhokam, *Vaiphei Pupa Chawndan*, Imphal: 2004, p.22.
9. Interview with Mr. Khuphau (88years) of K. Kotlian village, Churachandpur, Manipur, dated 04/07/08.
10. Kamkhanpau (ed.), *Op. cit*, p.13. Also see, Dr. Lalkhokam, *Op. cit*, p.21.
11. Interview with Mr. Kaitinpau (80years) of Lingsiphai Village, Churachandpur, Manipur, dated 20/06/2008.
12. Kamkhanpau (ed.), *Op. cit*, p.13.
13. *Ibid*, p.14.
14. *Vaiphei Chawndaṉ Bu (Custom and Culture)* is compiled by Mr. Kamkhanpau in 1997 under the supervision of *The Vaiphei Peoples Council*, the apex body of the Vaiphei people. It is the basic law book used by the Vaipheis till today, p.13.
15. Dr. Lalkhokam, *Op. cit*, p.21.
16. S. Prim Vaiphei, *Op. cit*, pp.8-9.
17. *Ibid*.
18. *Vaiphei Chawndan Bu*, *Op. cit*, p.14.
19. Dr. Lalkhokam, *Op. cit*, p.22.
20. T. S. Gangte, *Op. cit*, p.82. Also see, R. Brown, *Statistical Account of Manipur*, New Delhi 1886, p.50.
21. Kamkhanpau (ed), *Op. cit*, p.14.
22. Unpublished private papers Serial No.6 of page-3 of Rev. (Rtd.) Mr. Haukham. Also see, Lt. Col. J. Shakespeare, *The Lushai-Kuki Clan*, Tribal Research Institute, Aizawl: 1975 (First published in 1912), p.155.
23. Dr. Lalkhokam, *Op. cit*, p.23.
24. Bertham S. Carey & H. N. Tuck, *The Chin-Hills: A History of the people, British dealings with them, their Customs and Manners, and a Gazetteer of their Country*, Volume 1&2. Falam, Chin-Hills: 1896, pp.190-191. Also see, Dr. Lalkhokam, *Op. cit*, p.26.
25. *Vaiphei Chawndan Bu*, *Op. cit*, p.16. Also see, Rev. Khupkhawthang, *Namte Malai-Tulai*, L.Lawma & Sons, Churachandpur: 1996, p.72.
26. Dr. Lalkhokam, *Op. cit*, p.24.
27. *Vaiphei Chawndan Bu*, *Op. cit*, p.14.
28. Kamkhanpau (ed.), *Op. cit*, p.5.

29. *Ibid.* p.15
30. Interview with Mr. Kaitinpau, *Op. cit.*
31. *Ibid.*
32. Bertham S. Carey & H. N. Tuck, *Op. cit,* p.189.
33. Kamkhanpau (ed:), *Op. cit,* p.16.
34. T. S. Gangte, *Op. cit,* p.89.
35. In Vaiphei culture, the total bridal price could be given in the first stage. However, it has been given in three different occasions due to the reason that the parents of the bride refuse to part with their daughter. As such, as a mark of their love for their daughter and also in maintaining good relationship with the daughter's new family through generation, the last bridal price is even not initiated or accomplished during the life time of their daughter. It signified the last relationship and bonding a daughter had as part of the natal family.
36. Dr. Lalkhokam, *Op. cit,* p.26.
37. S. Prim Vaiphei, *Op. cit,* p.10.
38. T. S. Gangte, *Op. cit,* p.96.
39. S. Prim Vaiphei, *Op. cit,* p.11.
40. Bertham S. Carey & H. N. Tuck, *Op. cit,* p.209.
41. Dr. Lalkhokam, *Op. cit,* p.27.
42. Kamkhanpau (ed.), *Op. cit,* p.51.
43. Dr. Lalkhokam, *Op. cit,* p.17.
44. *Ibid,* p.52. Also see, C. A. Soppitt, *Op. cit,* p.16.
45. The in-laws of a man by marriage are referred to as Songgau relative while Tucha and Tute are the husband and children of a man's sister or daughter.
46. *Vaiphei Chawndan Bu*, *Op. cit,* p.25.
47. T. S. Gangte, *Op. cit,* p.69.
48. In the last few decades, the broad labels of 'Kuki', 'Naga' and 'Zomi' have become the symbol of ethnic re-alignment and re-grouping in Manipur. The formation of the Zomi Re-Unification Organization (ZRO) in April 1993 epitomized a significant movement in rethinking tribe identities which entailed geographical, political and socio-cultural re-unification. The term Zomi is conceptualized as an ethnic group having 'distinct culture, customs, traditions, values, dances, dress and folktales in juntaposition to the other surrounding and dominant plains people' In the context of the

Vaipheis, they have identified themselves since 1994 with other tribes under the nomenclature Zomi as their common identity where the name holds a wider appeal for other cognate tribe as the term 'Zo' means highlanders and 'Mi' signifies people.

49. R. Brown, *Op. cit*, p.50.

50. *Salam*- it is the second highest form of a Vaiphei's customary penalization given to a person for his/her misdeed. It constituted of one female swine. Both *Salam* and *Sialpi-Salam* are still uphold and in practice till date in Vaiphei society.

51. Kamkhanpau (ed.), *Op, cit*, p.20.

52. *Ibid*, p.37.

53. *Ibid*, pp.36-37.

54. Dr. Lalkhokam, *Op. cit*, pp.27-28.

55. *Vaiphei Chawndan Bu*, *Op. cit*, p.18.

56. Geraldine Forbes, *Women in Modern India*, Cambridge University Press: 1998. p.4

57. Revd. E. Storrow, 'Our Indian Sisters' quoted from Geraldine Forbes's *Women in Modern India*, New York 1998, Cambridge University Press. p.13

REFERENCES

BERTRAM S. CAREY & H. N. Tuck. (1896) *The Chin-Hills: A History of the people, British dealings with them, their Customs and Manners, and a Gazetteer of their Country*, Volume 1&2. Falam, Chin-Hills: 1896.

LALKHOKAM. (2004) *Vaiphei Pupa Chawndan*. Imphal.

GERALDINE FORBES. (1998) *Women in Modern India*, Cambridge University Press.

Interview with Mr. Khuphau (88years) of K. Kotlian village, Churachandpur, Manipur, dated 04/07/08.

Interview with Mr. Kaitinpau (80years) of Lingsiphai Village, Churachandpur, Manipur, dated 20/06/2008.

ROY, JYOTRIMOY ROY. (1858) *History of Manipur*. Calcutta: Eastlight Book House.

Singh, K. S. (Ed.) (1993) *Tribal Ethnography, Customary Law and Change*. New Delhi: Concept Publishing Company.

KAMKHANPAU. (ed.) *Vaiphei Customary Practice Book*. Hilltown, Churachandpur.

SHAKESPEARE, J. (1975/ 1912) *The Lushai-Kuki Clan*. Aizawl: Tribal Research Institute.

BROWN, R. (1886) *Statistical Account of Manipur*. New Delhi.

KUMAR, RADHA. (2002) *The history of Doing: An Illustrated Account of Movements for Women's Rights and Feminism in India (1800-1990)*. New Delhi:. Kali For Women.

KHUPKHAWTHANG. *(1996) Namte Malai-Tulai*. Churachandpur: L.Lawma & Sons.

STORROW, E. (1998) Our Indian Sisters In Geraldine Forbes's *Women in Modern India*. New York: Cambridge University Press.

VAIPHEI, S. PRIM. (1993) *The Vaiphei Tribe*, Chekon, Imphal: 1975.T.S. Gangte, *The Kukis of Manipur*. New Delhi: Gyan Publishing House.

Unpublished private papers Serial No.6 of page-3 of Rev. (Rtd.) Mr. Haukham.

Vaiphei Chawndan Bu (Custom and Culture) is compiled by Mr. Kamkhanpau in 1997 under the supervision of *The Vaiphei Peoples Council*, the apex body of the Vaiphei people. It is the basic law book used by the Vaipheis till today.

VUMSON. *(1986) Zo History: With an introduction to Zo Culture, Economy, Religion- and their status as an ethnic minority in India, Burma and Bangladesh*. Aizawl.

Chapter 8

Status of Simte Women in Manipur

Esther Lalremkim

Introduction

Throughout history, men have been by tradition regarded as superior to women in both power and status. To evaluate the status of women, one has to consider the role played by them in everyday life and work. The Simte women enjoy some amount of liberty in choosing a spouse in economic activities, household management, etc. Within the confines of their domestic arena they have full freedom and self expression. Family is largely managed by women who cater to the needs and demands of family members. In traditional Simte homes, much of informal education like cooking, weaving, knitting, farming etc. is imparted by mothers to their daughters. However, women are excluded from all decision making bodies in both social organizations and church life. They get no representation in the church administration in spite of playing a crucial role in the evangelical enterprises of the church.

Simte society is a patriarchal society in which males dominate in public domain. Women are not entitled to any immovable property other than those movable ones given at the time of marriage. Considering domestic activities, women work more than men and their domestic duties often made scholars from outside the community to refer to their roles as similar to the beast of burden. In productive activities, both males and females work together, but males work harder than that of females. Modernization, education, Christianity and development programmes are bringing changes which affect men and women differently. Despite the changes taking place in the society, they retain many things like language, traditional dress and cultural practices like traditional dances, greetings practices, food preferences, expected norms and values of the society etc.

1. The Simtes: Mapping of People and Culture

Simtes are one of the prominent tribes in the State of Manipur — a State strategically located in the North-eastern part of India. They are mainly concentrated in the southern part of the state. Etymologically, the term 'Simte' is a combination of two words, 'sim' which means 'south' and 'te' a suffix that denotes 'people'. In short, Simte primarily implies the 'southerners' or 'those who come from the south'. It must have been given to them by other tribes after they settled in Manipur, for there was no reference to be found regarding the use of the term (Leivang, 2011). According to the census of India (2001), the total population of Simte tribe is 11,065, and they constitute 1.49% of the total population of Manipur. They are recognized and known as Simte (*Khuangnung mite*) in India and Ngaihte in Myanmar. In the Indian state of Manipur, they were recorded by the Europeans as "New Kuki." However, the Simtes identified themselves as one of the tribes among the Zomis and had lately united with other tribes under the nomenclature "Zomi" since 1994 (Ginneiching, 2013).

Originally Simtes are Tibeto-Chinese of Mongoloid race. By criterion of affinity of language they are classed as "Tibeto-Burman." In fact, their physical features such as yellow or brown skin, prominent cheek-bone, brown-eye, straight black-hair, slanted narrow eye, flat and short nose, wide nostril, broad and flat face explicated indisputably that they are of

Tibeto-Chinese origin (Ginneiching, 2013). Considering genetic and physical features, the average stature of Simte population falls in 'lower medium' class following Martin's classification. They have higher frequency of A (+ve) blood group as compared to other groups, no individual having Rh (-ve) was encountered in a sample of 300 individuals. Majority of the population have dry type cerumen (79%) and taste sensitivity to phenyl-thio-carbamide (75.67%). The Simte males and females are 'short' and 'lower medium' respectively. They possess brown skin (64.33%), black straight hair (81%) and medium forehead height (64.9%). Simte spossess dark brown eye colour (48%) and straight nasal bridge (86.47%) according to Martin's classification (Lalremkim, 2012, p. 191). These characteristics which are all common characters of mongoloid population showed and proved that the present Simte group belonged to mongoloid race.

Mythologically, the Simte traced their origin from the *Khuul* (Caves). The history of the Simte people can be traced back to the beginning of their settlement in *Zuangkhua,* Burma around the year 1200 AD (Ginneiching, 2013). From Burma, they moved to the Lushai hills of the present day Mizoram state. After settling for around 30 years in Lushai Hills, the Simtes' had to move again due to the hostility of the tribal group known as the *Pawis* (ibid). These continuing processes of migration made them realize that they need to be under the protection of a powerful ruler in order to be safe (ibid). Accordingly around the year 1850, the *Khuangnung* people under the leadership of Khamzahen Thangsing went and submitted themselves to the Moirang king Maharaja Chandrakirti Singh and his son Senapati Koireng Sana, the latter more popularly known as Bir Tikendrajit Singh (ibid). It is said that the Maharaja was kind to the *Khuangnung* people and maintained a good relationship with them. The goodness of the Maharaja could be indicated by the fact that the Maharaja in order to show affection to the Simtes presented 30 single barrel guns to them. Further, the Maharaja recruited *Khuangnung* people in his Royal Army and named them the "*Khuangnung* Army" (ibid).

The Simtes have been a distinct tribe having separate socio-cultural tradition of their own. They remained hidden and unrecognized tribe in the pre-independence period of the Indian nation. Nobody, neither the Simte nor the outsider seem to bother about maintaining any written record on their life and culture. However, with the emergence of independence movement in India, nationalistic idea arose in the mind of some thoughtful people among them. Following this, since, 1948, re-unification of the Simte began (Lianzira, 2008).

In 1956, an assembly was held at Khuangnung village, Churachandpur with Khaikam Thangsing as its convener. Simte National Council was formed with Pumkhothang Thangsing as the first President. The formation of the Simte National Council was followed by a demand for recognition of the Simtes as one of the tribes under Indian Constitution of the Government of India. As a result, in the same year Simte became a recognized tribe listed as one among the Scheduled Tribes of Indian Union under the central Government of India, Order No. 1956 Vide SRO-24774 Gazetteer of India, Part-II Section-III, No.-316/A, and New Delhi, India and under the Indian constitution Article 330-342 (Lianzira, 2008, p. 47). The clans of Simte tribe according to the list submitted to the Government consisted of (1) Ngaihte (2) Hangnung (3) Taitom (4) Seldou (5) Tonsing (6) Hangsing (7) Thangsing (8) Leivang (9) Vangkot (10) Khumlai (11) Tlaulual (12) Munluah (13) Vanghan (14) Vangngoh (15) Sona (16) Hatsing (17) Haukhup (18) Hangluah (19) Luahki (20) Biangtung (21) Naulah (22) Suhte (23) Julom (24) Buansing and (25) Saute-Shoute (ibid).

2. Focus and Method of the Study

The essay would like to determine the extent of the status of inequality of men and women in socio-cultural, political and religious life of the traditional and contemporary Simte tribe of Manipur. Clearly women are biologically different from men. Their characteristics are genetically based; in particular they result from differences between male and female hormones (Tiger et al, 1972). In earlier life, the Simtes were a nomadic tribe, who were largely hunters and food gatherers, often engaged in inter tribal wars. Men being physically stronger became the bread earner and protector whereas the female were mainly confined to their home and were considered to be more suited to domestic roles. Because of his role as the protector and bread earner of the family, men dominate over women, and women consider themselves inferior and subordinate to men and accordingly judge the value of their contribution to the family. Such idea of inferiority complex remains the same even today.

Although the constitution of India guarantee certain right and privileges to women and confer equal right and opportunities with men as given in Article 14 of the Indian Constitution.[1] The Simte women are powerless in political, socio-economic and religious life. Status of women cannot be examined in isolation as it is interlinked with the socio-economic condition, inequalities inherent in the traditional social structure, its norms, values, customs and rituals. The traditional cultural norms continue to dictate the society in which women think of themselves primarily as nurturer and home maker. The role and status which the Simte women play in the society will be subsequently discussed in the essay. The study was conducted in the state of Manipur. It relies heavily on both primary and secondary sources. Methods used to collect primary data relating to the present research are observation method and in-depth and unstructured form of interview.

3. Womanhood and Culture

The Simte women have different qualities depending on the place and need of the society and family in which they are bought up. Everyone has their own idea of what a good and ideal woman is like or how a lady should carry herself in the society. This is influenced by the socialization process which a girl child experienced first in the family and then outside in the wider society. Famous quotes about women by Khurana[2] as "Reams of paper and reels of films have been dedicated to describe a woman. Numerous researches have been done on women so far. Women oriented books promise to reveal 'the secret' underlying womanhood. Biologists have spent their lifetime decoding the mystery of women. But the women continue to be an enigma. Her enigma embodies her beauty. And this beauty is not skin deep but qualities present in her". This shows that the qualities of women go further than mere look of shallow immediacy.

Some of the ideal characters and qualities considered desirable that was obtained out of the survey conducted are: self-esteem, independence, responsible, kindness, trustworthy, patience, gentleness, humility, assertiveness, cleanliness, etc. Beauty along with such character makes perfect women. But the characteristics that make a great woman can differ, depending on what qualities respondent value in a person. However, elements of a personality that most people would deem as great are found within a person of strong character. Wives, mothers, daughters, sisters and grandmothers are important people in everyone's lives and are greatly appreciated especially by those related to them.

4. Girl Child

Simte society prefers sons over daughters but do not discriminate against girl by female infanticide as done in some of the mainland Indian societies. The Simte society does not practice child-marriage or dowry but they practice bride-price. Many cases on honor killings have been reported in Northern region of India, mainly in the Indian state of Punjab, Rajasthan, Haryana, Utter Pradesh as a result of people marrying without their family's acceptance and sometime for marrying outside their caste or religion (Sharell, 2010). In contrast, honor killings are almost non-existence among Simte society. Though girls are not considered equal to boys in many aspects of life; they are not abused, hated or subjected to strict social norms. They are free to participate in any social events and recreational programmes. They are not considered a burden because of their economic value in an agricultural society. In fact they are made to assist the mother in the household chores at an early age.

5. Inheritance

Do women have equal property rights under Simte customary laws? Being patriarchal and patrilineal in nature, boys and girls do not have similar inheritance law. Women enjoy very little control over immovable properties. They hardly inherit land. According to their oral customary laws they are not entitled to receive and share the ancestral properties other than those given at the time of marriage. Lalhriatpuii (2010) writes about the Mizo women in Mizoram that they are extremely discriminated against with regard to the inheritance of property as they were never given rights over the landed property. If there is no son in the family, the family property including ancestral home should go to the nephew of the father. This condition is also true in the Simte society of Manipur. In matters relating to the new reformulated law of inheritance, only men are recognized as legitimate heirs and women do not legally have any rights in the family in spite of their tremendous income in their family. This is due to the fact that modernity itself is a patriarchal construct and the changes it brought about are also deeply concerned with the affairs of men. As long as the male-biased customary law of inheritance exists, gender discrimination will exist in the society.

6. Freedom in Selection of Life Partner

Traditionally, marriage is arranged by parents, sometimes without consulting the concerned person. The Simte women enjoyed very limited liberty in choosing a spouse. The prevalence of love marriage was equally very rare. As said earlier they preferred arranged marriage, and socially the most preferred form of marriage for a girl is with father sister's son (cross cousin marriage). This system of marriage is known "*ki neilah*". Sometimes her willingness is not even counted. She is forced to get married with her cousin. If she resist, her parents and relatives would beat her along the way till they reach the residence of the boy. This preference was a practice meant for strengthening brother-sister relation and to maintain purity of blood and avoid *kao* (human evil spirit) in the family. The women of today, comparatively, have a lot more freedom in choosing spouse. Girls and boys meet openly and have their say on selection of their spouse. The girl choice in selecting spouse is considered, after that all other condition needed for marriage has to be fulfilled by the groom's family. The case of marriage system "*kineilah*" is rare in the contemporary society. Simte women today are not coerced against their will. In Simte cultural practice, the bride price is transmitted from the father of the groom to the father of the bride.

7. Education

Does the Simte girl get equal opportunity for education? Even if they get education, do parents give the same importance to their education as those of their brothers? What about at the community level? Is the society open and encouraging to the education and over-all development of women? The education is a fundamental right that provides opportunity for socio-economic upliftment. The girl child was not the first choice for education in the traditional Simte society when schooling system was first introduced in the society. The common reasons were: financial constrains, women reproductive roles in child bearing and rearing, early marriage, submissiveness and societal attitude that consider investment on a girl child as a waste of money. This attitude is slightly changing in the present society though in poor families a boy is preferred over a girl for education and among the sons; preference for education goes to the eldest. The reason is that in the Simte society lineage is traced from the male line and the eldest son is by customary law the caretaker of his parents in their old-age.

The patriarchal attitude to women that defined family relationships is carried over to other institutions of society, including higher education and higher professional. Cultural norm continue to dictate over women and considered them as subordinate to men. Married educated women may enjoy better position than uneducated women in the family. Parallel explanation for the subordinate status of women is presented by Ortner (1974). She claims that it is not biology as such ascribes women to their society but the way in which every culture defines and evaluates female biology. She further believed, if the universal evaluation changed, then the basis for female subordination would be removed. Even the role of women in work place is seen as secondary to her role as nurturer and home maker. They experience helplessness in making new response within the culture to take charge of their own destiny considering themselves as professional in their mind but traditional home maker in heart. Though outwardly, the Simte women seemed to have moved forward, inwardly, they are still the same as in the past.

8. Pregnancy before marriage

When a girl becomes pregnant out of wedlock, they were stigmatized in the society. The matter is discussed in the village council or household council (*indongta*) and either the boy has to marry the girl or pay compensation to her family. The child is born in her natal family and must be under mother's care until the child attain the age of three. After this, the child becomes the exclusive right of the father. Sexual relationship before marriage may happen on mutual consent of both sexes, but if it involves the question of pre-marital pregnancy, the blame goes more to woman than man. Moreover, such women are considered to have an immoral character by the society. For all women, maintaining a good reputation is required as it is also connected with the prestige of the family. Promiscuity, rape, divorce etc. can tarnish a women's reputation. Once a women's reputation is tarnished, she is no longer respectable and society's respect cannot be regained. This is not true in the case of men. But, this pre marital pregnancy does not have an effect on her marriage prospect in future.

9. Married Women

Married Simte women in Manipur contribute positively to the local economy and participate along with men in subsistence activities. In reality women do more work than men. They participate in all kind of work done by the men and share major responsibility in the production process. Food processing and cooking is considered a women's job. In addition, they have to manage household chores, which is a stupendous task. Bearing and rearing of children is also the responsibility of women. Married women can be categorized into two categories: the wife and mother at home and the worker mother and wife. The tasks of the stay-at-home mom are never done. She works from the time she rises each day, until she retires to bed for the night. She is responsible for her children emotional, spiritual, mental and educational welfare.

On the other hand, women are turning out in large numbers in the work force due to economic necessity. The working married woman has the additional task of bringing income into the home. On top of juggling all her others duties as wife and mother, this women has to juggle employment as well. Whether she works in the home or out of it, she still has to work, play the role of a mother and a wife. Working mothers are often accused of not being able to give quality time to their children. According to a respondent "Playing dual roles are not easy, I come home tired from work and I have to look after the baby and cook and clean". According to the observation made in the current Simte society, many problems arise for the roles of mother because of undependable husband or death of husband. There are many female headed household in the present Simte society.

10. Bride price

With regards to marriage custom, the traditional practice of bride-price is still prevalent except the change in the amount of bride-price. Generally, price of Simte bride consist of seven mithuns including *'manlamkai'*. The bride-price of seven mithuns and *thaman* (the labour or service price) goes to the parents of the bride. Earlier *'manlamkai'* usually consist of a she-mithun and a young mithun or sixty rupees. In order to meet the standard of present day's life, bride-price has been modified which reduced *manlamkai* to three thousand and mithuns to a hundred each. A full payment of bride-price is completed within an amount of four thousand rupees. In addition to this, if younger sister get married before her elder sister, the bridegroom has to pay compensation known as *'ukaanman'*.

No one is exempted for payment of bride-price, on the condition that it is never paid up in full at the time of wedding. Even a rich man, who can afford to pay the bride-price, is not allowed to do so. A part of the payment is delayed and is meant to be paid later on. It is due to the fact that the man should always have love, respect and obligation, etc. for his wife and her relatives thereby enlivened a sense of maintaining constant and good social relationship with his wife and in-laws (Gangte, T.S., 1993, p.95). It may also be due to the reason that payment of balance installments gives a chance to both the parties, a kind of social contract which binds them together. Any items like precious stone (*khibah*), ornaments, and valuable assets like big gong (*dahpi or dahbu*) as observed for other tribes of Manipur were not required as Simte bride-price. The bride price of a Simte lady is lesser as compared to her neighboring tribes. Many are of the opinion that the practice of bride price has devalued a woman's position and status in the society as it presupposes that she can be sold and acquired like an economic asset. But, according to a respondent, higher bride-price is commendable as it shows the recognition given to women's position and status in a society.

11. Divorce

A divorce between a husband and wife is neither sanction nor allowed by custom. But divorce can take place due to adultery, issueless, unsound mind and body, family problem, misunderstanding, etc. The wife and the husband have equal rights to seek divorce but both are bounded by specific conditions of the customary law. The bride price is returned to her husband if divorce is caused by wife and she is not permitted to take back anything she brought. But if divorce is initiated by husband, wife is allowed to take back all the materials given by her parents in time of marriage. In addition to this, wife can imposed fine on her husband in case of infidelity. In case her husband dies, there is the practice of levirate wherein she is supposed to marry her unmarried brother-in-law. If she wants to remarry to a person other than the clan of the decease husband, she has to re-pay the bride price to her husband's family. According to Simte customary law, the children (if any) remain with father. This shows that women are considered inferior to men. It is generally believed that status and prestige of women can be upheld by giving equal right to have children to both wife and husband. Also, traditional saying "a women and broken fence can both be replaced" is an example of societal attitude towards women.

12. Political Sphere

The political life of the Simte as a separate institution cannot be studied in isolation. The institution is closely intertwined with other institutions, such as, social, economic, and religion. There was not much political consciousness among the Simte tribe of Manipur. There was "we-feeling" among them and their polity was village based. Each village has a chief who govern the whole village system. The chief decision in every matter was considered final. The law and order of village system is maintained by him and his elected village elders. There is no instance of a woman given space in the polity of the society except in cases where the husband dies and the wife take over the leadership temporarily during the minority of the son (Mangkhosat, 1996, p 88). Women were not consulted and excluded in all decision making at the societal level.

Now, education and Christianity have bought a sense of unity and political consciousness among the people. In the state assembly and district council elections, the villages play a great role. Even in the village authority election, the villager realized their fundamental right to choose a candidate of their liking. They often challenge the chief as they have the freedom to exercise their right in all elections within and outside the village. A numbers of factor have been suggested as explanation of why women are less likely to engage in politics. This is because the women are socialized toward a gender role that is more passive, private, rule abiding and compassionate while men are oriented toward leadership, public roles, autonomy and self reliance.

13. Socio-cultural Sphere

Status itself cannot be examined in isolation; it is interlinked with the socio-economic condition, inequalities inherent in the social structure, norms, values, customs and rituals. Patriarchy is still operational in the present society as effective as it was in the past. Women therefore, had no opportunities to go beyond the scope of the domestic sphere and it was only men who controlled and dominated the entire public sphere. Their words in public sphere were not given weight and simply considered as unimportant as the words of children. Numerous proverbs as recorded by Meirion Llyod (1991), expressed men's attitudes toward women in Mizo society are similar to men attitudes towards women in Simte society. These are: "a woman's mind does not reach across the stream"; "neither Crabs nor women have any religion; "a fence can be changed; so can a wife." A woman had no rights at all. Body, mind and spirit, she belonged from her birth to her death owes to her father, her brother, her husband. Her men folk could treat her as they like; and a man who did not beat his wife was scorned as a coward (Sitlhou, 2008).

An interesting example can be given on the attitude towards the wearing of traditional attires. Women preserved the culture of the traditional dresses by wearing the traditional

Simte wrap-around and shawl. On special occasions and days the women are compelled to wear the traditional dress. But, men are not compelled to uphold such tradition though '*Simte puan*' is also the traditional men's dress. Women's role as wives, mothers and organizers and as basic foundation of other dimensions of social life is of extreme importance. They are not only competent food producer and house maker but also the transmitters of rich local oral tradition. By and large, they are the only workers' who do not have regular time off. Within the confines of their domestic arena, they have freedom of movement and self-expression.

14. Religious Sphere

Religious practices of the Simte in the pre-Christian indicate the extent to which they live in fear of the spiritual world. Traditionally, they believed in the existence of one supreme omnipotent God. They practice sacrifice in times of sickness in the family, for the safety of crops, etc. to cure disease and to avert misfortune. According to Leivang (2011), a sacrifice for the propitiation of this spirits is done by the village priest who is known as '*Siampu*'. They try to cure diseases and to avert misfortune by offering cock, dog, pig, etc, in sacrifices. The most popular sacrifices among the Simtes is '*Sumtawng Bawl' or 'Pusa Bia*'. '*Pusa*' maybe interpreted as 'family God' and '*Bia*' means 'Worship'. In this worship a pig is killed in sacrifice and the head of the clan of the family acts as the priest for this worship. This worship is done once or more than once every year. They also recognized the presence of good and evil spirit and believed in life after death. But there is no separate role for women in traditional religion.

With the adoption of Christianity, women have their way to the path of public sphere through Christianity for they can equally participate with men in some of the church affairs. But women were considered to have no religion of their own. It was the religion of her parents or husband which was responsible for her continued welfare and existence. They were not supposed to have any independent religious loyalty, but were required to follow the religion of their husbands.

This also shows that Simte women were low in status. According to respondent Pastor Biangtung, majority of the religious view of the present Simte society is dominated by Baptist ideology. The Simte women were not allowed to speak in the church or to preach and teach publicly or be involved in the ministerial function. It is because, this is an act of power and authority, of rule and government so contrary to the subjection which God in his law requires of women unto men. A pattern is also set of male leadership so as the priest and kingly offices of the Old Testament were restricted to males. He was always a male until this dispensation, never an angel or female. In worship service, women need to cover head to show respect to God and males in accordance to the Bible. The scripture that determined the status of women can be seen in 1Tim. 2:11-15; 1Cor.11:3-12. Women are being excluded and are denied from ordination as pastor or elders. They get no representation in the church administration in spite of playing a crucial role in the evangelical work. For their welfare, they form a group among themselves called *'numeipawl'* playing active role in the Church in terms of outreach and hospitality. They get no representation in the church administration in spite of playing a crucial role in the evangelical work.

15. Economic Sphere

The status of women usually depends on the economic role they play. In the past, Simte tribe was mainly dependent on agriculture and food gathering economy. Slash and burn cultivation or Jhum cultivation was in vogue. Men mainly felled the trees and spread them around on the ground to dry before collectively kindling fire. Major portion of agriculture is done by women, engaged in broadcasting the seeds, weeding and harvesting. Women usually preserved the seeds at home and took the decisions about the crops to be cultivated. Besides, women work more than men; walk long distances to fetch wood and fodder. Fruits, roots and tuber, leaves, and all kind of vegetables were collected for self consumption as also for selling. Whatever income they have, they immediately spend it on meeting the basic requirement. Weaving is another common art of the Simte women. They usually weave in their leisure time and mainly for self consumption. Educated Simte women who reside in the urban area are office goers, either private or government offices but they are still responsible for domestic activities and child care. They have a "double burden" which does not allow them the time and energy to succeed in their careers. Taming of livestock which play an important role in the economy was done by women. Some important livestock are pigs, cattle, dogs, poultry, etc. These are reared for their meat as food and commercial dealings.

Discussion

The biological differences between men and women are used as a justification for coercing them into social roles which limit and shape their attitudes and behavior in Simte society. Some traditional discrimination of men toward women is still prevalent in the present day Simte society. They are discriminated in all social organizations and institutions. They are subjugated, dominated and exploited at work place and home. They are not consulted and under-represented in all decision making bodies. They were not allowed to inherit father's property in spite of tremendous contribution to family income.

With the positive impact of Christianity and modernity, changes are challenging the traditional institutions and practices. These progressive changes reconstruct social outlook and material culture, but this does not mean the complete changes in the conservative's ideologies of men toward women. Instead of encouraging women many people however, still opine that those women, who have entered the public sphere are making bold and aggressive claims. This is mainly because, the mindset of current society confines women's duties to the realms of the home and 'regards household activities as the most important duties for them; whatever knowledge a woman may acquire from her education, she hardly claims any rewards unless she is proficient in the management of household duties first'. In addition to this, concerned members of the society have begun to defend some of the old practices and intend to revive traditional values and customs in recent time. Thus, the women remain and act as a victim of social discrimination. This is due to the fact that modernity itself is a patriarchal construct and the changes brought about by it are infused with patriarchal ideology of the Simte society.

According to the survey of health, women and child development based on annual report-2011, the goals of human development are closely intertwined with development and empowerment of women. They constitute valuable human resource and their socio-economic development is imperative for sustainable growth of economy. Our law, development policies, plans and programmes are aimed at different spheres. The principle of gender equality is enshrined in the constitution, in its preamble, fundamental rights, fundamental duties and directive principles. It is high time to have full human equality among Simte society too. To have an egalitarian society women be treated as equal to men and laws, customs and education must be altered to encourage this as opined by Beauvoir's (1984) in the 'second sex'. According to Hmingthanzuali and others (2007), "Gender equality is a myth, whereas gender discrimination can be wiped out". For this, women need to join hand, develop consciousness and support each other wipe out the patriarchal dominated conservative attitude toward women. Once this is done, women will automatically transform themselves from a force in itself to a force for itself. Only then, thing will change for better and the old gender space can be discarded. "In addition, to build a socially equal partnership between women and men, we will also need to re-examine our assumptions about key social institutions, in particular the family, and about men's role and women's roles within the home and in society. To transform these roles and institutions might take decades and need to start at the individual (Sitlhou, 2008)."

Conclusion

It can be concluded from the above discussion that although women in the Simte society in Manipur enjoy a greater freedom to mix and move around, their social organizations and institutions are still discriminatory particularly with regard to the customary laws that guide the ownership of property and inheritance or also with regard to exercising authority both in the domestic and public spheres. It is high time to innitiate full human equality among Simte society. Women should come forward and fight traditional factors that influenced cultural differences of gender in order to achieved full human equality. Indeed, we need to change ourselves. Women need to change their outlook or orientation towards women. After all, as Zillah Eisenstein said, "*We must agree that most women want freedom and most women want equality as well. This is what makes us similarly human. That we may define these construct differently also make us uniquely human*".

List of Interviewees

Biangtung, C, (2013), *Interview on Religion* . Format: In person, Happy valley, Shillong, Aged 58, Dated: 11th March 2013.

Chingkhonuam, (2013), *Status of women*, Format: In person .Game village, Aged 62, Dated: 24th March 2013.

Dongkhogin, (2013) *Customary law of the Simte.* Format; In person, Game village, Imphal, Aged 65, Dated: 17th March 2013.

Hatkim,(2013) *Roles of working women*, Format: In person, Supermarket, Lamphel, Imphal, Aged 45, Dated: 12th may 2013.

Niangkhochiin,(2013) *Roles of Mother*, Format: In person, Lamphel, Imphal, Aged 59, Dated:24th March 2013.

Paudailou, (2013) *Bride price*, Format: In person, Happy valley, Shillong, Aged 75, Dated:11th March 2013.

Notes

1. Article 14 Equality before law: The State shall not deny to any person equality before the law or the equal protection of the laws within the territory of India Prohibition of discrimination on grounds of religion, race, caste, sex or place of birth.

2. Khurana, Simran. Famous quotes about Women. http://quotations.about.com/od/morepeople/a/woman1.htm . Accessed date: 1st July, 2013.

References

Census of India, 2001, Series 15 Manipur part VIII (II), Director of Census Operation, Manipur.

BEAUVOIR, SIMONE DE. (1984) *The Second Sex*. New York: Penguin Books.

GANGTE, T.S. (Ed.) (1993) *The Kukis of Manipur – A historical analysis*, Gyan publishing house, New Delhi.

GINNEICHING. (2013) *Genesis of the Simtes*, Simte people.com, [Online] March 16th 2013. Available on: http://www.simtepeople.com/genesis-of-the-simtes.html. [Accessed on: 29/3/2013].

HMINGTHANZUALI & VANLALHRUAIA, H. (2007) Women Issues in Mizo Society, [Online] July 28th, 2007. Available on: http://thangtharculture.blogspot.in/2007/07/women-issues-in-mizo-society.html. *[Accessed 1/3/2013].*

KIPGEN M. (Ed.) (1997) *Christianity and Mizo Culture: The Encounter between Christianity and Zo Culture in Mizoram*, Mizo Theological Conference, Aizawl, Mizoram.

LALREMKIM and SHAH S.A. (2012) *Prevelence and Gene Frequencies of four Genetic Markers among the Simte of Manipur India*, Frontier Anthropology, Journal of the Anthropological Society of Manipur India, Vol 1(3), p191-193.

LALHRIATPUII. (2010) *Economic Participation of Women in Mizoram*; New Delhi.[Online] Mainstream, VOL L No 12, March 10, 2012.Available on: http://www.mainstreamweekly.net/article3314.html. *[Accessed :1/3/2013].*,

LIANZIRA. (2008) *Simte History* (self publication, Lamka, Churachandpur)

LEIVANG, L. *(2011) A brief description of the Simte,[Online]* http://www.simtepeople.com/a-brief-description-of-the-simtes.html. *[Accessed 1/3/2013].*

LLOYED, J. MEIRION. (1991) *History of the church in Mizoram: Harvest in the hills*, 1991, Synod Publication Board, Aizawl, Mizoram

OAKLEY, A. (1974) *Housewife*. Allen Lane, London.

ORTNER, S.B. (1974) *'Is female to male as Nature is to culture?'* in woman, Culture and Society edited by M.Z. Rosaldo and L. Lamphere. Standford University Press, Standford.

SHARELL. (2010) *Honour Killings in India. In daily life in India* [Online]http://www.whiteindianhousewife.com/2010/06/honour-killings-in-india. *[Accessed:2/5/2013].*

SIMRAN, KHURANA. *Famous Quotes about Women; Capture the Essence of Women with these famous quotes about women.* About.com.quotation. [Online], Available on: http://quotations.about.com/od/morepeople/a/woman1.htm *[Accessed on: 1/3/2013].*

SITLHOU, H. (2008) *Women's Role in Community: In the Context of Kuki Society.* [Online], August 13th 2008. Available on: http://kukiforum.com/2008/08/women-role-in-community-in-the-context-of-kuki-society/. *[Accessed on: 1/3/2013].*

TIGER, L and FOX, R. (1972) *The Imperial Animal,* Secker & Warburg, London.

Women development, Survey of health& women and child development based on annual report-2011. Ministry of health, Ministry of women and child and development, Government of India. Chapter-2.p10-17.

ZILLAH, EISENSTEIN. (2004) *What's In A Name?: Seeing Feminism, Universalism, and Modernity,*"Wagadu Volume 1 : Spring. p.23.

Chapter 9

Health and Quality of Life: A case study among the Kuki women of Sapormeina, Manipur

Haokip Nemneivah

Quality of life (QoL) is a sense of well-being closely linked to one's own situation, or as some other combination of objective and subjective well-being. Health related Quality of Life is an individual satisfaction or happiness with various domains of life in so far as they affect health. On the other hand, a woman's health is her total well-being, determined not solely by biological factors and reproduction, but even by effects of work load, nutrition, socio-economic and migration, among others. This essay is based on the study conducted on health-related quality of life of women among the Kukis of Sapormeina, Manipur. The aim of the study is to evaluate the general well being of women in Sapormeina, which includes, but not limited to, obtaining a clear picture of different types of health problems such as gynaecological issues and other medical concerns prevalent there. It also explores different dimensions of QoL found in Sapormeina and examines the factors affecting these dimensions.

Introduction

The health of women everywhere is more vulnerable as they suffer from the diseases particular to their body mass. Women's health is generally considered to be weak and delicate. Some of the diseases found among most of the women include chronic anaemia, malnutrition and severe fatigue. Women also face unique reproductive health threats. Since the women in villages are mostly engaged in hard labour and work constantly at home as well, they are the ones who need health care most. Women generally require proper sleep, nutrient food and timely health care but these are left unnoticed since they are busy in various activities. Likewise, the women of Sapormeina are also found to have many health problems, and the present essay highlights the various kinds of health issues specific to them. Health seeking behaviour varies from person to person and according to the type of illnesses. When we say Quality of life, it is mostly the self-evaluation of a person and how much he or she is satisfied with the world around him/her. WHO in 1991 defined QoL as "an individual's perception of their position in life in the context of the culture and value systems in which they live and in the relation to their goals, expectations, standards and concerns". It can also be termed as an examination of influences upon the goodness and the meaning in life as well as people's happiness and well-being. Quality of life is generally measured with happiness, well-being and satisfaction. This essay is intended to discuss the physical, social, environmental and emotional or psychological aspects of the Quality of life. One limitation of this study is that the research done on Health and Quality of Life of these women in Sapormeina does not represent the whole of Kuki women in Manipur.

Universe of study

The study is conducted in a village called Sapormeina at Sadar Hills situated in the northern part of Manipur at a distance of around 28 kms from the capital. The village is close to National Highway no.39. There are 14 small villages which are clubbed together under the name United Sapormeina. The place is inhabited mostly by the Thadou speaking group of the Kuki tribe of Manipur and a few people belonging to different communities as well. But there is some kind of cultural homogeneity or cultural diffusion among them. According to the census of 2011, the total Thadou population in Manipur is 1,90,595, out of which 4000 people live in Sapormeina. The exact origin of the village cannot be correctly traced back but some data are collected from the village chairman. As narrated by them, it is believed that during the 2nd world war, the British soldiers landed in the present village in course of fighting the enemy. At that period of time the villages as well as the entire neighboring area were a dense forest populated by a variety of species and wildlife. Therefore, it became a proper place for the soldiers to hide. They dug trenches or saps for concealed approach to the enemy and planted mines. The diggers and layers of explosive devices are called sappers and miners. It is from the amalgamation of these two terms that the place got its name Sapormeina. After the British soldiers were defeated they left the place, but the settlers retain the name till date even after all these decades after independence. Till today, outsiders including the inhabitants time and again misspell the name Sapormeina and it is often the subject of wonder as it does not represent any meaning in the Thadou- Kuki dialect. The people have their own cultural identity markers with respect to their food and drinks, language, folklores, customs and traditions, dress and ornaments, material culture, etc. Christianity is now the religion of the people. Cultivation is still the main occupation, and the women folk are predominantly engaged in it.

Methods and data collection:

A representative sample of around 200 married women is selected from Sapormeina village, within the age group of 24 to 55 by purposive sampling method. Methods employed include: interview schedules, case studies and WHOQOL-Bref questionnaire. This questionnaire is made by WHO specifically for measuring women's quality of life. The questionnaire consists of 26 questions which comprise question on self-rating of QoL, satisfaction of health, satisfaction with physical, social, environmental and psychological domains of life. My study has also been carried out among various health givers such as traditional healer in the area and to different midwives on whom the women are dependent for their health. A study was also conducted on the Primary Health Care (PHC) center situated in the area. This health care institution is important to the people of all age group ranging from children to adult for obtaining treatment as its close proximity makes it the first destination for the people, and it also offers free medicines to the needy patients. Interviews were also carried out with the doctors and the staff of the PHC. Secondary data were also collected from the Government officials in charge of the areas concerned with the study.

Position of women in Sapormeina:

Since the community follows a patriarchal system, the role played by women is mostly determined by dos and don'ts that their menfolk prescribe. To some extent, women enjoy status and freedom but most often they are bound by certain rules laid down by their husbands, elders of the family and society. For instance, they are not allowed to participate in the decision making process and keep away from political issues that concern the village and the people. In some of the events such as prescribing punishments for individuals locally term as "Kileukham", the women are tabooed to participate in the meeting as well as to eat the meat of those events. There is inequality in religio-economic life of the people as well. For instance, women are not permitted to attain prominent posts in the church. The society has always been characterised by strict division of labour, and there are certain occupations into which women's entry is strictly prohibited. For instance, hunting is a sport meant for the men and women's place is confined to the more domestic or private spheres of the society.

Women in this tiny, hilly region carry the usual burdens that rest of the women in several parts of the country carry on daily basis: house-keeping, procreating, rearing children and so on. The main roles they play in their domestic setting include: cooking, washing clothes as well as utensils, cleaning, taking care of their husband, children and in-laws, working in the field, rearing cattle, etc. Only in some very exceptional conditions, the women folk enjoyed certain rights and freedoms equivalent to those of men. Women outside the formal employment run their own businesses like stitching clothes, weaving, knitting, etc in order to support their families financially. The status of women is also connected with their childbearing and child rearing functions; and as mothers they always receive respect and special treatment. In the same vain, a barren woman is stigmatised in the society. Widowers are normally allowed by social norms to remarry but widows are not really encouraged, for a good woman is consider to be the one who is devoted to the family even after the death of her husband. They are not entirely deprived of their basic privileges either, as they enjoy certain freedoms such as freedom to mingle with their friends and families, right to raise the children in their own way, etc.

Women and Health

Concept of Health: "Health is a state of complete physical, mental, and social well-being and not merely an absence or infirmity" (WHO, 1948). But recently this statement has been amplified to include the ability to lead a 'socially and economically productive life'. So health covers a large realm of a person's well-being, and we cannot judge a person by only the physical well-being. Therefore, is the popular proverb, "when health is well everything is well". Every society has its own concept of health. The women of Sapormeina perceived themselves as healthy as long as they can work in the field, carry out their daily routine and are in good shape in outward appearance. Headache, stomach-ache, cold and cough are minor cases that are not taken seriously enough either affecting them in their working or restraining them from performing their daily routines. For them a person is considered unhealthy only when she falls seriously ill and loses stamina to work. According to them, a healthy woman is believed to be the one who has clear skin, a strong body and a good appetite. Most of the health problems of the women here are seasonal in nature. While waterborne diseases are quite prevalent in summer, airborne diseases are common in winter. Anaemia, diabetes and high blood pressure are diseases which are found in most of the women. But the women here, however, assume that they acquire these types of diseases with increasing of age and they therefore try to accept them without much of a complaint.

These women had different notions about the causes of illnesses, and they can broadly be classified into two medical systems proposed by Foster and Anderson in Medical Anthropology (1979). They are: the naturalistic medical system and the personalistic medical system. Naturalistic conforms above all to an equilibrium model; health prevails when the insensate elements in the body, the heat, the cold, the humors or dosha, the yin and yang, are in balance appropriate to the age and condition of the individual in his natural and social environment; illness results when there is a disequilibrium. According to Foster and Anderson (1979:53), "a personalistic system is one in which illness is believed to be caused by the active, purposeful intervention of a sensate agent who may be a supernatural being (a deity or a god), or a human being (such as ghost, ancestor or evil spirit), or a non-human being (a witch or sorcerer)". Most of these illnesses are primary due to seasonal change, intake of unhealthy food and physical stress like headache, stomach-ache, cold, cough, fever, etc. These conditions are mostly treated in primary health care center located in the village or in a mission hospital at Kangpokpi or in the hospitals at the capital. They also approach the herbalists and traditional healers of the area.

Among the people of Sapormeina, there are still those who still believe in supernatural powers. With the coming of Christianity, the existence of supernaturalism or personalistic medical system began to take a back-seat, but it suddenly assumes significance when they suffer from psychological ailments, and particularly when the allopathic doctors fail to explain the problems at hand. Many of my respondents believe that the people living in and around the village of Sapormeina are liable to become the victims of illness caused by supernatural powers like ghost or evil spirit. To the west of the village there is a mountain range called Koubru and it is considered being the abode of deities. Thus, many non-Christian pilgrims come every year to pay respect to these deities. But the villagers have a different perception of who reside in the sacred mountain. The people of Sapormeina assume that it is the abode of malevolent and benevolent supernatural beings. In the cosmology of the people of Sapormeina, they believe that there are agents who affect people psychologically and bodily. The most vulnerable of this kind of attack are grown up boys and girls. Girls who are just attaining puberty in particular are susceptible to these kinds of supernatural attacks. The basic symptom of supernatural ailment affliction is somatic ailment with visions and hallucination. It is believed that no medicine would be effective unless the supernatural affliction gets fade away on its own accord. Whenever they face these problems they turn to the local healer who deals with supernaturalism.

Another belief is in the existence of evil eye. An evil eye is a look that is believed to cause injury or bad-luck for the person at whom it is directed for reasons of envy or dislike. Those who are possessed by this bad spirit are capable of causing evil to others. This occurs generally because of jealousy and grudge. The effect can be in the form of making someone sick, miscarriage, skin rashes etc. They believe that the one who possesses evil eye can even eat the body parts of the stomach of a person. According to my respondents, these people mostly enter a weak person and terminal patients. There is also a belief that sometimes even though a person passes away his/her body remains alive due to the intervention of these evil spirits through the ones who are possessed by them. The most common way of creating evil eye is through the mechanism of food. Therefore, they used to keep some portion of their food separately for the spirits before eating, but the practice is not much followed nowadays. Most of the respondents admitted that with the coming of Christianity all these believes are eventually fading away and that those who are believed to possess this negative personality are also losing their power – thanks to the intervention of the new faith.

Gynaecological problems of the Kuki women: Almost all of the world's women are struggling with one or other kind of gynaecological problems. The past decade has witnessed a significant shift in the study of health problems of women. There is a growing recognition that gynaecological problem is an important health concern for women. Most of the women in Sapormeina village have complains about their gynaecological problems. Some of the gynaecological problems found in the village includes Dysuria, menorrhagia (prolonged menstrual period), irregular monthly periods, white water discharge, amenorrhea, menstrual cramps, eclampsia (complication in pregnancy), miscarriage, sterility, uterine prolapsed, dysfunction uterine bleeding, anaemia and STD.

Women of Sapormeina are known for their hard work and they are always the earning members of the family. Therefore, they have less time to take care of themselves. Anaemia is one problem which is most prevalent among the women of this village. White water discharge is one of the main leading gynaecological problems of the women in Sapormeina. Most of my respondents below 35 yrs of age said they are coping with this problem. They feel reluctant to visit doctors for this purpose and therefore there is no proper cure. Though they face many gynaecological problems, most of them neglect them until they become too serious. These problems of women are found to be somewhat similar to the word 'caught' coined by Victor Turner while writing about the Ndembu of Africa. According to Victor Turner, "Being 'caught' means to be afflicted with bad luck at hunting in the case of men, with reproductive disorder in the case of women, and illness in both cases" (1957:292). For this treatment, the women of Sapormeina sometimes rely on allopathic medicine or consult the herbalist or traditional healers. The rituals performed by the traditional healers in treating gynaecological problems also shows some similarity with that of the rituals performed among the Ndembu of Africa. There are few cases of infertility among my respondents. There is a saying that the links between the moral order and reproductive health are particularly marked in cases of infertility. The inability to bear a child is understood to reflect moral status and in particular is usually blamed upon the woman who may suffer abuse and ostracism. It carries a grave social stigma and shame. In reality also this happens among the women who are infertile in Sapormeina. The blame is always on a female partner and she has to bear this social disgrace throughout her life time.

In Sapormeina, deliveries are done mostly at homes either by the midwives or by nurses employed in the Primary Health Care Center. However, the younger generation prefer to go to hospitals for deliveries. In many cultures, the postpartum period is defined as one of vulnerability for both mother and child and is characterized by a reduction of household and work responsibilities, minimal social interactions and support from female kin. Appropriate actions taken through the postpartum period are also believed to ensure a woman's continued reproductive health, strength and beauty in many cultures. This process of postpartum treatment generally involves dietary restrictions. But in Sapormeina, however, all these are lacking and women don't have proper rest both before and after their deliveries and they continue to carry out their daily workload. They failed to follow strict restrictions of dietary behaviour and they eat cold food, strong smelling foods which are believed to affect the quality of the breast milk. This also often leaves them with many problems in their health in the future.

Health seeking behaviour and various healing mechanism: With the onset of diseases, the women have fully developed their own way of diagnosis and curative systems, procedures and techniques in the treatment of diseases in their emic way therapy. The existence of primary health care center in the village helps the women and people of the area to get accessible to treatment and free medicines. Medical pluralism

– broadly implying the coexistence of various healing systems – is readily found in the village. The following are various health seeking behaviours and adoption of different healing systems of women.

Ethnomedicine: The traditional beliefs and practices of folk medicine are generally influenced by respective socio-cultural environment. According to Hughes 1968:99, ethnomedicine means "those beliefs and practices relating to disease which are the products of indigenous cultural development and are not explicitly derived from the conceptual framework of modern medicine, is the lineal descendant of the early interest of anthropologist in non-western medical systems". The uses of ethnomedicine are given in the following:

a) Home-made remedies: With the process of socialization, many people in the world are capable of having some medical knowledge and basic curative system which can be applied on the onset of illnesses. Thus, sometimes any specialists or expert are not needed but it can be practiced at home and this can be called 'home-made remedies' which can be practiced by every household as a tradition. Most of their household remedies are from plants, either fruits or vegetables. Sometimes they consume non-vegetarian diet which they consider as containing lots of vitamins that are good for health. When an illness first shows its symptoms, people initially approach the elders or an experienced member of the family for inquiring about the right kind of treatment. The villagers or peer groups may also play an important role. Being a steep and hilly place, most of my informants complain about having joint pains or arthritis. The cases are more severe for people who undergo surgery. Most of the time they hardly consult doctors for curing of it, and my respondents believe that using hot water therapy in the form of hot water bag or steaming makes them better. Some of the home-made remedies are while having cold and cough they massage their body with the mixture of garlic and hot oil. For ear pain, they put a tinge of mustard oil inside the ear. Menstrual disorder is one of the most leading health problems found among women. Sometimes there is excess of bleeding and sometimes only meagre amount of blood flows during menstruation. They also frequently witness cramps in their stomach. During this period, women abstain from eating hot things like spices and they rather take boiled vegetables. Some of them use hot water bag to relieve the pain. They eat lots of honey, brown sugar which they believe are capable of reducing the pain.

b) Supernaturalism and traditional healing: There are still believers in the intervention of supernaturalism in sickness. They acknowledge the supernatural causation of illness. For instance, when there is sudden misfortune happening in the family or strange illnesses developed, the villagers thought that it will be the work of supernaturalism. This kind of belief seems to closely resemble to that of Ndembu tribe in Africa. According to Victor Turner (1957:301), "Misfortunes, illness and reproductive troubles among Ndembu, if severe enough, are associated with the activities of spirits, witches and sorcerers". They believe that some illnesses are caused by the wrath of God as a sign of punishment for the bad deeds they did in their life. They also believe in the existence of witches and feel that those diseases which take time to be cured easily by allopathic medicine are done by witches. When they face all these kinds of illnesses they turn to their local healer or herbalist. The people of Sapormeina own only one herbalist who is also a traditional healer in the village. His name is Paokhongam (Ngampu) Kipgen and brought up in a Christian family and every step he takes in his work is done according to the will of God. Since the people also acknowledge the supernatural causation of illnesses, they rely on him for curing the diseases caused by supernatural powers. The healer deals with all kinds of diseases starting from simple illnesses to the one which they believe to be caused by supernatural powers. He was taught this traditional way of treatment from Pakho Sitlhou who was a pastor in the church and gifted with the making of herbal medicines and treating of illnesses that is believed to be caused by supernatural powers. After he passed away his work is continued by

Ngampu Kipgen, the local healer of Sapormeina village and the tradition is still carried on today. Though in this contemporary world allopathic medicines are gaining more and more significance, the use of traditional medicine, too, persists in many lives.

The herbs he uses are not found adjacent to the village, and he therefore gathers them from the inner part of the forests. He integrates them for making herbal medicine. Since he does not reveal the type of herbs he uses for his work, the substance of his treatment is not known to others except to his close ones. The medicines he prepares are generally in the form of syrup, tablets and pastes. Sometimes he even sacrifices animals like dogs and chickens for curing illnesses which he believes are serious enough and are caused by supernatural powers. He is a registered traditional healer under Health and Medical Research Welfare Union. Therefore he has authority to treat any diseases he is capable of, according to the needs of the people in and around the village. The main types of illness as he deals with comprise of epilepsy, injuries, abdominal pain which he terms as *Kaobol,* psychological problems which he terms as *Gambol,* and various gynaecological problems like infertility, miscarriage etc. Most of the cases he deals with are psychological problems. The first ritual performed for treating *Kaobol* and *Gambol* is by chanting a prayer and then killing a dog. The blood of the dog is then sprinkled on the patient. This is done to know the exact cause of the illness, and the real treatment is then followed by giving the medicines of his own making. Another major area of his treatment is infertility. He said that there are many barren women who are healed by him. He revealed that he massages the womb of the barren woman which, according to his assessment, is sometimes filled with many filthy things and sometimes it is not in a proper place. It is only after putting the womb in a right place and driving away all the unwanted substances from it that a barren woman becomes pregnant.

Primary health care center: The center is located in the north-eastern side of the village. It is open from 9:00 in the morning till 4:00 in the evening on all working days. There are daily OPD services and around 15 to 25 patients attend for check-up every day. Awareness programmes on tuberculosis, leprosy and HIV and AIDS are done twice each year. Polio vaccination is given to children every now and then. Free medicines are distributed to the patients. Some of the medicines routinely distributed include: antibiotics, vitamins, drips like IV fluids and dextrose, metron anti-diarrhoel. National Rural Health Mission has distributed various medicines and conducted awareness campaigns. Most of the patients who comes for treatment are female and children.

The health care center provides many medical facilities to the people in and around Sapormeina, especially for those who cannot have easy access to other hospitals for treatment. According to the medical officer of the center, a large percentage of the diseases registered are seasonal in character. Besides these, the highest cases that have been registered in the center so far pertain to tuberculosis. This is followed by respiratory tract infection (RTI) and gastro enteritis. There are cases of leprosy and lung cancer as well. Malaria is one of the most common diseases during the summer. The medical officer says that since there is high rate of smoking in the area there are high cases of chronic obstructive pulmonary disease (COPD). The center also keeps an account of patients having prolapsed inter vertebral disease (PIVD). There are records of low cases of people suffering from heart disease or diabetes because they go to different hospitals for treatment of these diseases. Conjunctivitis is a common case both in summer and winter.

The frequent visitors of the health care center are pregnant woman. They come for regular check-up and get the necessary injections and other medicines. Newborn children are also brought for monthly check-up, and they are usually given injection like Bacillus Calmette Guerin (BCG), oral polio vaccine and Diphtheria Pertussi Tetanus (DPT). Every month there are approximately 40 natal check-ups, and around 15 children are given such injections as: BCG, DPT and polio. As the center does not have a proper delivery room, the nurses usually go door to door for home deliveries. There is an account of around 10 new born babies every month. There is an Accredited Social Health activity in the center and they organized *Janana Suraksha Yojna* for the children. According to the medical officer, the life expectancy of the people in Sapormeina is around 60-70 years and women have a longer life expectancy than the male members. It is found that there are low cases of AIDS patient registered in the center among all the diseases. Most of the common diseases of female registered in PHC are malnourishment, anaemia and gynaecological problems like white discharge, STD, etc. These occur primarily due to unhygienic conditions, early marriage, ignorance, injury or infection. Migraine is a common problem among women caused mainly due to psychological problems or stress.

Women and Quality of Life

As it has already been suggested in the preceding pages, quality of life means the degree to which a person enjoys the important possibilities of his or her life and also a person's sense of well-being, satisfaction or dissatisfaction with life or happiness or unhappiness. 'Quality' can be said to refer to the level or standard or degree of goodness or excellence possessed by someone or something; or it can simply represent a summation of a thing's attributes (Schmadt and Bloomberg, 1969). 'Life' on the other hand, includes the entire state of functional activity of a person consisting of one's behaviour, development, sources of pleasure and displeasure and overall manner of existence. The QoL of women in Sapormeina varies from person to person, different age groups, their position in the society, etc. There are various factors on which one's own QoL depends upon, and such factors affect an individual both positively and negatively.

Factors affecting and contributing Social, Physical, Psychological and Environmental dimensions of QoL: When we say factors affecting quality of life, it generally means something that is negatively upsetting or disturbing the person's well-being. In short, physical aspects of QoL include excessive use of tobacco and drugs, lack of physical activities, imbalanced nutritional intake, unsafe sexual activity, polluted environment, natural resource depletion, dangerous work, overweight, poor hygiene, etc. Socio-economic aspects include poverty, low social status, discrimination in terms of sex, race, disability, steep power hierarchy within a community and workplace, etc. Psychological aspects include isolation, lack of social support, poor social networks, low self esteem, high self-blame, low perceived power, loss of meaning or purpose, abuse etc.

Physical factors affecting QoL include physical health, personal health, personal hygiene, nutrition, exercises, grooming, clothing, and general physical appearance. Diet and nutrition is an important aspect that determines the well being of the person physical health. These are the factors that contribute to the enhanced QoL and health. Proper diet and nutrition are of utmost importance for the physical well-being of a person. These entire factors can put a person away from sickness and doctor. Of my respondents, some them are conscious about their health and exercise regularly. These people believe that they are healthy and now have a good appetite when compared to those days when they did not exercise. They said that exercise reduce their weight and make their body feel light and fit. Non-vegetarianism being their staple diet, one finds a continuous consumption of meat, and it results in accumulation of bodily fat among the people. This in turn leads to overweight and cholesterol growth in the body mass. Many women thus suffer from high blood pressure, diabetes, heart disease, indigestion etc. For few of them who are in proper diet said that they have less complains.

Environment is also one dimension that affects the physical being of a person. Housing, sanitation, climate and pollution of air, food and water are the aspects of environment. A variety of life style or health related habits are tremendously affecting health. Behavioural attitudes and other habits that have major impact on health include smoking, diet, nutrition, alcohol, poor diet leading to obesity which reduce life expectancy or alternatively malnutrition, sexual behaviour leading to infection or teenage pregnancy and problems resulting from drug taking. The above mentioned physical factors are one of the major dimensions that physically affect the women's health or quality of life of Sapormeina. My informants are clearly aware of the fact that environment extensively contributes to the deterioration of their health. Residing alongside a national highway, the villagers are subjected to the continuous noise and air pollution resulting from the passing of vehicles. The ones living adjacent to the road in particular are exposed to the sound of vehicles in the nights, spending sleepless nights throughout their life. The emission of dirty gases from the vehicles also pollutes the air, and it is harmful for the villagers. Smoking and alcohol practices are another great dimension affecting the health of the village. There are women who are also indulged in these habits.

Social and economic factors play a vital role in shaping and re-shaping peoples' lives everywhere. Health practices and beliefs are strongly influenced by a person's economic level, life style, family and culture. For example, while the low -income groups are less likely to strive for health care, take steps for the prevention of diseases and seek the timely treatment for their ailments, high income groups, who are generally more prone to stress-related ailments, are quick to get the right medication and proper treatment. The family and the culture to which the person belongs determine patterns of living values about health and illness that are often unalterable. The type of house one lives in, the region and neighbourhood are some of the extraneous factors directly responsible for one's own well-being. Culture and ethnicity also act as the socio-economic factors that can contribute to one's own thought and expression. Both can have an impact on how people shape their core values, manage their families and cope up the norms of tradition. Among socio-economic factors education is one important variable. One's level of education can shape how he/she views the world and contribute to his/her social growth. It can lead to increased earning capacity, which in turn contributes to quality of life. Education can also contribute to decision making abilities that alter the paths people take in life. One's income and corresponding occupation are factors that can contribute to socio-economic status. Almost all my respondents admitted that social life extensively determines their well being or quality of life. Some of them have the urge of meeting their acquaintance everyday and the type of affiliation they share is quite important. This is one factor that determines their social dimension of their QoL. Since chatting with their acquaintances is a kind of routine for some of them, having a poor relationship brings discord within them. Therefore, living in peace and harmony with the other members of their social contact is considered essential for the women of this village.

When we say psychological factors, they include adjustment, cognitions, feelings, self-esteem, self-concept and self-control. It is measures by how an individual fulfils an active role in the society interacting appropriately with others, and overcoming difficulties without major distress or disturbances in behaviour. Participation in civic activities and social engagement, strong social networks, feeling of trust, feeling of power and control over life decisions, supportive family structure and positive self-esteem are enhancing psychological quality of life. It is also measured as the evaluation of happiness and satisfaction with life. According to my respondents, their psychological quality of life is affected by lack of social support, poor social networks, low self-esteem, high self-blame, abuse etc.

Analysis and interpreting of different dimensions of Quality of Life:

Table 1: Showing the total mean score of Quality of Life among women in Sapormeina, Manipur.

Mean	*Rate of QoL*	*Statistic of health*	*Phy. QoL*	*Psy QOL*	*Soc QOL*	*Env QOL*
Total	2.94	2.82	22.5	18.7	9.7	23.2

Table 2: Showing Marital Status wise QoL among women of Sapormeina. (Mean score±standard deviation.

Marital status	*Rate of QoL*	*Statistic of health*	*Phy. QoL*	*Psy QOL*	*Soc QOL*	*Env QOL*
Married	2.85	2.87	22.28	18.86	9.97	23.46
Widow	3.09	2.63	23.27	18.81	8.90	22.27
Total	2.94	2.82	22.5	18.7	9.7	23.2

In table 2, it is found that the overall mean score of QoL in Sapormeina is better for married women than for widow since they score higher in satisfaction of health, psychological dimension of QoL, sociological dimension of QoL and environmental dimension of QoL. The reason that married women score higher in most of the dimension of QoL is that since their partners are alive, there is sharing of most of the workloads and burdens among them and the women also have feeling of more self-esteem.

Table 3: Showing quality of life and educational qualification in Sapormeina. (Mean score±standard deviation)

Educational Qualification	*Rate of QoL*	*Statistic of health*	*Phy. QoL*	*Psy QOL*	*Soc QOL*	*Env QOL*
Illiterate	2.2	2.6	21.20	16.7	9.6	20.4
Upto 8th	2.75	2.56	21.75	17.56	9.3	21.25
Beyond 8th	3.32	3.0	23.40	20.12	10.04	25.44
Total	2.94	2.82	22.5	18.7	9.7	23.2

In table 3, it is found that in all the dimension of quality of life, the women with higher educational qualification beyond class 8th always recorded the highest in all dimensions of QoL. The reason is that since they have higher educational qualifications, they have better employment opportunities and job options. For instance, if they don't have government job they can still work in private firms or run their own business. This makes them financially better than the other women with less educational qualifications, and they are likely to have tension free, psychologically satisfying life chances.

Table 4: Showing quality of life and occupation among the women of Sapormeina. (mean score standard deviation)

Occupation Qualification	*Rate of QoL*	*Statistic of health*	*Phy. QoL*	*Psy QOL*	*Soc QOL*	*Env QOL*
Housewife	2.76	2.80	22.04	18.04	10.14	23.00
Govt.Job	3.54	2.90	25.00	20.90	9.72	27.0
Private	3.25	3.25	21.75	18.5	9.5	25.0
Entrepreneur	2.5	2.62	20.25	16.62	9.0	19.25
Others	2.83	2.66	23.0	19.83	9.15	21.0
Total	2.94	2.82	22.5	18.7	9.7	23.2

In table 4, it is found that the mean score is highest among those women who have government jobs. In physical, environmental and psychological domain, they score the highest. The reason could simply be that they had constant salary that meets their basic needs, and this makes their living conditions relatively better, and they eventually come to occupy higher status in the society. In self rating of quality of life and health satisfaction, women working in private sector score the highest. The reason could be as most of the work of private firms is demanding and hectic they feel healthy as they are capable of working in private firms and helping their family. In social domain, housewives score the highest which means that they have much leisure time in socializing with people.

Table 5: Showing correlation (r) of age with various parameters of the quality of life among the women in Sapormeina, Manipur

Age x Self Rating of QoL	*Age x Satisfaction with health*	*Age x Physical QoL*	*Age x Psycho-logical QoL*	*Age x Social QoL*	*Age x Environ-mental QoL*
- 0.39	- 0.24	0.26	- 0.09	- 0.17	-0.04

In table 5, it is found that except age physical domain of QoL (0.26), is found to be negatively correlated with all the other dimensions of QoL as it is found while correlating Age with self-rating of QoL (-0.39), Age with satisfaction with health (-0.24), Age with Psychological QoL (-0.09), Age with Sociological QoL (-0.17), Age with Environmental QoL (-0.04). This shows that as age increases, self rating of QoL, satisfaction with health, psychological QoL, sociological QoL and environmental QoL is decreasing. This means that age plays an important role in the women life.

Table 6: Showing correlation (r) of education with various parameters of the quality of life among the women in Sapormeina, Manipur

Education x Self Rating of QoL	*Education x Satisfaction with health*	*Education x Physical QoL*	*Education x Psycho-logical QoL*	*Education x Social QoL*	*Education x Environ-mental QoL*
0.521*	0.260	0.201	0.362*	0.086	0.429*

In the table 6, it is found that education is to be significantly correlated with self-rating of QoL (0.521*), psychological domain of QoL (0.362*) and environmental domain of QoL (0.429*) which is shown by the star mark (*). This means that as the educational level is higher among the women, the self rating, psychological domain QoL and environmental QoL also increases. We can also say that the self-rating of QoL, psychological domain QoL and environmental QoL depends greatly on the educational level. The correlation is statistically significant as shown by * mark. This shows how education is important in the life of women in coping with the society, family and within self.

* Correlation is significant at the 0.05 level (2 tailed).

Discussion

The study shows the different notions of women in determining their health and their quality of life. They defined their illnesses into personalistic and naturalistic in their own terms and conditions. Accordingly, they opted for different medical systems during their illness whether to go for traditional medical system or western medical system. There is presence of medical pluralism among the people based upon their cultural and ecological settings. People have various concepts of health and illness. The belief in evil eye and the effects caused by them still prevail among the people of Sapormeina. They still relate some of the illnesses and diseases to be the effect of some unseen powers. People believe that many of the misfortunes happening to the person or the family are caused by supernatural powers. This shows how these women are still rooted in the existence of indigenous believes and practices of black magic and supernaturalism though they are witnessing the western medical system. It is found that many of these illnesses are also caused due to the food habits and unhygienic conditions. This gives a need for women to maintain their health with proper diet and practice cleanliness. The presence of herbalist and midwives in and around the village ease the people to get treatment of various illnesses as well as their deliveries. The women of Sapormeina, like women from different parts of the country are also found to be engaged in more work than the men. They look after the household chores, work in the field and also they are one of the bread earners of the family. Their busy schedules give them less time to take care of themselves. Inequality of health in socially stratified societies is not surprising. The poor usually have more exposure to disease because they live in more crowded and remote conditions. And the poor are likely to lack the resources to get quality care. For many diseases, health problems and death rate incidence, relative frequency varies directly with social class. It is normally found that people with more socio-economic and political power are generally healthier

This is the first time that research on QoL is being introduced among the Kuki women. Analysis and interpretation are done according to the data collected. The result shows that women in this area have different QoL on the basis of multiple variables like education, occupation marital status, age group, etc. The result of the present study shows differences and relations of background variables and quality of life. It is found that education is one driving force which makes a good quality of life for women and this shows how formal education is needed in one's life. Besides this, occupation is another factor which enhances their QoL. Age was also an important variable which measures a good quality of life. Age and QoL are negatively correlated. As age increases, QoL of the women seems to get decreases. According to my research mostly women who are economically lower are psychologically down comparing to those who are economically sound. This affects the quality of life and therefore creating differences in the QoL economically. Therefore, we can say that QoL depends largely upon the socio-economic factors. Satisfaction with all these dimensions of quality of life will positively contribute to having good health.

Conclusion

From all the above discussions, it can be concluded that the concept of health and illnesses of the women of Sapormeina are determined by their own believes and developed their own health care system. They diagnosed their illness in their emic way therapy and accordingly they adopt the type of medical system of their choice. The study also concluded that differences found in the scoring of QoL of women in Sapormeina are due to the differences of variables among the women. The dimensions of QoL are interwoven with all the variables like occupation, marital status, education, age group, etc. All these variables have a definite influence QoL. It can be said that education is the most important variable for giving good QoL to women as it is found to be positively correlated with all the four dimensions of QoL. Increase in age group is negatively influencing the QoL. We can also conclude that QoL is also directly related to their socio and economic conditions. Therefore, we conclude that QoL depends on all the four dimensions namely physical, socio-economic, psychological and environmental well-being.

References

BURY, MICHAEL. (2005). *Health and Illness.* Cambridge: Polity press.

DALAL, K. AJIT and RAY, SUBHA. (2005). *Social Dimensions of Health.* Rawat publications.

DEB, SIBRATH. (2009). *Reproductive Health Management.* Akansha publishing house, New Delhi.

DECKER, JENNY. (2009). *Women's Quality of Life affected by lack of health care.* www.emaxhealth.com.

FOSTER G.M. and ANDERSON, B.G. (1979). *Medical Anthropology.* New York: John Wiley and Sons.

GANGTE, T.S. (1993). *The Kukis of Manipur: A Historical Analysis.* Gyan Publishing House, Delhi.

HUGHES, CHARLES, C. (1968). *Ethnomedicine. In International Encyclopedia of the Social Sciences.* New York Free Press.

KHANNA, RAJESH and KAPOOR, ANUP, K. (2007). *Ethnic group and health dimensions.* Discovery Publishing House, New Delhi.

KOBLINSKY, MARGE, TIMYAN, JUDITH and GAY, JILL. (1993). *The Health of Women: A Global Perspective.* Westview Press, Oxford.

MELIES, I. AFAF. (2001). *Women's Work, Health and Quality of Life.* The Haworth Medical Press.

MUKHERJEE, RAMKRISHNA. (1989). *The Quality of Life, Valuation in Social Research.* Sage Publications India.

OLIVER, JOSEPH; HUXLEY, PETER; BRIDGES, KEITH and MOHAMAD, HADI. (1996), *Quality of Life and Mental Health Services.* Routledge, Oxon.

TURNER, V.W. (1956). *Schism and Continuity in an African Society: A study of Ndembu village life.* Manchester University press.

WHITE, KEVIN. (2009). *Introduction to the Social of Health and Illness.* Sage Publication, New York.

Chapter 10

Women's Health and Healthcare Accessibility: A Case Study of Kuki Women in Gelnel Village of West Sadar Hills

Ruth Nengneilhing

"The test of civilization is its estimate of women" – George William Curtis

Introduction

If health is defined 'as a state of complete physical, mental and social well-being and not merely the absence of disease or infirmity' the health condition of women remains a far cry from the standard of this definition. Many studies have been conducted worldwide which have highlighted the active participation of women in promoting their health so as to realize their own potential as human beings though issues such as this is still a less travelled discourse of the Kukis in the public sphere. Doyal (1995) in her book, 'What makes women sick', explored and documented on the infinite variety of activities that constitute the fabric of women's lives. She wrote extensively on women's right to health. She also puts forward that the formulation of appropriate strategies for the realization of women's right to health must be a central concern not just in feminist politics but in wider campaigns for sustainable development, political freedom and economic and social justice (ibid. p232).

Women's health is often limited in the context of women's child bearing functions which only reflects a fragmented view of women's health. It often almost neglects the socio cultural contextual in which women's ills develop such as the background of poverty, patriarchy, and other life stresses. Mukhopadhyay (1998) stated that unequal access to nutrition, healthcare and education-early marriage, low autonomy in most areas of operation, the social responsibility for bearing and rearing of children, maintaining the household and ensuring family survival combine with a heavy workload to generate a state of endemic anemia and poor health for the majority of women.

Similar is the case with the Kuki women whose health concerns are compromised with several confounding factors such as poverty, overwork, and social inequality. The health of women fails to take priority due to the various demanding roles and obligations in the family. In most cases, they tend to visit the doctor or seek proper healthcare only when they had more than one complaint of ill health. The demand of managing a house, taking care of the husband and children, and going out to work to bring in extra money tend to place the women's own health quite low on the list of priorities.

(1) Conceptual Framework

The conceptual framework of this essay is within the social model of health theory embracing the context of health and illness beyond the biological model. The social model suggests that individual and community health results from complex cultural and structural influences affecting particular groups of people - ethnic minorities, women, the elderly, etc. This interpretation thus incorporates the wider social perspectives that affect an individuals' well-being. It focuses on the barriers and difficulties that prevent the 'ill' person from having access to health and 'normality'. These include lack of information or education on health care, lack of transport facilities to enable contact with doctors, hospitals etc.; difficult access to medical buildings; lack of support from and contact with others; limited protection by legislation; lack of funds or limited access to financial support; limited work opportunities.

The theoretical understanding of the study will be beyond the social model of health theory embracing the whole context of health and illness beyond the biological model (Nettleton, 1995). The underlying philosophy of the social model of health framework is that the health of individuals and communities is the result of complex and interacting material, structural and behavioural, cultural factors. The dynamic interplay of social and environmental factors has profound implications on the health of women in particular.

While the focus of the medical model is on pathologies, clinical interventions and patient behavior, the social model focuses on environment and collective measures. Social determinants of health are the economic and social conditions that shape the health of individuals, communities, and jurisdictions as a whole. Similarly, the barrier to attain maximum utilization of healthcare by the Kuki women is the result of the interplay of many factors which needs to be dwelt upon at an in-depth manner. Apparently, a vicious cycle of factors influence the health of the mother which unfortunately is often overlooked.

(2) Objective and Methodology

The essay is a study of women health issues in a rural setting. The main objective is to dwell on the underlying issues that pertain to women's health reflecting on Kuki women in Gelnal village of West Sadar Hills. Aligning to this objective, the sub-objectives are to explore the social, political, cultural and economic domain of women's health and also to examine the prevalent healthcare services and its limitations to women's health care needs. In a nutshell, the essay attempts to emphasize the significance of women's health in the setting of the Kuki society albeit based on a micro study.

The method of study is exploratory in nature and the source of data collection is based on observation and interviews. Fifty households were selected from systematic random sampling and the women from these households were taken for the study. The women's role in the social, religious and political field, the cultural influences and their economic conditions are being considered in the study.

(3) Profile of the Study Area

Gelnal is a Kuki village located in Sadar Hills sub-division of Senapati district. A roadway connecting Imphal to Tamenglong passes through the village. Gelnal village was established in the year 1928. It was earlier known as *Lammatek*. The place was filled with oak trees which created a landscape picturesque scene. As such, when Pu. Gouthang and Pu Chongkhosat Lhangum, the two brothers built the new village, they renamed this place as *Gelnal*. When Pu Gouthang passed away in 1964, his son Pu Thangkhosat Lhangum who was about 20 years old then took over the chieftainship.[1]

Under the Chieftainship of Pu Thangkhosat and his wife (L) Mrs. Neikhokim[2] , the village grew and prospered. It is worth mentioning the determination and perseverance of the people of Gelnal even at times of tragedies. The village faced a ghastly experience on the fateful day of 13th September 1993 when it was attacked by the NSCN (IM).[3] Human lives were lost and about eighty houses were also burnt down. The school building and the Church were also not spared. Seventeen persons died and about ten persons were severely injured. When the village was attacked, the men were engaged in defending the village; the women were in charge of taking care of the aged people and children. They took refuge in the nearby village called Tujang Vaichong while most of the men stayed back to guard the village. Despite experiencing such hardships, the village recuperated and rebuilt their lives with sheer grit and strength. According to the Village/Town Population by Sub-divisions and District of Manipur-2001 Census, Gelnel village has a total population of 986, out of which 508 are male and 478 female.[4]

(4) Women's status as defined by her daily routine

In conducting the study in Gelnel, the author experienced mixed reactions from the people which probably reflect the general attitude towards women. While some were appreciative of the determination of the author towards the work and studies undertaken, some could not find the essence of pursuing such work by a woman. Even the appreciative words come with a preceding clause *"numeicha hijongle chun"* which literally translated means *"despite you being just a woman"*.

The status of women in the society is low both in the social and the political spheres. They hold no significant role in the societal domain in terms of participation in the planning and decision making process. Their only participation is seen in the religious domain where they have leaders among themselves when they come together for worship every friday of the week. This is a gathering specifically for the married women in the village. The women grouping within the church is governed and managed by the women members themselves. So, all in all, women do not hold any leadership role in the village administrative structure as well as in the church fellowship, except for the leaders whom they elect among themselves in the women department of the church.

Women contribution to the domestic sphere is paramount but unrewarded and unrecognized. Usually her day starts at dawn when she would begin her daily chores. It is important to note that the workload of women depends on their standard of living. Women from households who possess better amenities and modern domestic appliances such as LPG and having running tap water in the house have lesser workload as compared to those women from poorer families who depend on firewood for fuel and fetching drinking water from the village well or pond or river. A few years before, all the women in the village were compelled, due to the lack of an alternative method, to fetch water with pots on their head from the public water source. However, in recent years most households have now possessed running tap water in their house compounds which brings much ease for the womenfolk as the duty of fetching water is and was considered a women's job.

Generally in most families women are the first among the whole households to wake up in the morning. A woman's first chore is to light the fire and boil a pot of water which is used for making tea, cooking etc. As mentioned earlier if there is running tap water in the house, it makes her work much easier. Otherwise she has to go and fetch water from nearby source. She would then prepare food for the entire family.

After accomplishing all her morning chores and taking her meal, if she has to go to agricultural field, she changed herself into some old tattered clothes which are usually hung in one corner of the house. She would clean up once she gets back home; prepare dinner for the family and the domestic animals. She would then retire to bed after the long day's work and resumes the same routine with the dawn of a new day. Some days she would be at home weaving clothes or shawl which she would either sell or keep it for use in the family.

It is noted that more female members in the houshold means lightened workload as most of the household chores are shared by all females in the house. However it cannot be ruled out that men do not chip in when required or demanded. At one instance, during one of the visits to the houses at Gelnal, the head of the household was busily preparing food for the family as his wife was away from the village for some work. Apparently in most cases when a man performs some household chores in the family it appears like a big favor while the work rendered by the woman in the house is considered part of her obligation. At the same time men who engage in such chores are often dubbed as 'hen-peck' or 'spineless' by his friends.

Apart from cleaning and maintaining the house, she also busies herself with other activities, in and around the house. This is where the womenfolk contribute immensely in the economy of the family. Most of the households in Gelnal have kitchen gardens where they grow different kinds of vegetables. Often she spends time growing and tending vegetables in this garden. She shares the products from the garden with her neighbors and other households too. Apart from kitchen gardening she also occupies herself with rearing pigs, poultry and other domesticated animals. Piggery and poultry are the two most common practices among the households in Gelnal mainly for commercial and consumption purposes. Majority of the women in the village depend on agriculture for their livelihood. Women also actively engage in the National Rural Employment Guarantee Scheme (NREGS) introduced by the central government[5]. However, the village has few resident female grduates. Due to limited work opportunities in the village, the more educated ones usually migrate to other bigger towns and cities for employment.

A few women also open small shops, tea-stalls etc. Women also practice 'Chit funds' also known as *Marup*. It is the practice of contributing a specific amount of money monthly by a number of beneficiaries. Each month the collected amount is given to a beneficiary. The beneficiary who has received the fund of a particular month starts contributing a pre-decided premium over and above the specified amount from the subsequent month. The month in which a beneficiary is to receive the fund is decided through a draw of lots. However, sometimes, the fund is given to the person who needs it most urgently. The contribution continues till the month the last person is to receive the fund. *Marup* may not necessarily be in the form of cash, as this practice of investment is also carried out to possess certain items on installment basis. This form of informal savings comes as a great aid to them in times of emergencies.

(5) Gender perspective of Health

The issue of women's health may be studied from different perspectives. Zaidi (1996) adopted a gender perspective of understanding the ill health of women and pointed out five broad themes and the reason he stated for identifying the causes that affect women and their health is to find ways of removing the constraints that exist which restrict women from improving the quality of their lives. The themes are *firstly* the lack of resources and poor access. *Secondly* the legal constraints: a male-oriented legal system; property rights which do not recognize women as equal partners; laws which do not consider men and women as equal. *Thirdly,* the lack of participation: women not part of the health (or any other) planning and participatory process; most decisions related to women made by male health administrators and professionals. *Fourthly,* the gender discrimination: preferential treatment for food intake and medical treatment for boys. And finally the values and norms: Social values, customs, cultures, religion, traditional societies, seclusion, exclusion-all discriminating against and restricting the contribution and role of women in society (ibid, p723).

Most of the explanations that have been cited above for the women's poor health apply to the Kuki women too. Among the Kuki women, health in most instances tends to be considered as secondary in their effort to juggle their role as a wife and mother. Their accessibility to primary health care which is designed to reach even the remotest village with the slogan of "Health for all" gets further detached and complicated by the inefficient and dysfunctional nature of the public health care facilities in the rural areas. Regardless of their ill health, the demand of their role in the family cannot be compromised. Their condition is deteriorated by the dysfunctional healthcare services in the rural areas. As such, with the tendency to delay their health demands in most instances they drag on until they succumb to the complication of their illness.

The myriad of socio-cultural factors which are confronted by women negatively impinge upon physical well-being and accessibility to appropriate health care services. Governmental strategies of primary health care seemed to have very less impact on the healthcare accessibility of the people especially among the rural population when factors such as access to income, legal rights, social status, and education prove far more important in determining women's access to health care. Women must become agents of change to improve their situation by putting forth their ability to make an informed choice and decision that plays a vital role in women's health. Preference for sons and failure to beget sons, and familial pressure also stripped women of any say in their health. Many of the institutional interventions have failed in the face of a society steeped in patriarchal moorings. It often becomes difficult for women to retrieve women's agency over their own bodies and choices, when husbands and in-laws usurp their rights over them.

Table 1 Summary of causes and explanations for gender inequality in health*

Ojanuga and Gillbert[6]	Puentes-Markides[7]	Okojie[8]
- Women suffer poorer health, consume less health care resources - Significant disparities between men and women on health indices - Poor communication and transport system prevent women from going to the hospitals for delivery. - Lack of adequate pipe-borne water and low standards of living contribute to high maternal mortality - Few women seek medical care during pregnancy and childbirth - Poor prenatal care and home delivery cause high maternal mortality - Poor nutrition affects women health - Preferential treatment to boys in provision of food. - Poverty affects opportunities for education - Some social and cultural customs affect food intake - In Islamic countries women may suffer seclusion and exclusion - Culture occupies dominant position - Women not part of participatory process in planning and implementing health care interventions.	- Women's status affects access to health care - Women are the largest proportion of the population below the poverty line - Legal system male biased-lack of obstetric care in rural areas - User fees and capacity to pay determine access - Socio-cultural issues, values, education, religion, influence access to health care. Cultural factors determine utilization of facilities. - Results from research not considered - Health policies insensitive to needs of women	- Ideological foundation for gender inequality is patriarchy - Maternal morbidity amongst leading causes of death, largely due to lack of access to or non-utilization of health services. - Limited access to maternity care and to general medical care - Nutritional and other discrimination against girls, preferential treatment for boys. - Gender inequalities of health originate in traditional societies - Numerous cultural practices and customs affect perceptions of health in traditional societies - In Muslim countries use of contraceptive is low - customs prevent women to make decisions about seeking health care - Seclusion puts restrictions on women's mobility -Health personnel and especially physicians mainly male

* This table summarizes the main features of three of the four papers presented on health and gender in the third world in the XIIth and XIIIth International Conferences on the Social Sciences and Medicine (Source: Cited in Zaidi; 1996, p.724)

(6) Lack of resources

The study area shows lack of resources to meet the needs of the people. Those households in the village who can afford use hydroelectricity for power supply while others mostly depend on other sources like lanterns or candles. The means of transport and communication is very poor which is further elaborated while describing the healthcare accessibility. Due to this lack of transportation the prenatal, natal and post natal care of women in the village all gets affected considerably.

(7) Nutrition

Regarding their food intake, women in spite of the hectic work demands generally lack sufficient intake of nutritious food. Women in most instances are the ones who arrange, prepare and serve the family. The average eating habit of a person comprises of two to three meals in a day. The first meal is taken in the morning which is usually taken around 8 to 9am. There is also an afternoon meal which is called *sun-an,* which is usually the left-over or kept aside from the morning meal. And the other meal which is dinner is usually taken around 6 to 7 pm when those going to the fields are back in the house or when all the members of the households get back after the day's work. While generally the whole family partake in the morning and evening meal, *sun-an* is not commonly eaten or pratised by all. Sometime between the main meals, tea and snacks are taken. The consumption of eatables in between meals varies among the various income groups.

As found in the study, the dietary intake of the people rarely includes milk and its products. The consumption of dairy products is found to be very minimal. There is low consumption of fat in comparison to cereals, pulses and vegetables. Rice is the main staple food of the people here. The non-vegetable food items are fish, beef, pork, poultry meat etc., yet in most cases its intake is occassional which is found quite limited to ceremonial and festive occasions.

(8) Lack of proper formal education

Women's poor health is also attributed due to lack of knowledge and ignorance of basic health care understanding. Education is a determining factor in empowering women which further influences their participation in the social and political front. However, females face a number of hurdles in the field of education. Poverty is one big hurdle in attaining proper formal education. Apart from this, women face many other hurdles and obstacles. Majority of the women did not receive formal education as education was not considered necessary or they were required for household work or agricultural field. Other reasons include high cost of education, responsibility of looking after younger siblings and lack of proper school facilities. Also in some cases, women are not encouraged to pursue education but get married at a young age.

(9) Women in healthcare sector

Women's health does suffer owing to lack of availability of female medical personnel (Zaidi, 1996). Zaidi further states:

> Most underdeveloped countries not only have very few (male or female) medical personnel in the first place, but the lower education levels and discriminatory customs and traditions do restrict women from taking skilled jobs. One cannot empathize enough the need for female health practitioners, especially in rural areas where many of the diseases affecting women are more marked. But given social restrictions and the dearth of qualified women it is unlikely that women will be available, leave alone willing, to work in desolate areas. It is not just the few qualified women, who are unable to go to rural areas, but the male dominated medical and health profession itself has few representatives in rural areas (ibid, p726)

Similarly, it is evident among the general Kuki population a host of factors restrict women's entry into the healthcare sector. No doubt there is a rise in the nursing profession opted by a large number of women in the Kuki society. However, there is dearth of professional medical practitioners among the Kuki women despite the great demand and need. Further research into this field can be encouraged to find the gap between the demand and supply of female health personnel among the Kukis. In many instances, language barrier also keeps women at bay from seeking healthcare as many Kuki women face the problem of communicating their problems to the doctors speaking another language than their own.

(10) Poor Access to Healthcare Services

In the context of the study area, the health care services are identified and categorized under two categories: government and private services. Under the government services are included- (a) Government Hospitals such as District Hospitals or the Government Hospitals in Imphal (b) CHC (Community Health Centre) at Kangpokpi (Kanggui).[9] (c) PHC (Primary Health Centre) at Tujang Vaichong (d) Sub Centre at Makui (e) Anganwadi/ICDS Centre/ASHA. And the private health care services include: (a) Private Hospitals (b) Private Doctors/Clinics (c) Paramedics engaging themselves in private practice (d) Traditional Healers/ Village Practitioners (e) Pharmacy/Drug Store.

(a) ICDS

Various centrally sponsored schemes if implemented efficiently and effectively can go a long way in promoting the health of the women and also the children who comprise the future generation of the Kuki society. Integrated Child Development Services (ICDS) Scheme which is a cent per cent Centrally sponsored Scheme was introduced in Manipur on 2nd October 1975 with a pilot project at Ukhrul T.D. Block. The Scheme has been successfully implemented by the Department of Social Welfare as the nodal department.[10] The aims and objectives of ICDS Scheme are to: improve the nutritional and health status of children in the age group 0-6 years, lay the foundation of proper psychological, physical and social development of the child, reduce the incidence of mortality, morbidity, malnutrition and school dropouts, achieve effective coordination of policy formulation and implementation among various departments to promote child development, enhance the capability of the mother to look after the normal health and nutritional needs of the child, through proper health and nutrition education.[7]

In order to achieve the above mentioned aims and objectives, the following package of services are implemented : supplementary nutrition,immunization, health check-ups, referral service, treatment of minor illness, nutrition and health education, pre-school education (to children in the age group of 3-6 years) and convergence of other supportive services, like water supply, sanitation, etc. ICDS care for children below six years of age. It is also intended to take care of essential needs of pregnant women and nursing mothers residing in socially backward villages and urban slums. However, there is need for more accountability for the successful implementation of such program as in many cases it fails to cater to the health demands of the targetted population such as the case in this study area.

Based on the interview with the ICDS providers in the area, it is stated that the utilization of the ICDS scheme is found to be very minimal due to lack of enough supplies. The main service that is provided in the ICDS programme is the supplementary food. The anganwadi workers provide cooked food to the children from time to time depending on the availability of the food supplies, there is no such particular time schedule when this service is provided. An Anganwadi worker at Gelnal village stated that along with the ASHA in the village, the Anganwadi workers provide services like supplementary nutrition to children aged six months to six years, pregnant and lactating mothers; immunization to women and children. The main problem that the Anganwadi Centre in the village face is the lack of supplies due to poor transport system in the area failing to their effective and efficient functioning.

(b) ASHA

The Accredited Social Health Activist (ASHA) in Gelnal actively engages in attending to the health demands of the people in the village especially the women and children. She carries out child delivery in and around the village. She is also a traditional birth attendant who inherited skills from her father. She conducts immunization services, takes malaria slides, checks blood pressures and keeps the records of weight. She also provides medicines like iron tablets, vitamins, glucose and other medicines to treat common ailments.

The coverage of the healthcare services needs to be revisited with due consideration of the existing socio political scenario in this area. The CHC in Kangpokpi is playing the role of district hospital for a large mass of the Kukis in this area. As such there is a huge gap between the CHC and the district hospital at Senapati its referral point, as most patients prefer to rush to the private healthcare services in Imphal, the state capital. The patients would shell out extra money for a better and immediate healthcare.

(11) Healthcare coverage

The coverage and utilization of the public healthcare services in this area need serious attention, where the people are deemed to acquire the basic health care as rightful citizen of the country from the state agencies. There is a high call for accountability on the part of the state authorities for effective implementation of the various health policies at the grass root level. Primary Health care in the country has still a long way to go in terms of quality and coverage and the vast majority of Indians still live in rural areas. Absence of accountability, inefficient planning and inadequate resources have rendered PHCs and sub-centres built across the country in many ways non-functional; they often lack doctors and medicines.

The nearest government health centre for the villagers of Gelnal is the Primary Health Centre at Tujang Vaichong, a neighboring village which lies at a distance of about five kilometers. However the PHC fails to cater to the health demands of the people due to inadequate infrastructure and lack of health personnel. As such, at most times, to avail better health care services they travel to Kangpokpi which is about forty four kilometres away. The Community Health Centre, Kangpokpi (Kanggui) Christian Hospital and other private clinics are available in this town. Sometimes, in case of illness which requires major surgery or other complications they head towards Imphal which is another forty five kilometres from Kangpokpi. The means of transport and communication is very poor in this village and as such the people encounter much inconveniences. Until the time of the study there is just one passenger vehicle available in the village with a carrying capacity of about ten to fifteen people. However in most instances, it exceeds the usual load carrying capacity. The fare usually ranges from sixty to seventy rupees. There is also a bus service that runs from Tamei, a neighbouringvillage.

Apart from the travelling inconveniences, accommodation is another issue for people seeking treatment outside the village. They need to save enough money and also find a place to put up during the duration of the treatment in case of going to Kangpokpi and Imphal for availing the healthcare services in those places. Thereby, in most cases, when they are not able to raise the required amount for the treatment and other expenses, they take whatever health care that is available in the village and delay their visit to the bigger health centres until they can procure enough savings. There is a paramedic from Tujang Vaichong whose service the people mostly avail in times of illness as he provides allopathic medicines. At Gelnal village, there is a traditional healer though he no longer practices the traditional method of healing after his conversion to the Christian faith.

(12) Perception On Healthcare

In terms of healthcare, allopathy is widely practiced and used as compared to the almost non-existent traditional medicine. In the past people resort to traditional medicine and traditional healing before the introduction of allopathic medicines. With the conversion to Christianity, people began to refrain from the practice of traditional healing as the ritualistic practice began to be considered not befitting of the Christian faith. The allopathic medicines that were first introduced to the people were tablets like MB and Quinine which in local term was known as *'lou-eng'* meaning 'yellow-medicine'. Such medicines were consumed for treatment of any kind of illness and it was believed to have cured all kinds of illnesses. Many of the diseases which are found to be prevalent and common now were not known or even heard of then. Unlike the debate prevalent in other areas of the world which has a tendency to place medicine as a product of science and therefore opposed to religion, in this village allopathic medicine is seen as synonymous with Christianity as it was the missionaries who first introduced it to the people.

Overall, the peoples' perceive the government health care as beset with problems such as unavailability of facility, long distance to travel, an inadequate infrastructure, unavailability of doctor or nurses most of the time, health personnel often absent, poor quality of service, unavailability of drugs and other equipments etc. Lack of awareness among the people about their right to health, and lack of accountability on the part of the health personnel leads to the failure of effective implementation of many schemes and welfare programs. Healthcare workers also sometimes face threats and mistreatment by influential armed groups. Clearly, the overall health situation in Manipur is being affected by the ongoing political unrest that affects service delivery as well as the health infrastructure.

(13) Differential factors of women's health

In understanding the issues of women's health in the Kuki society, it is also pertinent to note that women do not constitute a unified and homogeneous group. They are differentiated by factors such as age, sexual preference, race, class and very importantly, the geopolitical status. As such the essay also highlights the need to understand the socio economic condition even among the women group and stresses the need to strengthen the health demands of the lower most deprived class in the society.

Indeed gender differentials play a determining role in the understanding of women health, though it is also imperative to note that women's poor health is not only reflected in the gender differentials but also within the differentials across classes and castes (Qadeer, 2006, p4) .

The narrative of the experiential reality of health problem of Kuki women would best describe the accessibility of women to health care amenities. This is the account of a woman[11] in her mid-twenties who narrated her health issues and the problems hindering her to access proper healthcare. She was heading for Kangpokpi to seek health treatment from the CHC and other private clinics located there.

I have experienced two miscarriages as I could not seek any treatment when the complications arose. I could not attend timely medical treatment in my first two pregnancies due to lack of financial resources. Our main income comes from our work as agricultural laborers and we barely manage to make ends meet. The nearest Primary health center fails to cater to the needs of the people in the area due to lack of infrastructure and health personnel. As such we need to save enough money and spare days of work to seek proper health care located in the towns and other bigger settlement areas. (She was carrying their third expected child and wanted to ensure safe delivery of the baby. Appalled and saddened by the previous experiences, with much struggle they collected and saved enough money to seek better health treatment for the mother and the expected child)

In the understanding of women's health from a gender perspective, Zaidi (1996) states that

> "It is neither gender nor patriarchy alone which is to be blamed, but the structure of health care based on the prevalent specific economic and social structure". He further argues that while gender perspectives and gender differentiation in the quality of care does exist, and since the cause for the maldistribution of health resources is the social and economic structure then, not just women alone, but both men and women suffer the consequences of an inequitable system. The problem of a lack of access to resources, poor nutrition, lack of education, poor basic infrastructural facilities such as water and sanitation, and a

> lack of preventive and curative health facilities are not only one of the most important causes of the ill-health of women alone, but of the ill-health of entire nations, regions and classes composed of both men and women. In fact, it is the maldistribution of resources that results in ill-health. Poorer nations tend to have fewer resources which affect men and women equally. Poorer social and economic groups suffer much worse discrimination in every country in the world. The rich and well-to-do in the third world often have access to the best health facilities of the world, while the poor in their countries suffer severe diseases and have little access to even the most basic of health facilities (ibid, p723).

In the light of the above argument, one can certainly contest that the Kukis whose majority of population inhabit in the rural area of the state are deprived of most of the basic health care while women even suffer the most. Belonging to an underdeveloped country and a state where prevailing socio political crisis and economic instability influences the stark difference in resource allocation, the plight of the Kuki women is explicit due to the scantily available health care services.

Conclusion

The essay concludes that while both men and women suffer the consequences of an inequitable system and maldistribution of resources, evidently unequal burdens of domestic labour, discrimination in the allocation of household resources, constraints on women's capacity to determine their own sexuality and procreativity, inequalities in waged work and political power, and the continuing epidemic of male violence against women is equally inevitable. And the well-being of women is affected by the multiple burdens of production and reproduction borne from a state of disadvantage and which needs to be revisited and restored. Improving health of women impacts positively on the health of other family members, especially children. Also investing in the health of girls' results in particular gains for the family and society.

The framework of this essay is narrowed down to the importance and hurdles among the Kuki women in attaining health and healthcare. The domain of women's health engulfs vast area and covers wide ranging issues which this essay has failed to cover due to its limitations. This essay is just an attempt to crack the nutshell in the domain of women's health in the Kuki society where more research needs to be encouraged and explored. The issue of women's health needs further exploration to improve the quality of life of the Kuki women in particular and the Kuki society in general. All women irrespective of their social and economic circumstances need access to a comprehensive, affordable and quality health care. Finally as advocated by the social model of health, the health status of the Kuki women needs to be addressed by understanding the various complex cultural and structural influences which have an impounding bearing on the health of the women.

> *"I measure the progress of a community by the degree of progress which women have achieved". B.R. Ambedkar*

Notes

1. Record file of the Chief of Gelnal, accessed in July,2010
2. The wife of Pu.Thangsat, (L) Mrs. Neikhokim who was lovingly referred by the villagers as Inpinu, passed away on 23rd December 2012. She was deeply loved by the people and her absence left a huge void in the hearts of young and old in the village.
3. 1990s in Manipur was a period of great upheaval which witnessed thousands of lives lost, injured and displaced. The most affected groups in the upheaval were the Kukis and the Nagas. Many lives and properties were lost on both sides. The animosity between the two parties intensified in the early 90s and the intensity subsided towards the end of the decade. September 13th is observed among the Kukis as Black day which is also known as *Sahnit ni* in local term, as 108 Kukis were killed on this day alone in 1993. Recently few militant groups opposed the observance of Black day in the spirit of forgiveness. They are of the opinion that the observance will do no good, so they urge the people to rather focus on peace and harmony. However, the apex body of the Kukis, Kuki Inpi, voiced and urged that the day is to be observed until the case of the killing several Kuki civilians in the nineties is settled amicably. It is a customary practice that *Sahnit* is observed when someone is murdered in a village and the observance is stopped only after the

murder case is settled amicably by the conflicting parties in the proper court of law. As such, the Kuki Inpi stated that abiding by the Kuki customary and cultural law, the black day will be observed as long as the Government of India fails to settle the matter amicably, as the killings were caused by those fighting for sovereignty against India and therefore it is the bounden duty of the GOI to deliver justice to the Kuki victims. (Source: http://e-pao.net/GP.asp?src=25..120912.sep12, accessed on September 14 ,2012)

4. http://censusindia.gov.in/PopulationFinder/View_Village_Population.aspx?pcaid=965867&category=VILLAGE accessed on May 4, 2010

5. NREGA is an Act to provide a legal guarantee of 100 days of wage employment in a financial year to every rural household whose adult members volunteer to do unskilled manual work. He/she will get the minimum wage rate notified for agricultural labour in the State until the Central Government notifies a minimum wage rate, which in any case shall not be less than Rs. 60 per day. NREGA came into effect on February 2, 2006.

6. Ojanuga D.N. and Gilbert C. (1992), Women's access to healthcare in developing countries. Cited in Zaidi S. Akbar (1996).

7. Puentes-Markides C. (1992), Women and access to health care. Cited in Zaidi S. Akbar (1996).

8. Okojie C.E.E. (Gender inequalities of health in the third world. Cited in Zaidi S. Akbar (1996).

9. The Kangpokpi Town Committee (KTC), Sadar Hils Chief Association (SAHILCA) and other social organisations of Kangpokpi in a meeting on February 22, 2013 iniated the processs of changing the present name of Kangpokpi to Kanggui.

   (sources: http://www.ifp.co.in/nws-12965-kangpokpi-bodies-meet-resolves-to-change-kangpokpi-to-kanggui/Accessed on 9th March, 2013).

10. http://socialwelfaremanipur.nic.in/icds_schemes.htm accessed on April 17, 2013

11. Mrs. Nengboi (Named Changed at the request of the respondent for confidentiality), interviewed on 15th July, 2011

References

1. QADEER, IMRANA. (2006), Gender and Health Beyond numbers. In: Desouza Shaila (Ed.). *Women's Health in Goa,* New Delhi: Concept Publishing Company.
2. ZAIDI S.AKBAR, (1996) Gender perspective and quality of care in underdeveloped countries: Disease, Gender and contextuality, *Soc. Sci. Med.* Vol.43. No.5, pp.721-730
3. NETTLETON, S. (1995) *Sociology of health and illness.* Cambridge: Polity press
4. MUKHOPADHYAY SWAPNA (Ed.). (1998) *Women's health, public policy and community Action,* Institute of Social Studies Trust. New Delhi: Manohar Publishers and Distributors.
5. DOYAL, LESLEY. (1995) *What makes women sick: Gender and the political Economy of Health.* Hampshire and London: Mac Millan Press Ltd.

Chapter 11

Representation of Kuki Women in Thadou-Kuki Films

K.C. Gabriela

I. Introduction

Manipuri (meitei) films have already made an impact on the national and international levels by bagging prestigious awards. On the other hand Thadou-Kuki films are still in their infancy and are way far behind from any accolades as they lack the fine tuning of film making in terms of editing or acting, even directing. Films are meant for entertainment and that's exactly what Thadou-Kuki films are intended to do with additional interests in making some money out of it. The intention of this essay is not to criticize the technical aspects of Thadou-Kuki films because the film-makers tried their best in transforming the real to the reel. With the kind of infrastructure the Kuki film industry had, it is commendable to see that there are more than fifteen films released till date. Thadou-Kuki films started taking shape in the early 90s with the purpose of producing films in the local dialect to be watched and enjoyed by a specific narrow group of audience. Letthang Doungel and the late Lamgin Doungel are known as the pioneer of Kuki films. Thus, began the onset of a new spectrum where the Kukis were introduced to their own kind of films to whom the audiences could relate to. They saw images of themselves on screen, people who racially looked like them and behaved like them. Music videos too started churning out at a very quick rate and the Kukis were experimenting with an art that had already existed but now they were producing their very own kind.

Although culturally the Kukis are different from the Meiteis, Kuki films are highly influenced by the Manipuri films in terms of music and film techniques. And since, Manipuri films too are influenced by the larger Indian cinema (Bollywood), Kuki films too has the popular song and dance sequence embedded in its script where one can see the lead actors running around trees singing songs to each other.

II. Images of Women in Kuki Films.

Every thadou speaking Kuki is familiar with films such as "*Kum Som Kilungsel*" (Ten years of love), "*Jonlhing*", "*Heno Neingailou hitam*" (Mother, don't you love me anymore) among many others. Kuki films can be territorialized under the sub-regional film category which means it stands to represent its society and culture. Mostly Kuki films can be seen as a depiction of real life as part of documenting the culture and traditions while mirroring the society. Reproducing our way of living into films for years to keep, from the time of its inception, Kuki films have strongly been rooted in contemporary social reality. Themes were based on social realism and characters were stereotyped. Kuki films can thus be perceived as what Kukis think of themselves and how they want to represents themselves to others. Malraux demonstrates this capturing of images as a cultural more than personal. Images today are thought to serve symbolic and aesthetic functions, not magical ones; they signify what is important to culture and they do so in styles that display values (Andrew, 2005).

The film scripts are very fond of conservative ideas and emphasizes on family roles especially that of a women. This essay intends to look into how Kuki women are represented in Kuki films. We shall examine the roles rolled out for women to portray and to what extent they are true. Also, we shall see in what way gender identities are constructed. Suppression of women is not new in the society, and the same has been projected on and on in films, be it Bollywood, Hollywood or Manipuri cinema or Kuki films for this matter.

Films after films we have been shown women being portrayed confined in the four walls of her household, especially the kitchen. Women are barely seen in dominating roles or as the protagonist of any story script. Women in Kuki films play second fiddle to male protagonists and are mainly casted as the love interests in most cases, sometimes the sole reason why the male protagonist fights for. In minor cases, we see them in the roles of nurses (*Lhalihjaan, 1996*) where the doctor is played by a male. There are barely any attempts at raising consciousness to create women of independent thought and action. The female characters are left to be dependent on their male counterparts. Kuki cinema resonates the Kuki tastes and aspirations. So, can one concede that in order to understand the contemporary social life of the Kukis, can this be read through its films? Almost all Kuki films have created the image of the women who loves to cook, clean and scrub utensils, cleaning rice and food items, watering the plants, basically, as someone who takes care of the house's chores and looks after the well being of the family. She is burdened with demands of an all encompassing, ever loving and compassionate mother as well as a dutiful and obedient wife. Correspondingly, we shall try to examine how much subjectivity towards the role of women comes from the opposite sex, since almost all the people behind the camera are men, written and directed by men. Since these roles of women are written down by men, does it mean that the interpretation of the social status of gender identities come from only one-sided point of view? Males perspective gets identified as the society's perspective. A woman earns the appreciation of a "perfect woman" with her "genteel silence" (Devi, 2012). More often than not, a woman who bears pain silently and does her work with no complains is considered as a "*numei pha*" (good woman) or "*numei ching*" (wise woman). Perhaps, this formulation in the depiction of the "ideal women" comes from this aspect of study. For this we need to study the social status of Kuki women in the society. Historically and culturally speaking the society in which they do well remain by and large patriarchal in which males have been traditionally assigned 'masculine' roles in the public arena and their female counterparts customarily expected to embody female characteristics by taking pride in running errands within the private/domestic spheres (Kipgen, 2010, p. 117).

Like any other tribal societies in Manipur, the Kuki women occupy the private domain of lighter domestic household chores such as weaving, cooking, rearing poultry and pigs. And the males engage with tasks in the public domain such as house constructions, felling of trees, manual labours, hunting and fishing. It is considered highly feminine for a woman to know how to weave. A Kuki woman who has good knowledge of hand-loom weaving techniques has a very high reputation in the community and is perceived as a good homemaker. Rice cultivation is one of the main sources of income and food for the Kuki society and it is common to see both men and women involved in "loukon" (working in the fields). Nowadays there are many educated Kuki women who are working in Government offices and bringing in equal amount of wages as their male partners to run their families. The advent of cultural movements such as the Second wave feminism brought in the consideration to accept a working woman. The Kuki society is a patriarchal society; this means the women have no say over the property matters. The society is male-dominated and women have no say over almost everything. Women are rarely consulted over society matters. Education brought about some changes, although earlier, gender inequality existed where sons were given more weightage to pursue education over daughters. Daughters were expected to stay at home and help with the household chores. Along with education, Christianity played a major role in configuring the roles of women. The bible provided a manual handbook to how women are supposed to behave in the society.

When it comes to gender studies in films, there have been many discourses about the male gaze (in terms of how men look at women) and the stereotyped image of a woman as a sex objects or scopophilia[1]. Kuki films have barely emphasized on this aspect. Because the Kuki society is a conservative society, elements of sexual titillation is completely absent. Camera angles are limited to movements and facial expressions and do not go beyond. The concept of gaze is not employed in Kuki films. The focus is seen more on how femininity is constructed in the film with signs and languages. A woman is often portrayed as someone who takes pleasure in serving her man, the man she loves or her husband. So, are Kuki films perpetuating femininity as a social construct by projecting women in a specific role of making her behave a certain way in the way she dresses.

Unconsciously, the projection of females as demure beings can be the public dream, the female lead as a romantic ideal, gentle, timid gait and submissive traits might come from the film-makers' psyche. The Kuki film industry are mostly written and directed by men. It could be that the projection of women are a construction of how the auteur (usually a director who exercises creative control over his/her films with personal inputs) perceives woman as or what he expects how an ideal women should be. The section of people involved in the making of films asserts their own identities in the way they perceive the society. The female leads are often younger than the male lead in age. It is safe to say every thadou-kuki film has the female lead calling the "hero" addressing him as "heo" (brother). The term "heo" is a reference to someone who is older and senior as a mark of respect. In reality, people do not strictly follow this; one would rarely find a girlfriend calling her boyfriend "heo". But it is regarded disrespectful to call one's husband by name once married.

This article has taken about four films to analyze how women are portrayed in films in coherence with their position in the society. These movies are chosen on the basis of random selection and all of them belong to the early Thadou-Kuki films in the 90s and early 2000s. Co-incidentally all the movies below are directed or produced by Letthang Doungel who can be considered as the pioneer of Kuki films. Another common factor to most of these films is the lead hero, mostly played by the late Mangboi Doungel popularly known as Dehjamang. The actresses do not appear to repeat appearances in any other films; this is conclusive of the idea that the male actors have a longer shelf life than women actors.

III. Case Studies of Selected popular Kuki Films

1. *Lhalih jaan* (Full moon night)
   Year of Release: 1996
   Written and produced by Letthang Doungel
   Starring: Mangboi Doungel, Jamchong Hangshing

Lhalih jaan is a love story between Mangboi (Mangboi Doungel) and Lhingnu (Jamchong Hangshing). The film begins with the death of Mangboi's parents survived by him and his elder sister Hatneo. Hatneo earns a living by weaving and selling pons (traditional wears) while Mangboi goes to college. One day, Lhingnu is abducted by some goons, Mangboi comes and saves her and thats how they meet and fall in love with each other. She's rich and he's poor and thus begins the story of forbidden love. The girl's father makes it clear that he does not want her mingling with people below the level of their economic status. Despite the restriction laid out by her father, she continues to be in a relationship with Mangboi. She is grounded for breaking her father's rule so she initiates to elope with him by sending him a letter telling him to meet her at dawn to run away and get married. Somehow the letter does not reach Mangboi on time and Lhingnu returns home disappointed adding to her earlier disappointment of feeling double-timed by Mangboi on an event that was in reality not true. It is interesting to note how the economic status of Lhingnu who comes from a well-off family is not shown doing any household chores at any point of the film. The mother in one scene is shown scrubbing utensils and in another offering tea to the guest. Mangboi and Lhingnu finally managed to elope away and get married in the woods. They had started to live together but their happiness did not last long. Lhingnu's father sends a group of people to bring her daughter back at any cost. In the process, Lhingnu is shot dead and Mangboi too takes his last breath next to her body.

2. *Ngaidam* (Forgiveness)
Year of Release: 1992
Directed by Letthang Doungel
Produced by Lunkhojang Haokip
Starring: Paozathang, Manglun, Kimhoichong, Lhingboi, Ngamsei

Ngaidam is a story about an estranged son (Hegin) who runs away due the ill-treatment by his step-mother. Hegin's mother passes away when he was a little kid. His father remarries so that his son can have a mother who can love and take care of him. She ends up treating her own kids (Lalboi and Chongneo) and her husband's kid, from his first marriage, differently. The step-mother here is stereotyped as an evil inconsiderate ill-treating the child of the first wife to the point that she drives away little Hegin out to the streets. Her intention is to let her own blood Lalboi take over the family assets which Hegin is entitled to. The film tries to projects the patriarchal system of the Kuki society emphasizing on the roles of mi-upa (eldest son) in a family and the society at large. On the other side, a young girl called Boinu lives with her father. There is a scene where Boinu is seen watering the plants and her father comes to tell her that if she behaves and listens to him like an obedient daughter than all his properties and will be given to her for he does not have a son and treats her like one. The role of the venomous step-mother is later asserted when Lalboi's girlfriend's mother warns her about his mother, how she could not keep the family together and these are signs of a atrocious women. Lalboi finds out from his grandpa about his estranged step-brother who is the real heir to the family's properties. He demands from his mother that she apologizes to Hegin and ask him to come back home. The film ends with Hegin forgiving his step-mother.

There is a scene in Ngaidam where Chongneo is being chased and attacked by a drunk man, and Hegin comes on time to save her, who realizes that it is his step-sister when he goes and drops her home. The director must have meant to show that Hegin is a good guy by making him save his (step) sister but to do so he added the element of a weaker women being attacked by a man and is protected by another man and making her feel indebted to him for it. Basically, the good triumphed over evil.

3. *Kum Som Kilungset* (Ten years of love)
   Year of Release: 1994
   Produced and Directed by Letthang Doungel
   Starring: Mangboi Doungel, Themneihat, Chochong

This is a love story between Hoinu and Len who meet during one Christmas in a village where the former lives. Len's mother passes away early in the film. Len professes his love for Hoinu which is reciprocated back. One morning, Hoinu goes to the woods to collect firewoods and is possessed by the ghost of a tree and becomes ill. On hearing the news, Len who lives in a town comes to pay a visit. Meanwhile, Hoinu disappears into the woods; Len follows her and somehow manages to get rid of her illness. These films inculcate the intricacies of a relationship of what could happen when lovers make promises to each other.

Even though Hoinu's parents were aware of her relationship with Len, they arranged her marriage to a suitor they found suitable for Hoinu. She tried to contact Len but fails and thus gets subjected to her parents' wishes. So, what happens is that, due to the vows made between them to be together was not fulfilled; Hoinu is unable to conceive and leads a barren life. She confesses to her husband that she and Len had made vows to marry each other if that doesn't work out then the trees and nature are witness that she will not bear any children. Her husband requests Len to free her off the vows by letting her go. Len meets Hoinu and wishes her a happy married life, only after which she immediately conceived. Len is still binded by the vows, he is unable to attain any achievements due to that and comes back to Hoinu to free him off the impediment. She wishes him success and helps him get rid off of the promises they had made. Ten years go by till the time they fully separate from each other. Hence, the name of the film is "*Kum som kilungset*" (Ten years of love).

4. *Heno Nei Ngailou Hitam* (Mother, don't you love me anymore)
   Year of Release: 2000
   Written and Directed by: Letthang Doungel
   Starring: Mangboi Doungel, Lhingkhonei Haokip

The film begins with the female heroine (Neinu) migrating from a village to another for reasons unknown. The next footage shows the male hero (Thangboi) as an inspector in a police station working. His masculinity is put forward as he beats up a culprit in jail. The lead heroine is shown selling vegetables and this is where the two leads first come across each other. She is a single mother who lives with her daughter Boikim. She is shown as someone who is dedicated mother and homekeeper. Boikim, on the way to school comes under the vehicle of Inspector Thangboi's Jeep. He immediately takes her to the hospital for treatment. He meets with Neinu officially when he drops Boikim at her house. After meeting Neinu, he deeply thinks about remarriage for the sake of his little son Lenboi who was still a baby when his mother left home. Hatnu is Thangboi's first wife who was having an illigetimate affair with another man. When Thangboi caught her red-handed, and later confronted her, Hatnu left home. He narrates this story of his past life to Neinu and ask her to consider marrying him. In the next shot, Neinu is giving a hard thought to her earlier conversation with Thangboi interrupted by Boikim who wants to know where her father was and Neinu tells her that he was killed in a war. Neinu agrees to get married to Thangboi and goes to live with him and his family.

Meanwhile there is another plot to the story where there is a gang of goons who are busy plotting to get their leader out of jail who Thangboi has captured and kept in jail. Ngaltun, the captured gang leader manages to escape from jail with the help of his gang members. He intends to seek revenge by killing Thangboi who is responsible for his misery in jail. Neinu is given a hard time by her mother-in-law who ill-treats and calls her "numei chavei" (immoral women). Nei is the quintessential silent sufferer who does not mouth a word against her mother-in-law, even though we as audience only know she has not been at fault.

Ngaltun is plotting against Thangboi and wants him dead. He traps him by kidnapping Boikim and in the exchange of firings; Thangboi succumbs to his injuries and dies in the hospital. The mother-in-law is afraid that Neinu might take over Thangboi's properties, so immediately tries to change the will to his grandson's name. Paocha who was helping her out with the papers cheated them by changing the will to his own name instead.

They are compelled to move out of their house and live in a smaller place. The mother-in-law comes to accept Neinu and asks for forgiveness and passes away. Neinu cannot afford to send both the kids to school anymore and chooses Lenboi to be sent to school instead. She takes Boikim to labour work at the factory with her. A rich couple wish to adopt Boikim and Neinu agrees to give her away for adoption in exchange for some money that could help her pay the school fees. Boikim.

Heno Neignailou hitam is the hallmark of a woman's sacrifices. Every aspects of femininity has been applied to Neinu's character. She is soft-spoken, she is a homemaker who cleans, washes, and single handedly takes care of her daughter. Widowed, she takes care of herself and her child by selling vegetables house to house. She does not retreat back when her mother-in-law ill-treats her. Let us take an instance where Lenboi comes home with a torn shirt and blames it on his step-mother Neinu, the mother-in-law (Lenboi's grandmother) scolds her and calls her numei chavei (immoral woman), yet she remains silent even though we as audience know that she is not at fault. When Boikim intervenes by saying that Lenboi's shirt had gotten torn on the way home while playing, Neinu asks her to remain silent. The mother-in-law is portrayed as a disgruntled, pouring out her frustrations on the newly arrived bride but these events only take place when the son (Thangboi) is not at home. Neinu never complains a thing to her husband; instead she suffers without an iota of protest as if self-sacrifice is the only path to redemption. A clear distinction is created between the bad and good woman. The mother-in-law later repents for all her wrong doings and asks Neinu for forgiveness. This film is a good example to show how films work on the idea of how ultimately good triumphs over evil. We have discussed how sons are preferred over daughters when it comes to affording education for the kids. She lets Boikim drop out of school saying she's a girl and can follow her to work while Lenboy can go ahead with studies so that he can get a job and get back their father's house. Bigger responsibilities are made to carry by males.

Most of this paradigm of women is designed by men because they are the ones writing the script and screenplay of the films. Female characters are created and directed by men. They are principally given the role of a wife or mother. And most often than not, these women are to play the role of a quintessential idea wife who is demure and fragile. She does not oppose her husband and stays at home and takes care of the wellbeing of the family. She is mostly confined to the kitchen and cooking with her mother, sister or mother-in-law. Kuki films have stereotyped women. In Lha lih jaan, when the father hears the news of his daughter had eloped, his wife worries about their reputation but he asks her not to bother about it. Her opinion is suppressed where he takes it upon himself to fix the situation. Lhingnu's mother does not have much screen space in the film, comparatively Ngamsei, the comedian had more lines in the film.

The concept of damsel in distress is seen in almost every film, where a girl is chased or attacked by goons. This concept is used to establish the male hero in the story. The male hero is mostly cast as the "good guy", one who protects and fights off villains. In Ngaidam, the step-brother comes and saves the sister from a drunkard man who was trying to snatch her handbag. In Lha lih jaan, there are two instances where in the beginning Lhingnu is being chased by a group of boys and in the second instance she is abducted. Mangboi runs after her to rescue her from the goons. All Kuki films project the male protagonist as the good guy. The side role varies from character to characters. For instance in the same film, HeoLal, Hatneo's husband plays an unfaithful shameless husband who brings girls into their home and drinks alcohol. He beats her up and splashes alcohol into her eyes leading to blindness. In the immediate next scene, he is seen to repent for his deeds and changes for the better. Hatneo forgives him easily even after being subjected to domestic violence by her husband overlooking the fact that he has physically abused her.

In *Heno Neingai lou hitam* (2000), the gang of goons lead by Ngaltun which I have already talked about earlier has a female member names Chongneo. She is considered to be an important member of the group who initiates most of the plans carried out by the gang. She was the main help behind Ngaltun's escape from jail. After the success, Ngaltun sits down with his gang and thanks them for helping him out. He praises the members, especially Chongneo because he implies that even though she is a woman, she has managed to execute the gang's plan properly. "*Chongneo jong numei ahivanging, kapahchatlheh jenge*"-(I really appreciate Chongneo's effort even though she is a woman).

IV. Conclusion

In conclusion, this essay was an attempt to study the roles of women portrayed in film and how close or far is it related to reality. There are not too many Thadou-kuki films to fully be able to precisely talk about realism and reelism. For now, what we can understand is that the Kuki film industry's main effort is to duplicate our society onto images that can be kept and looked back at, in the process documenting our cultures and traditions and communality. When it comes to representation of women in thadou-kuki films, the roles are highly centred on the idea of femininity making women appear fragile. This study of representation is important today because of the problems faced by woman in real life somehow comes from the notion of the 'imagined' women (Pillai, 2010) that is constructed by the various social and cultural practices in the society.

Selected Bibliography

1. Kipgen, G, Tingneichong. (2010) Women's Role in the 20th Century Manipur: A Historical Study. Gyan Publishing House. New Delhi. pg 117
2. Pillai, T, Meena. (2010) Women in Malayalam Cinema- Naturalizing Gender Hierarchies. Orient BlackSwan Private Limited. New Delhi.
3. Butler, Judith. (1990) Gender Trouble: Feminism and the subversion of Identity. Routledge. New York.
4. Mulvey, Laura (1989) Visual and Other Pleasures. Bloomington: Indiana University Press.
5. Lauzen, M., Martha. (Ph.D). (2011) It's a Man's (Celluloid) World: On-Screen Representations of Female Characters in the Top 100 Films of 2011. It's a man's world exec summit, 2011.
6. Andrew, Dudley (New Foreword). (2005) What Is Cinema, Vol I by Andre Bazin". University of California Press ltd. London. Pg. Xiii
7. Devi, Ahanthem, Anita. (2012) Repetition of Manipuri Women's Tattered Existence? Shanghai Express. 25 january 2012. [Online] Available from http://e-pao.net/epSubPage Extractor.asp?src=features.Spotlight_On_Women.Repetition-of-Manipuri-Women-Tattered-Existence [Accessed on: 20th June 2013]
8. *Lhalih jaan* (Full moon night). (1996) Film. Directed by Letthang Doungel. [VHS] Niso Films Presentation.
9. *Ngaidam* (Forgiveness). (1992) Film. Directed by Letthang Doungel. [VHS] Niso Films Presentation.
10. *Kum Som Kilungset* (Ten years of love). (1994) Film. Directed by Letthang Doungel. [VHS] Niso Films Presentation.
11. *Heno Nei Ngailou Hitam* (Mother, don't you love me anymore). (2000) Film. Directed by Letthang Doungel. [VHS] Niso Films Presentation.

Chapter 12

Changing Pattern of Marriage System among the Thadou-Kukis of Manipur

Arfina Haokip

Introduction

Marriage is a legally recognized union between a man and a woman in which they are united sexually, cooperate economically, and may give birth to adopt or rear children (Kaur and Chhikara, 2006, p.3). Due to the changing needs of the people in a dynamic society the purpose, motives, and functions of marriage have kept on changing and evolving with the demand of its constituent member. In the Thadou-Kuki society marriage is a lifelong commitment between wife and husband. It is an act of finding a soul mate and a fulfillment of the purpose of life for both men and women without which both gender are considered a complete human being. Even with modernity, both gender, more so in the case of women, who married late are the subject of much discussion and sometimes scorn in the society.

In the past, the institution of marriage in the society was more a negotiation and coming together of two families, but now it is entirely at the discretion of the individual concern. The most common reason cited as the function of marriage are: social security, physical security, need for belonging to a husband or home and children to fulfill one's sacred and social duty, for mutual love to mutual companionship, material comforts, satisfaction of emotional and physical needs etc. The introduction of Christianity and the spread of education closely followed by modernization of the society have also affected changes in the marriage system of the Thadou-Kuki of Manipur. The present work tries to analyze the changing patterns and ideologies of the concept of marriage in the present Thadou-Kuki society in order to bring out the position of the women.

(1) Contextualising the concept of Marriage

Although social scientist felt that it was not easy to define the institution of marriage, we would examine some of the definitions of marriage. According to Westermarck, "marriage is a relation of one or more men to one or more women which is recognized by custom or law and involves certain rights and duties both in case of the parties entering the union and in case of children born of it... marriage always implies the right of sexual intercourse"(Westermark, 1921, p.1). Stephens considers marriage as a "socially legitimate sexual union... it is assumed with a more or less explicit marriage contract, which spells out reciprocal rights and obligations between spouses, and between the spouses and their future children" (Stephen,1963, p.5). Linton has defined marriage as "a socially recognized union between persons of opposite sex" (Linton,1936, p.173).

The ideology of marriage among the Thadou-Kuki simultaneously differs and run parallel to the Hindu and Muslims ideology of marriage. Marriage is necessary in the life of a Hindu because of the following reasons: (1) marriage is a religious sacrament and it is indissoluble, (2) he cannot enter the stage of a householder (grihastha asrama), (3) there can be no offspring (without a son, release from the chain of Moksha or the chain of birth-death-rebirth is not possible) and (4) it has been designated as the body sanctifying ritual which every Hindu has to perform (Majumdar et al, 2002, p.81).Unlike the Hindus, marriage for the Muslims is more of a civil contract rather than a religious sacrament. The similarity between both types of marriage is that it put the women in a very precarious and vulnerable position. There are practices like sati, dowry, child-marriage etc. in Hinduism and practices like polygamy and Talaq system (where divorce is easily obtained by men) in Islamism. The essay tries to understand the case of the Thadou-Kuki society. How does marriage system define the status and role of Thadou-Kuki women? There are changes in the Hindu marriage and Muslim marriage today where women are empowered to re-marry and sati and child marriage are banned by the Indian constitution. What are the changes brought about by the advent of Christianity in the Thadou-Kuki society? In order to understand this, let us first discuss the traditional system of marriage in the Thadou-Kuki society.

(2) Marriage System in the Thadou-Kuki society

Marriage is considered as one of the most vital duties in the life of a man and a woman among the Thadou-Kukis. It is the first step to the establishment of sexual relationship between a married couple as husband and wife or a web of mutual relationship to provide for the procreation and upbringing of offspring. Marriage is an institution which leads to the social recognisition of both the partners involved as also an arrangement for building a network of social relationships in the society. Spinsters are generally looked down by the society.

William Shaw mentioned four type of marriage among the Thadou-Kuki i.e *Chongmu (mou), Sahapsat, Jollha (h)* and *Kijammang* (Shaw, 1929, p.57).

(a) Chongmou

Chongmou (cross cousin) marriage is the most preferred and the most expensive form of marriage associated with the marriage of mother's brother's daughter called "*Nei*' or '*Neinu*'. When the parents find that their son has attained marriageable age, they discuss about his marriage. Once it is finally decided to go ahead with marriage proposal to a girl of their choice, the parents of the boy discussed it with their family's *Becha* and *Tucha*. In the Thadou society, there are three sets of relatives- the *tucha,* the *becha* and the *songgao*[1] who play an important role and constitutes the strongest strand in the fabric of the constitution of the society. These relatives are possible mainly because of the practice of marriage of mother's brother daughter or *'neinu'* by way of preference (Gangte, 1993, p. 46). A *Tucha* is selected amongst the father's sister's family, sister's family or daughter's family known in the local terminology as *'pu-te'* family (ibid, p. 52). The *'Becha'* is termed as a representative or spokesperson who has been vested with the full power and authority of an ego (ibid, p. 52). It is not mandatory for a *'becha'* to be chosen from amongst one relative or be a product of marriage alliance. They can be also be selected from one-clan members, a close friend or any person with the ability to shoulder the responsibilities required of the title (ibid).The boy's parents, their *Becha* and *Tucha* went to the girl's parents with their pot of rice beer known as *Ju bel* to ask the hand of the girl. They offer a *Ju* to the girl's family, and if the girl's parents agreed to it, they will drink the *Ju* but if not, they will not drink but instead they offer back their *zu* to the boy's family. Their acceptance and non-acceptance of the marriage proposal is not spoken in word. In the event of acceptance of the proposal a second visit is agreed upon and a date is fixed. As was done earlier the boy's family offer *Ju bel* to the girl's family. At this stage village Chief is invited by the girl's family and thus the proposal for the marriage negotiation becomes public.

During the third visit, the boy's parents is accompanied by their *Becha, Tucha* and the Chief of the boy's village come to the house of the girls parent for the final round of negotiation. At this negotiation they settle the terms and conditions of the marriage as to how much bride price has to be taken by the bride's family and fixed the date for the marriage. Once the terms and conditions are accepted, the next morning the boy's parent kill one mithun in the house of the girl. This is called *Sum-Tan-Sa*. It is a kind of witness meat for the consummation of the marriage negotiation (Gangte, 1993, p.81). Once this ritual is performed the negotiating parties are bound to adhere to the terms and conditions merely agreed upon. Any breach of the terms and conditions by any one of the parties result in imposition of penalties (Goswami, 1985, p.33). The penalty is to killed one mithun by the parties who breached the negotiation (Misao,1970, p.69).

If there is death in either of the families of the negotiating parties the negotiations have to begun afresh from the first stage. If no misfortune happened, the bridegroom's party comes on the fixed date at the bride's house. They come along with the people or friends of the groom's family. Along with them they bring bride price and a pot of rice beer as a token of gratitude and also for showing respect (Gangte, 1993, p.81). After the arrival of the groom party wrestling bouts and other merry making took place. At night the bridegroom's *Becha* and *Tucha* present the price and other articles to the bride's family. After satisfying with the presentation ceremony, the bride family prepared for the send-off in the next day. On the send-off day, the bride's family killed the pigs and a mithun. One of the killed animals is cut into halves to be taken to the bridegroom's house. This is called *'Sahap'* or *'Chanu sa'* (Gangte,1993, p.82).

Before departing from her natal family, the bride family presents a gift to their daughter. Such gift to the daughter at the time of her marriage is called *'sumken'* or *'thilken'*. This is equivalent to the term 'bride-price' or 'bride-wealth' as against the dowry gift in Hinduism. "Both bride price and dowry involve the transmission of property between the two families linked by marriage (Randeria et al, 2005, p57)". They differ in terms of the direction of gift giving. Bride price is considered to be transmission of goods from the kin of the groom to the kin of the bride where as dowry is technically referred to as the groom price where there is transmission of goods from the kin of the bride to the kin of the groom (ibid). The definition of brideprice or bridewealth is best put forward by Srimati Basu, "...Levi-Strauss argued that women and bridewealth were the most significant of 'gifts' exchanged between cultural groups, and delineated marriage as the site where the gift of women traveling in one direction and bridewealth traveling in a counter direction was put into play between groups, the combination helping to cement intergenerational exchange" (Basu, 2005, p.v).

The following are the Bride price or *Man* of some major Thadou-Kuki clan (Crawford, 1984, p.2-3).

Clan	Price
Doungel, Sitlhou	10 Mithun
	2 Large gongs
2 White gongs	
	2 Ear beads
2 Necklaces	
Singson	15 Mithun
Haokip and Kipgen	10 Mithun
2 Gongs	
2 Necklaces	
2 Ear beads	
Chongloi and Hangsing	7 Mithun
1 Gong	
1 white gong	
1 Bead	
1 Necklace	

If 30 Mithun is the bride price for the Singson, there will be no other items like gongs, beads and necklaces (Gangte, 1993, p.95).

The gifts to the bride consist of:-

1) A female mithun-*Selpi Khat*

2) A female attendant-*Soh Numei* (This is only for the Chief's daughter)

3) One big gong-*Dahpi Khat.*

4) A bamboo comb and hair oil

5) A bamboo basket (Goswami,1885, p.48)

6) A big basket

7) A small basket meant for sowing seeds

8) A hoe

9) *Sumbel* or pot usually made of copper

There are certain social norms that the married lady has to follow.

1) Ideally the bride should leave her parent's house before sunrise. This timing is dependent on the type of marriage performed. For *Chongmou* she leaves after sunrise, and for *sahapsat* she leaves before sunrise (Chongloi, 2013).

2) The priest gives the last rite of farewell to the girl by letting her sit in the middle of the house where the main pillar of the house stands.

3) When she is about to cross the door of her parent's house, she crosses the door with her left leg first (Gangte,1993, p.84). The reason behind this act is to indicate that, the girl once she left her natal home ought not to think in terms of coming back via divorce or dispute with her spouse and from that day onward think of her conjugal home as her real home (ibid).

After arriving at the bridegroom's house, marriage ceremony is performed the same day. The bride opens the door with her right hand and enters the house by first placing her right foot across the threshold (Goswami, 1985, p.56). "The priest lets the boys and girl sits together in the middle of the house called '*sutlai*'. They are made to sit on their legs, the priest too sit in the same fashion facing them with one cook in his hand. He then begins to tie up each string made of cotton called *'sa aw'* separately around their necks with one knot each. Thereafter, he takes the ends of both the string of the boy and girl and holds them together and starts propitiating. In doing so, he uses ginger. After completion of all propitiations, he ties the second knot separately one after another; with this the marriage ceremony is formally close (Gangte, 1993, p.86-87)." After the marriage is solemnized, the couple assumes their role as husband and wife in the society.

On this occasion several pots of rice beer are served to the entire guest. The bride offers the boiled rice and meat to the guest. Various sorts of entertainment will be held on this day. The bride, with the help of her mother-in- law, presents what she brought from her home to the family member of the grooms. She also presents necklaces and woven clothes to the relative of the bridegroom family. Many a time this is the place where many disgusting scene happened. If the gift is not attracting, especially in the eyes of the groom's aunt, they immediately create a scene that she is not expecting to get this and should be replaced by another. If it is replaced and satisfied it is okay but if not, it becomes one of the main causes of family discord. According to the groom's aunt, is she is not given a gift worthy enough it is considered an insult. Sometime in order to avoid such scene all the groom's aunt are allowed to choose the gift which should be presented to the family relative.

The bride's first visit to her natal home after her marriage is very important. For this visit a date is fixed and certain rituals are observed. This first visit of the bride to her natal home is called *'sulle'* or *'kituine*h' and the ritual is called *'thing khosuh,'* till such time the bride cannot take food, nor can she drink even water in her natal home.

(b) Sahapsat Marriage

This form of marriage is also done through negotiation. *Chongmou* and *Sahapsa*t is more or less similar except on the following points.

1) In *Sahapsat* marriage after two rounds of negotiation the marriage agreement is finalized.

2) Only one pig is killed whereas one Mithun and three pigs are killed in the *Chongmou* type of marriage.

3) In *Sahapsat,* the practice of bringing boiled rice and boiled meat in a basket is not observed.

4) The bride must leave her parents house before sunrise where as in *Chongmou f*orm, the bride may leave her parents house three or four hours after sunrise and reached the house before sunset.

5) The bride is not provided female attendant as in the case of *Chongmou* system (Goswami, 1985, p.63-64).

(c) Jollhah

In Jollhah marriage, there is no negotiation for marriage. This form of marriage takes place in certain exceptional exigencies. Sometimes it so happen that the girl's parents are reluctant to give their daughter in marriage to a particular boy even when the parents of the boy are very eager to get the girl as their daughter-in-law. In such case the boy's parent contrive to take away the girl to their home without her parent's knowledge. The girl is then married to the boy. Sometime *Jollha* marriage happens when the girl chosen has an unmarried elder sister. This is because in the Thadou-Kuki custom, unless the elder sister is married the younger cannot be given in marriage (Goswami, 1985, p.68). In case if a boy married the younger sister leaving one or two elder unmarried sister, the boy has to pay one mithun for one sister. This penalty is called *Unu-dalhah-man.* Also sometime this type of marriage happen when the boy family did not like to indulged in the long process of marriage negotiation due to certain circumstances like poverty, pride of the girl's parents, then the boys parent would asked the girl directly, and if the girl agreed to it, they would take the girl as their bride (Sitlhou, 1967, p.127).

(d) Kijammang/elopement

The fourth type of marriage is *kijammang* or marriage by elopement. When a boy and a girl fall in love and their parents or one of them raise strong objection to union, then the boy and girl resorted to elopement. Sometimes it so happen when the boy impregnates the girl, in order to hide their clandestine affair they resorted to *kijammang*.

In the last two forms of marriage the parents or relatives of the boy immediately go to the house of the girl to inform the girl parents of the misdeeds of the lovers. For this they carry a jar of *Ju* with them. This is called *'kiphon'* or declaration. This is done with the aim of apologising to the girl's parents with a request to condone the mistake committed by their son and also to give their daughter in marriage to the boy. If the girl's parents agreed a day is fixed for further negotiation regarding the bride price, and after the agreement a further date is fixed for the boys parent and their relative to come. On this day the boy's parents come with the bride price and a jar of *Ju* along with the bride. This is called *'in lut'* (Gangte, 1993, p.90).

There are other forms of marriage practice by the Thadou-Kuki but are not popular among them.

(e) Doithugop

In this form of marriage, a person engages a magician to corrupt the intellects and mentality of an unwilling person. The magician chant incantations upon an edible item or rice beer and give it to the girl who subsequently come under the spell and ultimately gives her consent for marriage (Haokip, 2006, p.92) However this method is not always successful as seen in the folk love story of *Khupting* and *Ngambom*. *Khupting* and *Ngambom* is a legendary story in the folktales of the Kukis. Though both of them were in love, the mother of *Khupting* was opposed to the marriage. In order to change the circumstance in his favour, *Ngambom* use magical spell on *Khupting* by pulling off a strand of hair from *Khupting's* head.

He then collected some sediments of honey or beeswax called *Khoigip* and moulded the wax into a small statue and sticks the piece of hair on its head. *Khupting* became terribly ill. When he removed Khupting's hair, she would recover from her illness. *Ngambom* kept doing this for a period of time hoping that *Khupting* parents would eventually consent to the marriage. One day, there was a heavy downpour and the statue was carried away by the river. *Khupting* died and *Ngambom* could not do anything to save her beloved *Khupting* from death (Goswami,1985, p.368-369).

(f) Guhmang/Pumtho

It means marriage by kidnapping the unwilling party. In many instances, it is the groom party who forcibly captures the chosen maiden. This often is the result when either of the girl and parents of the girl do not agree for the union (Haokip, 2006, p.92).

(g) Monogamy and Pologamy/*Jikop*

Although monogamy is the common practice of marriage in the Thadou-Kuki society, there are also cases of polygyny which is the social arrangement in which social norms allow the husband to keep more than one spouse at a time. The main reason for having more than one wife is often due to inability of the wife to conceive. Another reason is that if a man is rich enough and had capacity to give bride price. The chief of the village can take anyone as his rightful wife in traditional Thadou-Kuki society. However, polyandry is prohibited and the wife is to commit herself to her husband even if he is impotent or ill treats his wife.

(h) Dana (ill-fated marriage) Levirate

Uthinaodana and *Naothi udana* is senior and junior levirate practice. The Thadou Kuki practices both senior and junior levirate marriage but it is not popular in the society. *Uthinaodana* is a form of marriage in which a man is to marry his deceased elder brother's wife and *Naothi udana* is the reverse form of *Uthinaodana* (Haokip, 2006, p.93). Soppitt also mentions that "A man if not married, is bound to marry the widow of a deceased brother (Soppitt,1893, p.14)." However, a widow is free to remarry other man other than her deceased husband's elder or younger brother. But it is not a general rule. It depends wholly on the decision of the widow and her deceased husband's brother (s). If a widow remarries, her bride price is reduce to half of her original price at the time of her first marriage (Misao, 1970, p.41). A widower can also marry his deceased wife's sister. But this form of marriage is not popular or obligatory.

***(i) Kong lo* (Marriage by probation)**

Probationary marriage was practiced in the traditional Thadou society. "They permit a young man to live with his sweetheart in the latter's house for weeks together, after which, if they so decide, they marry each other. In case the couples do not find each other's temperament to be suitable and compatible, they separate, and the young man pays cash compensation to the girl's parents (Majumdars et al, 2002, p.75)." When a man fancies a lady, he offers *Ju* (rice beer) to her parents and discusses the matter with them. If they agreed to accept him as their son-in-law, the boy has to stay with the prospective in-law and render necessary help by working in and around the house and also in the jhum fields. After the end of the stipulated period he is allowed to marry the girl. However, he still has to remain for another two years in order to ascertain the ultimate approval of the girl's family. After five years, he is free to build a separate house and start life on his own (Soppitt, 1893, p.14-15). In case of any breach of the contract before marriage vows, the defaulter has to pay a heavy penalty.

(J) Jolgai

Jolgai is the case of pregnancy out of wed-lock; the partners involved are obliged by social norms to marry. But there are certain social prescriptions as to how to go about it so that such activities are not encouraged in the society. If the boy remains aloof after seducing her, the girl goes and stays with him disregarding opposition from the boy's parents (Haokip. 2006, p.93). If he refused to marry her, he should pay a fine of one mithun to the girl's parent or her next-of-kin (Misao, 1970, p.63). He should also pay a mithun after three years and claimed his child, for meeting the management or the cost of child maintenance. It is called *Chavahman* (ibid, p.64). The child that is born in this unwanted fashion is called '*kholaicha*' of 'children of the community' also used to refer to cases in which the father of the child refused to claim responsibility over the child. However, if the couple marries without any hassles, the misdeed is forgotten in course of time.

(3) Bride Price

Bride price or *man* is a must in all type of marriage mentioned above. *Man* or bride price consists of seven to ten mithuns depending on the clan of the bride. *Lutom* (clothes for the bride's father), *laisui* (clothes for the bride's mother), *dahpi* (large gong), *dahbu* (set of trio gongs), *khichang* (ear ring made of cornelian beads), *khichong* (necklaces made of cornelian beads) (Shaw,1929, p.59). Bride price among the Thadou-Kuki is a socially accepted norm. It is never regarded as trading of woman, but rather compensating the family for parting with a daughter, symbolizing a new relationship between the two families (TJ, 1976, p.105-136). The central idea behind this custom is to act as a reminder to the groom's family that the new bride has her own family background and that they cannot ill-treat her (Gangte, 1993, p.95). This ideal is further evident by the way bride price is paid. The bride price is never paid in full at once at the time of wedding. The rest is paid in easy instalments for more than twenty years or so. The underlying motive is to compensate the girl's parent for the loss of their daughter who was an asset to the family both in cultivation and household work. Thus, the practice of paying bride price indicates that girls are precious and are economically viable.

In all marriage negotiation, the family *Becha* and *Tucha* play important roles. The *Becha* is the person upon whom a family has absolute confidence and given the charge of all the social functions as also liaisons with other families is negotiated (Goswami, 1985, p.19). Thus, *Becha* of one's family performs the jobs of a general manager of the family shouldering the managerial responsibilities in all social functions of the family. A man's *tucha* will be his sister's son or father's sister son, whereas mother's brother or mother's son is his *songgao* (Das, 1985, p.51). The *tucha* of the family will do all the necessary work of the family activities relating to marriage, birth and death. At the time of marriage negotiation, *becha* will speak on behalf of the boy's father and the *tucha* will carry the rice beer pot and serve the *Ju.*

(4) Kida or Kikhen (Divorce)

Once married, no divorce is allowed except for adultery and even in this case, if there be children, it is rarely resorted to (Soppitt,1893, p.15). If the husband divorces without proper reasons, a mithun is fined as a divorce price or *daman* (Misao,1970, p.38). If the divorce is initiated by the wife, all the paid bride-price or *man* except *sum-tan-sa* must be returned to the aggrieved husband. In the case of barrenness, divorce is done on mutual understanding, only half of the price is returned to the wife family (ibid). It is customary for the husband to call back his wife if she ran away from him. If he does not do so then it is obviously a case for *Kikhen* or *kida* and forfeiture of bride-price or *man* (Shaw,1929, p.63). If she refuses to return in spite of the request to do so, then *man* is returnable to the aggrieved husband (Crawford,1984, p.7). As far as divorce is concerned women were simply the victims of men's decision (Kipgen,1982, p.24). Because, divorced woman is not allowed to take her children with her, she has to leave her children and any property she may have. The case is similar to the widow, if the widow is to re marry another man; she has to leave her children and any property she acquired with her late husband to the relative of her deceased husband. Therefore, Thadou-Kuki women find it difficult to be separated from their children and opted to stay back with her husband and endure the humiliation she suffer from her husband. Thadou-Kuki widows are also in the same situation; if she has a son, it was thought to be proper to remain in the house of the deceased husband and look after her son and his interests. But if she has only female issue at the time of her husband's death, all the properties should go to the next of kin of the husband (Misao,1970, p.41). Thus customary law of divorce among the Thadou-Kuki favours men and gives privileges to men by promoting traditional gender roles (Kipgen, 2010, p.85). Although, there is space for women to end the marriage, Thadou-Kuki women hardly resorted to divorce since they are the one who suffer the most. Despite this, they are condemned or disdained by the society and sometime even disown by their family.

(5) Mate Selection

For the Thadou-Kukis, the most suitable age for a boy is between twenty to thirty years; for a girl between fifteen to twenty years. The society has certain guidelines for marriages. This is knowledge is passed down from one generation to the next. Formal rules are concerned with the proscriptive, prescriptive, and preferential stipulation. The proscriptive rules include instructions on inappropriate mates or whom one should not marry. The society is endogamous in the original sense of the term. They practice both village and clan endogamy. However, exogamy was maintained at the sub clan level (Das,1985, p.47) and no marriage with outside their groups, religion and race are advisable. Although marriages with the mother's brother's daughter (MBD) are the most preferred mate for the son, marriage with father's sister's daughter (FSD) (*tunu*) is regarded as taboo and regarded as incest. The question of marrying any girl from father's side does not arise except if the distance of this relationship is no less than three generations (ibid). Also marriage with one's direct blood relation is prohibited. The prohibited marriage for a Thadou-Kuki male are as follow: his mother or grandmother; his daughter or granddaughter; his sister whether full or consanguineous or uterine; his niece and his great niece; his aunt or great aunt; one's wife's mother or grandmother; his sister's daughter (Misao,1970,p.37).

The preferential rules determine the closest possible relative as the most desirable mates. The closest relative in this regard is cross cousin (MBD) marriage and this cannot be incestuous as the bride belongs to her father's lineage. Those who don't have cross-cousins as favoured mates are considered unlucky. This kind of mate is so favoured that they go even to the extent of engaging a new born baby girl by undergoing the ceremony of '*kikhaokhi*'. This is done with the idea that, when the girl reaches the marriageable age, she should be given in marriage to her father's sister's son. The practice is more or less an obligation on both sides (Das, 1985, p.47). Marriages to such close relatives are believed to strengthen the relationship between brothers and sisters. This also considerably reduces the chance of conflict in marriage too. Conflicts arise from failure to abide by obligations involved in affinal kinship. When cross cousin is not available efforts are made to find out a suitable bride from a mother's side (Das,1985, p.47).

In selecting a mate for the boys, the boy's parents are chiefly concerned with certain consideration. The qualities of a girl to which the boy's parents give prominence are: good physique which the Thadou-Kuki consider as beautiful and healthy. Because it is believe that such girl could work hard in the fields and house. If she is a good tillers of the soil she is a good match (Carey and Tuck,1896, p.189). Girls are sometime enquire how quickly and thoroughly she can clear a hillside of weeds or how long it takes her to plants a patch of millet (Carey and Tuck,1896,p.190). Another attribute was their skill on the spinning wheel and loom. Girls had to be proficient in the pros and cons, the ins and outs of the art (Nunthara, 1996, p.87). These things are taken into consideration because housewife is supposed to shoulder the economic responsibility of the family. Unless the girl is hard working and strong, she could not shoulder all the responsibilities of the family. Other important criterion is that the girl should always be younger than the boy. The idea is that, the wife has to bear and rear the children, in shouldering economic responsibilities of the family and in maintaining a level of happiness of which the subservience of woman to man and younger to older is practical. Unless the bride is younger than the groom, this ideal cannot be realized. There are two unique ways of testing the girl's personality while considering a suitable mate for the son. First, they see that the girl urine does not flow too much forefront or backpack for such girl would disintegrate her husband's family or her parental home. Second, the breast of the girls is closely watched. They prefer pointed breast or broad breast than those of hanging type (Haokip, 2006, p.91).

Virginity of the girls is also considered. The honour of a girl involves sexual chastity. Once this is lost it cannot be regained. If the lost of virginity of a girl becomes known, no one of the appropriate group will come forward to marry her. The Chief would never consider his subject of the village as his daughter-in-law; he would consider only the daughter of the other village Chief and also the daughter of his *Semang-Pachong* or council of minister. Never would he consider the son or daughter of the widow or the poor as their daughter-in law or son-in-law. There are many tales of folklores of love between the son of the Chief and the daughter of the widow or Chief's subject. Thus, the boy's family prefers girls of equal economic and social status. The parents are also careful in selecting their daughter or son's mate in order to prevent the inclusion of a type of social outcast called *'Kao'* or *'Kaose'*, or person possessed by evil spirit (Carey and Tuck,1896, p.200). They are excluded and are not allowed to attend the community feast or if attended, they are allowed to have first. The girl from affluent family is also not preferred by a poor family for fear that she would look down on her husband family.

The Thadou-Kukis also considers certain attributes of a boy in choosing a husband. One of the qualities of a boy that are considered important are: good physique, industriousness and hard working nature as to ensure that he is able to support a family. Economic and social statuses of the boys are also considered by the girl's parents. But, they put more emphasis on the individual character of the boy.

(6) Courtship

Courtship usually took place at *Som in* or young men dormitory. The dormitory has a separate place for girls and boys. If one particular boy belonging to her *Som* is attracted a girl, he helps her family in all possible ways including cultivation to prove himself worthy of the lady he likes (Gangte,1993, p.140). The *Som* boys would accompany her to the field and at night, the boy would sit beside the girls while weaving cloths. The girl would sometimes have many suitors after her and she is to choose among them. Wooing between the boy and the girl took place at the residence of the girl in the evening. The boys and girls used to communicate in a meaningful folk. There is no restriction of boy courting girl at night.

(7) Some Aspects of Change in the Marriage System

British administration, the advent of Christianity and introduction of education caused changes in the pattern of marriage system in Thadou-Kuki society. The type of marriage system followed by the Thadou-Kukis still remains the same except the discontinuation of wrestling bout and other merrymaking at the time of marriage. These are replaced by singing of Christian songs in *Chongmou* and *Sahapsat* type of marriage. Social gathering is often hosted by the groom's family at the night of the marriage day. In this social gathering all sort of entertainment like singing of love songs by popular singers of the community and other entertainments are organized by the youths of the village. Usually, it goes on till late at night. In towns and urban areas, this practice has stopped altogether. An effort was also made to minimize the number of animal killed at the time of marriage or to substitute with tea and snacks. Instead of taking pot of rice beer, a tea pot *(Chabel)* is being served during the negotiation of marriage. The role of priest is being taken over by the church pastor who officiates the marriage ceremony following the religious tenets laid down by the doctrines of the particular church in which the couple choose to get married. However, there is a remarkable change in the wedding dress. In olden days the bride and bride groom wear the traditional dress but this has changed after the acceptance of Christianity by the Thadou-Kukis in which western wedding gowns and suit and a tie have become popular.

However, with modernization marriage system gradually came to be modified or rather simplified. The first two type of marriage viz. *Chongmou* and *Sahapsat* became corrupted and are taken as the same. People generally used *Chongmou*, which was associated with the marriage of a son marrying the mother's brother's daughter, but today all the negotiation type and arrange marriage type is regarded as *Chongmou* type of marriage. The use of the word *Sahapsat* started diminishing and gradually died down. The formalities followed in marriage arrangements have been modified to adjust to the changing times. For example the rule of visiting the bride's house three times for marriage negotiation is sometimes followed, and sometime it depends on the negotiating parties. Moreover, the bride can leave her parental house at any time of the day in an informal way. The traditional ritual priest has lost significance in the marriage rites today.

The church took an important role in trying to simplify the process of marriage negotiation and an effort was made to do away with the bride price and other expensive presentation done at the time of marriage but this has not met with much success (Vaiphei,1997, p.185). The reason behind the curtailment by the church authorities is that following all the traditional practice has become an expensive and irrelevant affair in the present day. It was also thought that the long procedure of negotiation, high bride price often leads to many cases of elopement which is not favoured by the society. The church often organized a youth camp on the theme 'Holy Marriage'. Kuki Inpi, the socio-political apex body of the Kukis, from time to time dictate the general rules on bride price. They also fixed the amount of bride price, but uniformity is lacking in the Kuki society. At the end of the day, it depends on the agreement between the two families concern. The church too strongly advocates minimization of the amount of bride price as a result of which the bride price has changes in the present day. Value and the amount had changed, but the principle and practice has been retained firmly in the Thadou- Kuki society (Vaiphei,1997, p.186). "The Christian marriage Act 1872, lays down elaborate procedure for the solemnization of marriages. Three sets of authorities are provided for the solemnization of marriage, viz, minister of religion, marriage registrars and person licensed to solemnized marriage"(Diwan,2008, p.54). The procedure of notices of the intended marriage, publication of notice and a declaration by one of the parties to the marriage as essential procedural requirements are being followed by the Thadou-Kuki before the wedding. However, this type of requirement is essential only for the *Chongmou* or negotiation or arrangement type of marriage. Yet, the contractual nature of the Christian Marriage Act of 1872 is something that Thadou-Kuki marriage is not bound with it because marriage among the Thadou-Kuki is still regarded as a sacred union that a couple enter into. In the case of divorce, there is still continuity in the traditional practice and is still not encouraged in the society.

With the introduction of cash and the dwindling of mithun (*Sel*), bride prices are paid in terms of certain amount of cash or are replaced by buffaloes. Cash payment becomes more popular than fictitiously taken buffaloes as mithun. Sometime, one mithun is fictitiously fixed to Rupees ten or more during the British period. Subsequently increases in course of time. Nowadays, it becomes 10,000 to 20,000 for one mithun. The traditional customary apex body of the Kukis, the Kuki Inpi and church leaders made a conscious effort to fix the amount of cash for one mithun, but so far there is no unanimous decision. It is still depends on the whims of the family concern. *Lutom. Laisui, Khichong, Khichang* continue as it is in the past,and *Dahpi* and *Dahbu (gongs)* are replaced by a big pot preferably made of copper or cash fixed by the bride's family, but some insist the giving away of the real *Dahpi* and *Dahbu* which is an expensive affair.

With the change of the mode of payment of bride price, there are also changes of *'Sumken'* or *'Thilken'*, gift to the daughter at the time of marriage. Traditional gift like *Tucha* (Hoe), *Thilbu* (weaving implement), *Lel* (storing basket) are no longer hold much significance. They are also considered irrelevant as the Kukis in general have shifted to other means of livelihood other than farming. Gifts to the daughter become more elaborate, comprising of modern amenities of life and assets such as land, gold jewellery, vehicles, furniture etc. In fact, rich families are fond of giving lavish gifts to their daughters in order to show their wealth and status. This is also done with the intention of assuring that the daughter would be respected and treated well in the groom's family. This has led to a condition similar to the problems of dowry in which the girl's family is reduced to poverty. Thus, the value of the goods given by the bride's family to the bride and groom's family is several times more than that of the goods offered by the groom's family to the brides. Another similarity of the arrangement with the dowry system under Hinduism is that it is done because of the desire of the parents to have educated and employed bride grooms for their daughter.

The practice of *Sum-Tan-Sa* or the witness meat which was done after the negotiation of the marriage is also discarded in some area, but in some area it is still a compulsion. In the modern society, there is no hard and fast rule that one has to wait for harvesting as was considered as the most appropriate time for marriage. As regard the venue of the marriage, it happens in the church in which the groom's family has membership. The church pastor recommends the grooms for his eligibility of holy marriage and thus marriage is solemnized according to Christian principle. In *Kijammang* type of marriage, there is no send-off ceremony and no marriage ceremony is performed in the church. However, now send-off type of ceremony is being done at the time of *'In Lut'* or house entering day. Many relative and people were invited, many animal were killed and presented the girls with many gift, nothing less than the send-off of the bride in the negotiation type of marriage. Some people are of the view that if these trends continued, a time would come that there will be no different between the *Chongmou* or negotiation type of marriage and the *Kijammang* or elopement type of marriage (Letthang, 2012). The role and importance of *Becha* and *Tucha* remain the same even after Christianity and modernity. In fact this relationship is deeply rooted in the Thadou-Kuki society.

(a) Mate Selection

On the question of mate selection, questionnaire is distributed to six respondents from each group. One group represents the parents, 2) employed boy of above 28-38 year of age and 3) unemployed, 4) employed girls of above 25-35 years of age and 5) unemployed. The minimum qualification of the respondent is 10+2 or higher secondary school level.[2]

In mate choose by the elders, numerous ideal group interests come into play; the reputation of the girl, whether she can manage the family, love the family member, for that they still prefer their near relative who is known to them for a long time not necessarily mother's brother's daughter or brother's sister's son. But here the parent set condition that if the brother's daughter or the sister son is not compatible educationally, they would never consider as an ideal mate. The next preference is to look from another mother's clan. Here, many criteria comes in, educational background of the girl, preferably holding a comfortable job, social and economic background of the girl's family. Although exogamous to other tribes or community is favoured, the rigidity that was in the past has no more in vogue. Girl's families also look to the educational background of the boy, preferably holding job, social and economic status of the family. However, girls family look to more on the personal character; none smoker, none drinker, not lazy, and not aggressive boys who can fulfilled social security, who can be a lifelong companionship, who can give emotional, material and physical needs of their daughter.

In the selection of a life partner, several individual motives come into play: mutual attraction and intimacy are important. However there are different motive for the youth of older age, say from the age of 28-35 years; their ways of choosing mate is considerably different from the youth of 18-27 years of age. The teenage or adolescent are attracted to more on the beauty of the girls and boy, whereas when they cross teenage, their perception dramatically change to more rational thinking about the ideal life partner. Economic security also plays an important factor in the choice of a life partner. Women in general prefer a man with a secure job as compared to one who is unemployed. The men too have their own criteria when it involved searching for a wife. The dominant choice is for a woman who is beautiful, soft-spoken, polite, submissive, educated, and younger to them. Some even take into consideration the social and family background of the girl's family. For these groups, as in Trobriander society, marriage brings economic advantage (Malinowski,1922, p.69). For fear that their wife would dominate over them, most men prefer women who are less educated or with a job of lower ranking than them. Thus, the process of mate selections has attained an ugly motive in the present generation.

Caution is also taken so that the chosen person is not involved in deviant behaviour like consuming alcohol or drugs and many couple are advised to undergo an HIV test before the marriage is agreed upon. They are regarded as the modern days *'Kao'* or *'Kaose'* (Ngainei, 2010). Courtship becomes easier than earlier. The boy and girls usually acquainted in schools, colleges, universities, etc. They date in the restaurant, park etc. Olden day courting at the house of the girls is still practice but no longer very common. The mode of courting has changed due to technology in the form of telephone, internet, mobile phone etc.

Conclusion

Marriage as an institution among the Thadou-Kuki has continually evolved since time immemorial. Along the road it has changes it forms, norms and practices. Like all institutions in the society it adjust itself to the changing times and is influenced by external factors like British Imperialism and the new religion and education system that it tags along. Changes are made when traditions is seen to hamper development or is irrelevant. Marriage is solely based on the choice of the partners involved and the network of kinship relations accommodates the decision instead of the other way round as was practice in the past.

References

BASU,SRIMATI.(2005).*Dowry and Inheritance*,New Delhi:Women Unlimited.

CAREY,BS. and TUCK,HN.(1896) *The Chin Hills*.Vol-1.Delhi:Cultural Publishing House.

CRAWFORD,CG.(1984) *Hand Book of Thadou Custom*.Imphal:Directorate for Development of Tribal and Backward Classes,Government of Manipur.

DAS,RAJAT KANTA.(1985) *Manipur Tribal Scene.New* Delhi:Inter-India Publication.

DIWAN,PARAS.(2008) *Family Law*.Delhi:Allahabad Law agency.

GANGTE,T.S.(1993) *The Kukis of Manipur:A Historical Analysis*.New Delhi:Gyan Publishing House.

GOSWAMI,TARUN.(1985) *Kuki Life and Lore*.Assam:North Cachar Hill District Council.

HAOKIP,DL.(2006) *Historical Traditions and Customary Laws of the Chassad*.Un published Ph.d Thesis,Department of History:Manipur University.

HAOLAI,THANGKIM.(2006) *Kuki Culture in North Cachar Hills*. Guwahati:Director.assam Institute of Research for Tribals and Scheduled Caste.

KAUR,PRAVEEN.AND CHHIKARA,SUDHA.(20O6) Mariage and Family in Diverse and Changing Scenario.New Delhi:Deep and Deep Publication Pvt Ltd.

KIPGEN,KHAIKHOTINTHANG.(1982) *The Thadou Kukis:A brief Account of History andCulture*.Manipur:Th Thangkhochon,Motbung.

KIPGEN,TINGNEICHONG G.(2010) *Women's Role in the 20th Century,Manipur*.Delhi:Kalpaz Publication.

MALINOWSKI, BRONISLAW. (1922) Argonauts of the Western Pacific.London:Routledge and Kegan Paul.

MAJUMDAR, DN and TN MADAN. (2002).*An Introduction to Social Anthropology*. Delhi: Mayoor Paperbacks

MIBANG,TAMO.and BEHARA,MC.(2007) Marriage in Tribal Societies (Cultural Dynamics and Realities).New Delhi:Bookwell.

MISAO,PC.(1970) History and Customs of the Thadou Kukis.Deulahland Imphal:Author.

NUNTHARA,C.(1996) *Mizoram Society and Polity*.New Delhi:Indus Publishing.

RANDERIA,SHALINI,LEELA VISARIA.(2005) 'Sociology of brideprice and Dowry' in Srimati Basu's (ed),*Dowry and Inheritance*.New Delhi:women Unlimited (Kali for women).

REDDY,K RAJA.(2001) *Dynamics of Family and Kinship*.New Delhi:Commonwealth.

RIZVI, SHH. And ROY, SHIBANI. (2006) *Kuki-Chin of Mizoram and Manipur*. Delhi: BR Publishing Corporation.

SHAKESPEAR, J. (1912) *The Lushai Kuki Clans*.Mizoram: Tribal Research Institute Aizawl.

SHAW, WILLIAM.(1929) *The Thadou Kukis*. Delhi: Cultural Publishing House.

SITLHOU, JAMKITHANG.(1967) *Thadou Puchon Pachon*.Imphal: BK Store.

SOPPITT,CA.(1893) *A short account of the Kiki-Lushai tribes on the North-East Frontier*. Mizoram: Firma-KLM Private LTD.

TJ KHOTHANG. and HK KHENTHANG. (1976) A Brief Introduction to Tribal Language and Culture of Paite. In Singh,KB. (eds).*An Introduction to Tribal Language and Culture of* Manipur. Imphal: MSKA

VAIPHEI,TH.LAMBOI.(1997) *Advent of Christian Mission and Its Impact on the Hill-Tribes* in*Manipur*.Imphal:Frontier Mission Society.

CHONGLOI, LALGIN. (2013) Impact of Christianity on the Thadou-Kuki Marriage. In HAOKIP, THONGKHOLAL. (Ed.) *The Kukis of Northeast India*. New Delhi: Bookwell.

INTERVIEW

Lhouvum, Kaitinsei (Age 50), K.Tuikun, Sadar Hills, interviewed on 10th September, 2012

Haokip, Letthang. (Age 55) Mongbung, Sadar Hills, interviewed on 25th June, 2012

[1] 1) What type of marriage do you prefer for your son/daughter and for yourself.

A) Arrange marriage

B) Love Marriage with arrange

C) Elopement

2) What is the ideal character of your mate? Arrange the qualities give in order your preference.

A) Polite

B) Soft spoken

C) Straight forward

D) Outspoken

E) Assertive

F) Humble

G) Quiet

H) Economically Independent.

3) Which one of this is given weight while selecting mate. Arrange it according to your preference.

A) Looks

B) Character

C) Educational background

D) Socio-Economic background of the family.

4) Which one of this is prefer for your mate? Arrange it according to your preference.

A) Medium education without job.

B) High education without job.

C) Holding third grade job.

E) Holding first and second grade job

5) Do you still prefer Cross cousin marriage?

Chapter 13

Language and Gender: The Linguistic Representation of Men and Women in Kuki Society

Ngaineiting Baite

Introduction

When a child is born, one of the first question that people ask is whether it is a boy or a girl. The question reflects how important the sex we belong to is, in our society, the social roles and opportunities which will be determined by our biological sex. The roles and opportunities of a person are predetermined by the society and there are certain expectations from our society depending on which biological sex we belong. And these expectations are often realized or expressed through language: from the way we use language, and from the way language is used on us. This makes us reflect about the relationship between the language we use and the world around us. It is a known and accepted fact that most languages of the world are sexist, and this, claimed by many, is because of sexism in society. The bias in sexist languages is mostly against women. Does Thadou-kuki (the language) discriminate against women? What was the reason behind the use of different languages for different genders? Is language a direct reflection of the world around us? Or, do we impose our ideas on our environment as a result of the language we have?

(1) Language

Language is the means of communication, either spoken or written, consisting of the use of words in a structured and conventional way. Not only written or spoken, speaking and hearing impaired people also communicate through sign language. The scientific study of language is called Linguistics. Language may be defined in two different ways, language in general and a language in particular. "Language (with uppercase 'L'), is the ability of humans to speak a (particular) language, it is the part of the mind or brain that allows a human being to speak; whereas, language (with lowercase 'l') is an instantiation of this, for e.g. English, French, Hindi, etc. (Carnie, 2006)".

The number of languages spoken around the world is estimated to vary between 6,000 and 7,000. There are 114 (18 Scheduled languages and 96 Non-scheduled languages) and 216 mother tongues identified within India, and these languages are found to belong mainly to four language families: Austro-Asiatic, Dravidian, Indo-European and Tibeto-Burman.

Our day to day activities involves communication. The purpose of communication depends according to the needs of individuals. Some may use it for sharing information while others may use it for building up relationships, between families or between corporations, and all these communications are carried out through the medium of language. Languages around the world differ not only in vocabulary, grammar or pronunciation, but also through having different cultures of speaking. Language is, in some way or the other, used as a way of signaling identity with one cultural group, or differences from other cultural groups. Not only that languages differ according to difference in speech communities, even among speakers of one language, several different ways of using the language may exist, and these linguistic differences may become salient markers of division between different social class, status or gender.

(2) Gender

It must be noted, first of all, that 'Gender' and 'Sex' have different meanings and usages. As noted by Goddard and Patterson (2000), "Sex is a biological condition that is defined as a set of physical characteristics, while Gender is a social construct, about socially expected characteristics. So, for instance, while possessing different physical features is about biological factors, seeing this as leading to certain forms of behavior is about gender". General usage of the term gender began in the late 1960s and 1970s, increasingly appearing in the professional literature of the social sciences. The term helps in distinguishing those aspects of life that were more easily attributed or understood to be of social rather than biological origin. "While the terms 'man' and woman' can refer to definitions based on biological differences, the terms 'masculine' and 'feminine' are always about expected gender characteristics - what men and women are supposed to be like. While 'man' and 'woman' are nouns and therefore suggest 'people', 'masculine' and 'feminine' are adjectives and suggest qualities or attribute. So, we could talk about 'masculine women' and 'feminine men' and be thinking about people who depart from the norm of what we consider appropriate for sex (ibid)".

(3) Language and Gender

"*Language and Gender* refers to the relationship between language and our ideas about men and women. 'Gender' as a term differs from 'Sex' in being about socially expected characteristics rather than biology (Goddard and Patterson, 2000)". Languages across the world are usually associated with a male world-view.

Language often reflects sexism in society. Language itself is not sexist, but it can connote sexist attitudes about social taboos or racism. English is claimed by many to be a sexist language, because they have different pronominals for male and female, for e.g. he, she, her, him; the label Mr. is used for every male, whether married or single, while the labels Miss,

Mrs, Ms are used for female, which indicates their marital status; the opposite counterparts of 'bachelor' and 'master' are 'bachelorette' and 'mistress', but these counterparts connotes negative meanings unlike the male terms.

Thadou-kuki is also a sexist language in some way or the other. The difference with the other languages is in the fact that other languages overtly mark the gender differences, like English mentioned above, but in Thadou-kuki gender differences are marked covertly, in the way it is denoted as well as connoted. The existence of sexist language is due to sexism in society. Deny it or not, everybody including men and women has a mindset that women are the weaker sex of the society, and that their existence is simply for support and nurture. "Women experience linguistic discrimination in two ways: in the way they are taught to use language, and in the way general language use treats them (Lei, 2006)".

(4) Thadou-Kuki: The Language

The language is given different names by different people. T.C. Hudson (1905), the colonial ethnographer was the first to call the language Thado, followed by the American Baptist Missionary Rev. William Pettigrew who named it Thadou, and finally the local pioneers of Manipur Longkhobel Kilong (1922) and Ngulhao Thomsong (Lekhabul, the Thadou Kuki first Primer 1927) called it Thadou Kuki, because the scholars of that time felt it necessary to add the word Kuki to indicate that the language in question is a non-Naga language. It is also usually called by the local people as Thadou *Pao* (Language). T. Lunkim in the early 1970s proposed the name of the language as Kuki, and was the first to translate the whole of the Holy Bible and identified the language as Kuki (Go, 1996, p. 81). Now, the Thadou-Kuki language is approved and prescribed by the State Government of Manipur and taken as MIL from classes IX, X till Graduation. However, the name of the language is not the concern of this essay, but the content and its use, because as the saying goes "a rose by any other name would smell as sweet".

Thadou, as recorded in the Linguistic Survey of India. Vol 3, Tibeto-Burman Family part 3 by Grierson (1903-1928), belongs to the Northern Kuki-Chin sub-group of Tibeto-Burman sub-family which in turn belongs to the Sino-Tibetan family of languages. It is spoken mainly in Manipur, Nagaland and some parts of Assam, Mizoram and Myanmar. Thadou follows the Subject-Object-Verb (SOV) word order. It is also a tonal language. "Thadou phonemic inventory consists of twenty nine phonemes, of which twenty one are consonants, eight vowels and three tones: rising (H), high falling (HL) and low falling (L) (Pauthang, 2008)".

(5) Linguistic Behaviour of Men and Women

The term Linguistic behaviour is sort of technical, so in this paper the term shall sometimes be switched to another term and call it 'conversational characteristics' wherever appropriate, so that it would give better accessibility for the layperson. Even linguistic behaviour is gendered, in a way that there are expectations from people, since earliest days, disparities in the way men and women should speak. And these disparities have been observed since time immemorial. Few of the conversational characteristics of Kuki men and women observed will be listed below, and we will go further and explain some conversational characteristics of Kuki women in particular. Here are some differences observed in the speech of Kuki men and women:

1) Men are more likely to interrupt others than women in most conversations except gossips, mostly to show power and dominance.

2) Women are more communicative than men. They tend to repair conversations after a silence.

3) Men see the purpose of conversation as information-gathering; women see it as a support mechanism, it is co-operative.

4) Men's language is mostly about status and independence; women's speech is of closeness and rapport.

5) Men do not give verbal recognition of a contribution made by women in a mixed conversation between men and women.

6) Women talk more with one another; men talk less with one another.

7) Men, if they do talk to each other, talk about work, sports, politics; women share with each other mainly for rapport

8) Men discuss temporal things; women discuss people and feelings.

9) Women gossip more than men.

10) Men speak more comfortably in public than women.

11) Men get more opportunity to speak in public than women; women get more opportunity in family matters at home.

12) Men mostly use commands; women mostly use requests and tags

13) Men contribute ideas in the form of orders; women contribute in the form of proposals.

14) Men make jokes; women do not, but rather laugh at the jokes made by men.

15) Women are more likely to frame their turns as questions in a conversation; men does not usually wait for others to finish, for their turns.

These features are not restricted to men and women in particular, the speech style of women is also observed in the language of powerless men, and that of male features in the practices of powerful women. When it comes to women's gossips, it is true to an extent that most women cannot sleep with a secret. Women are usually the source of rumours. As Coates has argued about all-women conversation building her argument on Deborah Tannen's ideas, the conversations of the Kuki women also falls under one of these categories:

a) House-talk: Women talk to each other about their female role as an occupation. The occupations of the Kuki women in the urban areas are mostly housewives, only few are government or corporate employees, while those in the rural areas play both the role of mothers as well as field laborers. They love exchanging information and resources regarding their occupations.

b) Scandals: Women tend to judge the behaviours of others, on the grounds of their domestic morality. They love talking about the private lives of others, and women in particular.

c) Bitching: Women undergo a lot of pressure in their own occupations, especially that of inferiority. But they do not complain about their anger to just anybody, they express it in private and to other women only, because they tend to understand each other. They do so not because they expect change, but to let their emotions free.

d) Chatting: Women love to indulge themselves in leisure talks, and chatting is the most intimate form of gossip. They love sharing and learning about their experiences and skills to and from each other.

(a) Epistemic Modality

When observed carefully, the speech of Kuki women seems to lack confidence and truth, since it contains lots of unnecessary sounds, or words which are not obligatory. These unnecessary sounds or words are termed in Linguistics as tags, hedges, etc. which altogether forms epistemic modals.

"Epistemic modal forms are those linguistic forms which are used to indicate the speaker's confidence or lack of confidence in the truth of the proposition expressed in the utterance (Coates, 1989)". It might also be alternatively used as a means to mitigate the force of an utterance for the sake of politeness. Since epistemic modality is commonly observed in the speech of women, some consider it as a sign of powerlessness or weakness. However, that is not true, it is used by women to save or protect both addressors' and addressees' face. Another function of epistemic modal forms is to facilitate open discussion. Epistemic modal forms are frequently used where sensitive topics are discussed. Few of the epistemic modal forms used or observed in the speech of Kuki women are discussed below in brief.

(b) Tag Questions

There is a peculiar feature that women use in most conversational situations than a man, which is called a tag-question. "Tag-question is a linguistic term used under certain contextual situation: not those in which a statement would be appropriate, nor those in which a yes-no question is generally used, but in situations intermediate between these. A tag, in its usage, is midway between an outright statement and a yes-no question: it is less assertive than the former, but more confident than the latter. A statement is made when one has confidence in what one says and is pretty certain that his statement will be believed; one asks a question when one lacks knowledge on some point and has reason to believe that this gap can and will be remedied by an answer by the addressee. A tag-question is an intermediate between these and is used when a speaker is stating a claim, but lacks full confidence in the truth of his/her claim (Lakoff, 1973)".

"Kim ahunge" Kim is coming/ Kim came		(a statement)
"Kim hung am?"	Did Kim come?	(a question)
"Kim hung chu na?	"Kim came, didn't she?	(a tag-question)

In a claim like the third, the addressor is already biased in favour of a positive answer, wanting only confirmation by the addressee. This is a very common feature found in the speech of kuki women.

(c) Intonation

Intonation is one feature which is commonly observed in the speech of Kuki women. The speech of women is more melodious than men. In Linguistics, intonation is the variation of spoken pitch, refers to the distinctive use of patterns of pitch and melody, not in the word but phrase or sentence level. In lay terms, it may be defined as the stressing of a word or words in a sentence, for instance for emphasis, to convey surprise or irony, or to pose a question. The main purpose of the use of intonation by women is for politeness, or an invitation for a response from the male participants in a conversation. Sometimes, intonation is often accompanied with few vocalizations such as short laughter or backchannel voices like *'ee...', 'umm...'*, etc. One other function of intonation is the attitudinal function, often used for expressing emotions or attitudes.

(d) Hedges

In the speech of Kuki women hedges are found in abundance. The use of these hedges may be perceived by some as a sign of powerlessness or lack of confidence, rather, it is found to be a means to facilitate open discussion, and sometimes not to offend the addressees. Hedges are words or phrases that make statements less forceful or assertive. They may also be known as uncertainty markers in a language. They are used as indirectness in a speech. Some of the common hedges used by Kuki women are:

"kagel dan a...."	(I think...)
"kaginchat dan'a..."	(I guess...)
"......hi di baha"	(...might be)

"......hile kilom (kasah)"	(...it seems)
"kaha hetchen lou, ahivanga..."	(I'm not sure, but...)

(e) Verbal Hygiene

Men and women face normative expectations about the appropriate mode of speech for their gender. Women's verbal conduct is important in many cultures. Women have been instructed in the proper ways of talking just as they have been instructed in the proper ways of dressing, in the use of cosmetics, and in other "feminine" kinds of behaviour. This acceptance of a "proper" speech style, described by Deborah Cameron as "verbal hygiene", is observed in our society. We have certain expectations of ways women of our society should speak. These are not just expectations by others, but also the linguistic behaviors of women of our society observed since years, as it has become part of our culture.

(f) Turn-taking

It is considered inappropriate for women to interrupt while men speak. Women are expected to wait for their turns. In most cases, women are expected to speak only if they are given chances, or to response to questions asked by men. If women interrupt a conversation between men, it is taken as a sign of disrespect. However, if men interrupt a conversation between women, women are expected to hold their conversation and listen to them. However, when the conversation is among women only, there is overlapping of turns amongst them. One reason for this overlapping of turns might be because, for most women, it might be the only platform where they get chances to express themselves freely, or alternatively because they want to dominate others since they are always dominated. On the other hand, in the conversations of older women, it is found the opposite. Since their main purpose of communication is for rapport, they do not interrupt each other and wait for their turns until one finishes, to show their support and encouragement.

(g) (Super) politeness

Women are expected to speak softly, in what they call 'the feminine way'. At least a small taste of melody is expected in the speech of a woman, as it is a known fact that the pitch of female's voice is higher than that of the male. If a man speaks loud, it is considered manly, but if a woman speaks loud it is considered aggressive. It is also considered inappropriate for a woman to swear, or joke.

Female children are taught since childhood to speak in a soft and low voice and not to rush words so that they can be the so called 'lady-like'. As children, women are encouraged to be little ladies. The traits expected of little ladies is that little ladies don't scream as vociferously as little boys; they are taught since childhood to sacrifice more often than boys; and they are rebuked if they throw tantrums or show temper because those are the expected traits of males.

(6) Portrayal of Men and Women in Thadou-kuki (the language)

The status of Kuki women is not only determined in the way they use language, but also in the way language is used on them. Women are portrayed as different images using adages, parables, folktales, etc. and even in our Naming system and use of Adjectives.

(a) Diminutive Marking

Woman is found to be diminutively marked in Thadou-kuki, along with children. This is an evidence of how women are considered as the weaker sex in our society. In order to explain this feature, I may be compelled to use some Linguistic terms. A diminutive is a morpheme or an affix that is added to a word to convey the meaning 'small' or 'unimportant', or to express affection. In Thadou-kuki, the diminutive marker is the morpheme '-cha'. This morpheme occurs in words like *'them-cha'* (few), *'neo-cha'* (tiny), *'chom-cha'* (very short), *'kot'* (door), *'kot-cha'* (window), etc. They intensify the smallness of the objects. This diminutive marker occurs only with woman and children but not with man. For example:

Numei cha hijongleh.... (Even if she is just a girl/woman...)

Chapang cha hijongleh... (Even if he/she is just a child/kid...)

*pasal cha hijongleh... (Even if he is just a boy/man...)

(Asterisk * stands for ungrammatical)

These words *'numei cha'* sometimes even occur with '–se' suffixed to *'numei'*, forming *'numei-se cha'*, which gives more diminutive meaning to women. According to the narration of some old people, '-se' means 'trash', as in *'nihse-ponse'* (torn clothes or patches; trash), and this was suffixed to women since women were considered to be worthless during olden days. But unfortunately, such utterances are still heard from the Kukis of the present day.

(b) Naming

To start with, let us look at some Kuki names.

Nenem ('Soft' reduplicated[1]),

Neneng ('Abundant' reduplicated),

Hoinu ('Beautiful/Pretty' + feminine marker),

Zouzam (Name of a flower),

Nunnem ('Behaviour' + 'soft'),

Hangpu ('Courageous' + masculine marker),

Thathang ('Famous' reduplicated),

Lelen ('Big' reduplicated),

Lalpu (Glorious + masculine marker),

Goulen ('Assets' + 'big'),

Gugun, ('Worth' reduplicated)

These are few names which are very common among the Kukis. By looking at the names, one is able to make out which ones are women names and which are men names. One must have thought that it's simply because of familiarity, but there is something more in it. Most people are usually ignorant about what their names actually mean until somebody belonging to other tribes or speaking other tongues asks them. It is observed from the different names given to the genders that the women names are associated with beauty, tenderness, politeness, sweetness (as few are named after flowers), while men names are associated with might, robustness, valour, etc.

(c) Teknonymy

Teknonymy is a term used for the labeling for people that identify them only through their relation to someone else. And the labels used are called teknonyms. Thadou is one language among many which uses teknonyms. One very interesting teknonym found among the Kukis is 'Hepu', which carries various relational meanings. "Among Kuki clans, 'hepu' is used for father's father; mother's father; wife's father; mother's brother's son; wife's brother; wife's brother's son. Thus, people of various age groups (generations) are designated by a single term (Majumdar and Madan, 2002)".

In every aspect of life, a woman is identified in terms of the man she relates to. Referring a woman through relational forms is very common in the Thadou-Kuki society. A girl is referred to as somebody's daughter or sister until she is married, and when she is married, she is referred to as somebody's wife, mother or grandmother. Women do not even have their own surnames, but bear that of the father until they exchange it for that of a husband. The very semantics of the language reflects women's condition. These practices of labeling de-emphasize the status of women.

Mention may also be made of the fact that in our society, as a sign of formality, parents are sometimes addressed as father or mother of the eldest son among the siblings, even though the eldest son may have a sister or sisters elder than him.

The notion of this teknonymy, the identification of women in relation to men, I believe, must have been an influence of our religion, in some way or the other. Our religion, whether it be Christianity or Judaism, accept the Old Testament. The story of Adam and Eve, and the Garden of Eden was one of the first stories from the Bible we learned as a child. The second chapter of the book of Genesis, verses 21-23, depicts how God created Eve from one of the ribs of Adam. To be more precise, let us cite from Gen. 2:23b. It reads *"she shall be called Woman, because she was taken out of Man"*, and Gen. 3:16c, which reads *"and thy desire shall be to thy husband, and he shall rule over you"* Another instance may be cited from the book of Matthew of the New Testament where the status of women is depicted. The verse from Matthew 14:21 reads *"And they that had eaten were about five thousand men, beside women and children"*. 'Men' is a generic term for human beings, yet women and children were not included in the counting. At the same time, women were considered to be in the same status with children. And these religious beliefs in turn shaped the norms of our culture, which is why women are given their identities in our society by virtue of their relationship with men. However, the Bible also depicts women in many of the parables and stories of the books as a symbol of love, source of life, and is even called a crown for her husband.

(d) Generic terms

Some names or terms which are meant to be used for both sexes are usually interpreted to indicate male alone. *'Mi'* or *'Mihem'* is a generic term for human beings; or people. However, we unconsciously sometimes use it as a male term. Let us look at some phrases or sentences I hope we all have heard or came across.

Ahung kikhom chu mihem 2000 ahi, numei le chapang simlou a.

(Two thousand people gathered, besides women and children)

Another instance may be cited from newspaper headlines:

Mi 9 kitongkha, 3 chu numei.

(Nine people injured, three of them women)

Let us again look at some professional terms like Doctor, Engineer, Nurse and Babysitter. We unconsciously associate some professional terms to belong to a particular sex. If somebody says, *"ka-U Police/Doctor ahi"* (My elder brother/ sister is a Police/Doctor), it will be assumed by everybody that the *'ka-U'* here is a male. But when it comes to professions like Nursing and Babysitting, it is assumed that the person talked about is a female. As such, we tend to use terms like *'Numei Police'* (female Police) or *'Pasal Nurse'* (male Nurse).

(e) Evaluative Adjectives

Adjectives, as everybody knows, are modifiers of noun. They attribute the noun, specifies the quality of the noun. In Thadou, there are few adjectives which are associated with female only; which would sound awkward if it occurs with a masculine noun. To mention few, adjectives like *pah silsel* ('Vibrant' + *morphological reduplication*[2] in expressives/ onomatopoeic word which gives a pleasant meaning to the colour), *nun-nem* ('Behaviour' + 'Soft'), *chon-nem* ('Character' + 'Soft'), *khoto-them* ('Considerate') are associated with feminine nouns. These adjectives just do not go right with masculine nouns, it rather sounds unrealistic. If these labels are given to a man, he will instantly be considered or thought of as a homosexual, or the so called powerless man.

(f) Colour terms

Thadou-Kuki has only five basic colour terms. They are *Avom* (black), *Akaang* (white), *Asan* (red), *A-eng* (for both green and yellow) and *Adum* (blue). The other shades of colours are termed by reduplication of the basic colour terms as in *Asan-a-san* (very red), by suffixing morphemes as in *Asan peh* (bright red), or by suffixing adjectives as in *Asan dup* (red+dark; maroon), or by using names of abstract objects as in *Vut machu/rang* ('Ash' + 'borrowed words for colour'; grey).

Like adjectives, different colour terms are also associated with men and women. Vibrant colours like pink, red, orange are called feminine colours, and associated with women, while dark and pale colours like black, grey, military colours are called masculine colours, and associated with men.

(g) Adages

An adage is a traditional saying which is accepted by many as true or partially true. It clearly shows the portrayal of women in the language since olden days. In Thadou-kuki adages, women are portrayed to be submissive and their presence or roles in the family or society are pre-empted by men. To mention few, instances are found in the very common sayings like:

'Numei le baalke alhah lhah na in apo e'.

Here, women are compared to Taro sprouts mainly because of their feature of adaptability. Taros can grow anywhere, but the capability of the Taro sprouts to procreate depends on the soil they are rooted. Taros sprouts in numbers if they are rooted in fertile soil, while it might either fail to reproduce, or produce deformed bulbs or corms if the soil is unfertile or grown in an unsuitable environment. Such is the life of women, as depicted in this adage. What the adage wants to convey is that women, like the Taro sprouts, grows anywhere but its qualities are dependent on where they are rooted. The nature of women is determined by the place or environment she is exposed to. This is another evidence of how women are considered to be the weaker sex of society, and are dependent on men, that their lives are determined and controlled by men.

'Numei leh bel kehbai'

In the olden days, pots were made of clay, and they were brittle. This adage is about the comparison of women to those brittle pots, because women get easily hurt, and easily fall a prey of empathy. So, women are portrayed as weak, emotional, empathic and vulnerable in this adage.

Conclusion

It is still unclear whether language is an influence of culture, or our use of language influence the way we perceive. However, it is universally accepted that every languages not only have different vocabulary or grammar, but also have different cultures of speaking. Even within speakers of a language, there may exist several different ways of using the language, and these linguistic differences may become salient markers of division, and one of them is gender. Most languages of the world are found to be sexist, and Thadou-kuki is also found to be covertly sexist, from the differences in the observed and expected linguistic behavior of men and women, and the portrayal of men and women in the language use. However, some of the features found in the linguistic behavior of women were earlier thought to be signs of powerlessness or weakness. But rather they are signs of politeness, not because they consider themselves as the weaker sex of the society, but to protect both the face of addressors' and addressees', to facilitate open discussions, to build up rapport. It is not a sign of weakness, but the nature of women. Therefore, the claim made by Deborah Cameron may be taken into account, that the conversations of men and women are not about being right or wrong, superior or inferior, they are just different, like differences in cultures, and she termed the languages 'Genderlects'. The fundamental differences in their linguistic behaviours arise from their purpose of communication; women have deep drive to seek connection, whilst men have a deep drive to seek status.

Notes

1. Reduplication in Linguistics is a morphological process in which the root or the stem of a word (or part) is repeated exactly or with slight change. (Wikipedia)

2. Morphological reduplication refers to the minimally meaningful and segmentally indivisible morphemes which are constituted of iterated syllables. Thus, the base and the iterated part together constitute a single morpheme, which is a lexeme (Abbi, 2001).

References

1. ABBI, ANVITA (2001). *A Manual of Linguistic Field Work and Structures of Indian Languages*, Lincom Europa.

2. CHESHIRE, JENNY and TRUDGILL, PETER (Ed.) (1998). *The Sociolinguistics Reader, Vol 2: Gender and Discourse*, Oxford University Press Inc.

3. CHESHIRE, JENNY and MEYERHOFF, MIRIAM (Ed.) (2003). *The Handbook of Language and Gender*, Blackwell Publishing Ltd.

4. FROMKINN, VICTORIA and RODMAN, ROBERT (Ed.) (1988). An *Introduction to Language*, Holt, Rinehart and Winston, Inc., Saunders College Publishing.

5. GO, KHUP ZA. (1996). *A Critical Historical Study of Bible translations among the Zo People in North East India.* Manipur: Chin Baptist Literature board.

6. GODDARD, ANGELA and PATTERSON, LINDSAY MEAN. (2000). *Language and Gender*, Routledge Publications, London and New York.

7. GRIERSON, G. A. (1903). Linguistic Survey of India Vol. III, Tibeto-Burman Family Part III, Calcutta: Government of India.

8. HAOKIP, PAUTHANG. (2008). Phonological Structure of Thadou, *South Asian Language Review*, Vol. XVIII, No. 1.

9. HOLMES, JANET. (1990). Hedges and Boosters, *Journal of Language and Communication*, Vol. 10, No. 3, pp. 185-205, 1990, Pergamon Press.

10. HOLMES, JANET. (1997). Women, Language and Identity, *Journal of Sociolinguistics* 1/2 1997: 195-233.

11. JULE, ALLISON (Ed.) (2005). *Gender and the Language of Religion*, Palgrave MacMillan Publications.

12. LAKOFF, ROBIN. (1973). *Language in Society: Language and Women's Place, Vol.* 2, Number 1, pp. 45-80, Cambridge University Press.

13. LEI, XIAOLIAN. (2006). Sexism in Language, *Journal of Language and Linguistics* Vol. 5 Number 1.

14. MAJUMDAR, D. N. and MADAN, T. N. (16th Ed.) (2002). *An Introduction to Social Anthropology*, Mayoor Paperbacks, Delhi.

15. THANGLIENMANG, PHILIP. (2006). *A brief historical linguistics of Kuki-Chin languages with special reference to diachronic linguistic studies of Zo language in India and Burma.*

16. THIRUMALAI, M. S. What *is in a Name? Everything is in a Name! Thadou Versus Kuki.*

List of Contributors

1. **Behind the Scene: Prejudice of Kuki Chin-Zo Women in Manipur**
Author: Hoipi Haokip
Assistant Professor
Department of History
YK College, Wangjing
Manipur

2. **Portrayal of Women in Folktales and Myths of the Kukis**
Author: Hoineilhing Sitlhou, PhD.
Assistant Professor,
Department of Sociology,
University of Hyderabad

3. **Weaving: the Traditional Craft by the Kuki Women**
Author: Ngamkholen Haokip
Research Scholar,
Department of Visual Arts
Assam University, Silchar

4. **Women in the Informal Economy: Unpacking realities of the Tribal Women Vendors of Manipur**
Author: Jaja Kipgen
Research Scholar,
Tata Institute of Social Sciences
Mumbai

5. **Women Organisations and Collective protest: Nature, Scope and Challenges**
Authors: Hoineilhing Sitlhou, PhD.
Assistant Professor,
Department of Sociology,
University of Hyderabad
and
Lamtinthang Haokip, Research Scholar,
Department of Anthropology,
Delhi University

6. **Customary Laws of the Chikims with Special Reference to the Thadous**
Author: Priyadarshni M. Gangte
M.A., LL.M. & Ph.D.
Associate Professor,
Department of History
Human Rights Study Centre,
Damdei Christian College, Manipur

7. **The Socio-Cultural lives of Vaiphei Women as defined by the Vaiphei Customary Laws**
Author: Mary Nengneichong Baite, PhD.
Research Scholar,
Centre for Historical Studies
Jawaharlal Nehru University
New Delhi

8. **Status of Simte Women in Manipur**
Author: Esther Lalremkim
Research Scholar
Department of Anthropology
Manipur University, Manipur

9. **Health and Quality of Life: A case study among the Kuki women of Sapormeina, Manipur**
Author: Haokip Nemneivah
Research Scholar
Department of Anthropology
Delhi University, Delhi

10. **Women's Health and Healthcare Accessibility: A Case Study of Kuki Women in Gelnel Village of West Sadar Hills**
Author: Ruth Nengneilhing
Research Scholar
Centre for Study of Medicine and Community Health
Jawaharlal Nehru University
New Delhi

11. **Representation of Kuki women in Thadou-Kuki films**
Author: K.C. Gabriela
Research Scholar
Centre for Film Studies
English and Foreign Language University
Hyderabad

12. **Changing Pattern of Marriage System among the Thadou-Kukis of Manipur**
Author: Arfina Haokip
PhD.
History Department
Manipur University

13. **Language and Gender: Linguistic Representation of Men and Women in Kuki Society**
Author: Ngaineiting Baite
Research Scholar
Centre for Applied Linguistics and Translation Studies
University of Hyderabad

Index

A

Accredited Social Health Activist (ASHA) 254
Ahsi 84
Aige-Hoh 62
Akuanlam-Inneipa 179
Akuanlam-Tuchabul 179
Anal 124
Ancient things are today 46
Army personnel 128

B

Bazaar in Manipu 141
Becha 165
Beedis 95
Behind the Scene 1
Bhadur 79
Birth Rite 162
Bride price 207
Buantual-Khaw 186
Burmese corruption 5

C

Changkhatpu 52
Changmai-mu 76
Chapman and Clarke 19
Child marriage 177
Chin Hills 5
Chin-Kuki-Mizo 152
Christianity 169
Churachandpur District 66
Colour terms 315
Contextualising the concept of Marriage 276
Courtship 292
Customary Law and Impact on women 7
Customary Laws 12
Customary Laws of the Chikims 148

D

Daughter 111
Dharmasastra 151
Diminutive Marking 311
Divorce 161, 208

E

Eagly and Dickman 3
Economic Sphere 212
Education 205
Emergence of women in Politics 25
Epistemic Modality 307
Exploitation and oppression 1

F

Formal education 251
Freedom in Selection of Life Partner 204

G

Gangte 124
Gender 303
Gender prejudice 3
Generic terms 314
Girl Child 203

H

Hapless condition 54
Haryana 150
Healthcare coverage 255
History of weaving 66
Home made remedies 227

I

Informal Economy 101
Inheritance 159
Islamism 277

J

John Stuart 2

K

Khalvomtepu 48, 50
Khul or Khur 84
Khulmi national Union 11
Khwairamband 104
Kijammang 284
Kileukham 221
Kineilah 205
Kinship 149
Kinthuijinang 17
Knitting 198
Koirao 124
Kong lo 286
Koubru 224
Kuki and Chin 5
Kuki Baptist Convention (KBC) 30
Kuki community 44
Kuki Films 267
Kuki tribes 160
Kuki women 265
Kuki Women Union 31
Kuki-Chin-Zo 1, 2, 7
Kuki-Chin-Zomi people 22
Kukis 9
Kukis of Manipur 64
KWHROs 136

L

Lammatek 244
Language and Gender 301
Lenchonghoi 47
Levi-Strauss 279
Lhingjaneng Sitlhou-Gangte 26
Linguistics 302
Lom Upanu 125
Lushai 124
Lushais 157
Lutom Laisui 157

M

Magnificent Boxing Champion 35
Manipur 16, 117
Manipur 199
Manmasi 67
Manpi 182
Marginalised 103
Marriage System 275
Mate Selection 289
Meitei 79
Method of the Study 201
Mirrors Society 56
Mission English Schools 18
Mizo or Zomi women 6
Mizoram 16

Mou-kham 183
Mukhopadhyay 242

N

Naga 79
Nagaland 16
National Rural Employment Guarantee Scheme (NREGS 247
Nau-Vakman 191
Neingailou hitam 263
Nemcha Kipgen 27
Ngulhao Thomsong 304
Non-governmental organisation (NGO) 32
Non-tribal vendors 107
Numei jummoh 23
Numei leh bel kehbai 316
Numeipawl 212
Nutrition 250

O

Ordained Minister 29

P

Paigen 154
Pandit Jawaharlal Nehru 129
Papad 95
Patriarchal notion 110
Phenyl-thio-carbamide 200
Pi Chaiching 55
Piggery 15
Political Agent in Manipur 156
Political Sphere 209
Ponchial Rulpuiyek 74
Pondum/Puandum 78
Portrayal of Woman 43
Poultry 15
Pregnancy before marriage 206
Protest Movement 142
Punishment 228
Purum and Monsang 124

R

Religious Sphere 211
Rural areas 21

S

Sadar Hills District 130
Saipi-khup 76
Sampi/Saipi 76
Sapormeina 218, 230
Sawng-Satha 181
Selkeng-liding 157
Senhut 166
Sialkhau-Thun 180
Sialpi-Salam 191
Siamang-Pachong 176
Siamang-Upa 176
Simone de 8
Single term 313
social status 3
Socio-cultural Sphere 210
Som-nu 65
South Africa 149
Street vendors 106
Sumlom 114

T

Tag Questions 308
Talaq system 277
Tale of Jonlhing 51
Thadou-Kuki Films 262
Thadous 155
Thangal 124
Thempu 164
Themthu 14
Thepthak 185

Thi-pha 166
Thi-sie 166
Thiempu 184
Thilbu 70
Tucha 278
Turn-taking 310

U

unemployment 105

V

Vaiphei Customary Laws 175
Vaiphei society 176

W

Weaving 61
Weaving 198
Western Education 16
William Shaw 63
Womanhood and Culture 202
Women and Health 222
Women in the Informal Economy 94
Women's development 98
Worship 211

Z

Zous 157